THE FIRST RULE OF COMEDY..!

THE FIRST RULE OF COMEDY..!

MEMORIES AND MOMENTS

JEFFREY HOLLAND
WITH ROBERT ROSS

*To my darling wife, Judy,
and to my children, Lucy and Sam.
I am blessed.*

First published 2025

The History Press
97 St George's Place, Cheltenham,
Gloucestershire, GL50 3QB
www.thehistorypress.co.uk

© Jeffrey Holland, 2025

The right of Jeffrey Holland to be identified as the Author
of this work has been asserted in accordance with the
Copyright, Designs and Patents Act 1988.

All rights reserved. No part of this book may be reprinted
or reproduced or utilised in any form or by any electronic,
mechanical or other means, now known or hereafter invented,
including photocopying and recording, or in any information
storage or retrieval system, without the permission in writing
from the Publishers.

British Library Cataloguing in Publication Data.
A catalogue record for this book is available from the British Library.

ISBN 978 1 80399 639 4

Typesetting and origination by The History Press
Printed and bound in Great Britain by TJ Books Limited, Padstow, Cornwall

 Trees for L𝑖fe

CONTENTS

Foreword by Su Pollard   7

The First Rule of Comedy…
… You Must Have Integrity   9
… You Must Have Reality   39
… Don't Antagonise Your Audience   95
… Never Telegraph a Joke   119
… Pretty Girls Aren't Funny   151
… Always Have a Great Finish for Your Act   203

Afterword by Roy Gould   243
Acknowledgements   245
Index   249

FOREWORD
BY SU POLLARD

The clue is in the title. 'The First Rule of Comedy' intimates 'be funny', and Jeff certainly fits that bill. When David Croft and Jimmy Perry wrote *Hi-de-Hi!* he was the first and best choice for the role of Spike. Indeed, his subsequent roles of Mr Twelvetrees (*You Rang, M'Lord?*) and Cecil Parkin (*Oh, Doctor Beeching!*) cemented their faith in him. I have known Jeff for a fantastic fifty years (flippin' 'eck, where's that gone?!) and it has been my real pleasure to have him as a friend. Paul Shane (Shaney, as we all called him) nicknamed him The Vicar, and I always refer to him as the 'R' man – reliable, because, for me, there is no higher praise than that. We have worked with each other in various shows over the years and always had the biggest fun. Jeff has one of the bestest laughs ever, hearty and guttural. You always appreciate him being in the audience, on or off stage. I cherish our friendship because when you have Jeff around you know you're in safe hands, just as you will be when you read his book. Enjoy yourselves.

Much luv, Su Pollard xxxx

THE FIRST RULE OF COMEDY...
YOU MUST HAVE INTEGRITY

'Hi-de-Hi!' (*pause for audience reply, 'Ho-de-Ho!'*) 'Jeffrey can't hear you ... Hi-de-Hi!' (*audience reply again, 'Ho-de-Ho!'*) 'Thank you!' As my old mate Paul Shane used to say, 'There's a few more years left in that yet!'

You know, it's been well over forty years now since we filmed the pilot show for *Hi-de-Hi!* and I have counted my blessings every single day since. I'm very proud to have had a long and diverse career on stage, screen and radio ... and it's not over yet. Still, that idiot character, hapless holiday camp comic Spike Dixon, is the one that everybody seems to love. He's certainly the one everybody seems to remember me for!

I've honestly lost count of how many people have shouted 'Hi-de-Hi!' at me in the street, and it still happens. Not to mention the thousands of people who have asked me, 'How many times were you thrown into that Olympic-sized swimming pool?' My answer is invariably, 'Too many times!' To be honest, I don't remember. If anybody wants to watch all the episodes again and jot down the number, I'd be fascinated to know. Mind you, that wouldn't include the retakes and dry runs. Dry runs? What am I saying? There were none – once I was wet, that was it!

The First Rule of Comedy..!

For me, *Hi-de-Hi!* remains a special, nay crucial, part of my life. I forged many important, lasting friendships during the making of that show. The most important, of course, was with Paul Shane.

I can remember our first meeting as if it were yesterday. I was called to the read-through for that *Hi-de-Hi!* pilot show, as was Shaney, who was cast as the camp host and top comedian Ted Bovis. The truth is, Ted wasn't that good a comedian at all. Like all of the entertainment staff at Maplin's, he was a failure. Still, he was a big fish in the tiny pond of the holiday camp. So big, in fact, that he didn't even wear the soon-to-be-iconic yellow coat. He wore his civilian clothes: a very loud, checked suit. A proper working men's club comedian!

Not only was Ted Bovis vital to the running of the camp, the character was vital to the success of *Hi-de-Hi!* He could be a deeply furtive and shady bloke, and he was always on the fiddle. The writers knew that they needed someone brilliant and extremely likeable to play the part. You had to love this rogue.

Jimmy Perry, who had been a Redcoat at Butlins and put all his personal experiences into the scripts, was co-writing with that sublime director, producer and unstoppable star-maker David Croft. Both knew that the casting of Ted Bovis was key.

Paul Shane was a stand-up comedian from Rotherham and had worked those self-same working men's clubs for over twenty years, winning the Club Comic of the Year award on many occasions. He had started to get some extra work on TV, filling in with the odd line or two, most notably in a play by Alan Bennett in 1972 called *A Day Out* about a Halifax cycling club. He was given a kind of catchphrase in this and kept saying, 'Me bum's numb!' at every available opportunity. It must have worked as he eventually found himself in *Coronation Street* playing the part of Alf Roberts' boss. This was when Jimmy Perry happened to be watching one night and, during the commercial break, rang David Croft and said, 'David, are you watching *Corrie*?' David replied in the negative and Jimmy said, 'Well, put it on. I think we've found our Ted Bovis!'

That's why, in the pilot show, in that first scene with me and Paul in the train compartment, Ted is going on about this TV series he's going up for, all about 'this mucky street'. 'Apparently I'm dead right for it!' He *was* dead right for it. Our show, of course, was set in 1959. *Coronation Street* started in 1960. A lovely homage from our fantastic writers.

Anyway, I digress. I do that sometimes. You must try to stop me!

Back to the rehearsal rooms and my first meeting with Paul Shane. When they called me in, I walked into the room and there was Paul, standing in the middle of the floor looking rather overwhelmed, so I walked over to him and introduced myself. We shook hands and as we did so he gave me a very strange look. He said, 'Have we met before?'

I said, 'Oh no. Never. I would have remembered!'

Paul said, 'I have this really odd feeling that we have worked together before.'

We really hadn't, but I could feel the same immediate chemistry between us, which was to manifest itself so obviously in all the work we did together.

That was the beginning of almost twenty years of blissful comedy together, and a friendship that lasted for the rest of Paul's life. It was an uncanny bonding. A short-hand, if you like, for how to play these hilariously funny scenes together. It never left us. It was magic. Alchemy. 'The First Rule of Comedy'!

I may not have met Paul Shane before that first *Hi-de-Hi!* read-through, but I had certainly met and worked for Jimmy Perry and David Croft before. Many, many times ...

The Day I Met Croft and Perry

To my shame, looking back on that first, monumental meeting with David Croft and Jimmy Perry, not only was I not interested

The First Rule of Comedy..!

in the potential job – a life-changing one, as it turned out – but I was also in the foulest of moods. I've never been a poker-faced sort of bloke, so I'm sure it must have showed.

Allow me to set the scene. It was on a day in mid-June 1975 that I got the call to go to London. It was a call that should have filled me with excitement ... but it didn't. The call was to audition for the *Dad's Army* stage show.

Now, I had been a huge fan of *Dad's Army* since it was first on TV in 1968. It was a wonderful show and hugely popular. So popular that it was being adapted as a musical show for the stage. What's more, Roger Redfarn, the director, with whom I had worked in repertory theatre at Coventry, was staging the show and had asked for me particularly as he knew I could be very useful to them. He knew me and my work, as did the choreographer Sheila O'Neil, but everyone had to be approved by Jimmy Perry and David Croft. As I said, at the time *Dad's Army* was one of my all-time favourite TV shows – but I was not a happy man! Let me explain.

You see, I was working at Chichester at the time, doing the first half of the Festival season. I was playing parts in only the first two plays of a four-play season, as there was nothing for me to play in the second two. That's the way it was and I knew that from the outset.

I was sharing a house, though, with two other actors at the time, and these two were staying on as they had been cast in the other two plays of the season. It was a beautiful summer and we were all having a very happy time, but I had to leave and I simply didn't want to. My mood could not have been blacker. I was preparing myself to leave the company and, when that happens, your mind races about whether you are ever going to get another job. Frankly, I got very down in the dumps about it and became quite morose.

The day came for my trip to London and I was still in denial about my future in showbusiness. Even having this audition for

Dad's Army didn't raise my spirits. Lord alone knows why not! I was so despondent that I had nothing at all prepared and certainly no song ready to offer them. I didn't care. I thought, 'Well if they want me to sing, I could always sing "Hang Out the Washing on the Siegfried Line". Everybody knows that. What the hell?' I just didn't want to go. I *did* go though, of course, and I duly caught the train to London. I should have been thrilled, but I couldn't have cared less. I was stuck in permanent doldrums. What an idiot I was! I didn't even wear anything decent, like I would have usually. I was wearing just a shirt without a jacket as it was such a lovely day and the view from the train of the Sussex countryside was gorgeous, but I didn't care a jot. It was just one of those days when I had to go somewhere I didn't want to be and, as I said, I had nothing prepared at all.

I arrived at Waterloo Station and rather sluggishly made my way to the Mermaid Theatre, where the auditions were being held. I was still in a foul mood when I got there.

I went rather unenthusiastically to the stage door, where I was given a piece of the script to look at while I waited to be called in to see the producers. I skimmed through it with very little enthusiasm and then something caught my eye. It was a song that looked quite promising. It was a parody of that old wartime favourite 'Yes, We Have No Bananas', which was to be sung by Private Walker, the spiv. The show was to be quite a musical extravaganza and Walker had this very funny routine in which to promote all his black-market goods – you know, the sort of thing that dear old Jimmy Beck used to hawk around Walmington-on-Sea: knicker elastic, nylons, watches all up his arm and inside his big overcoat. He had the lot – all the nigh-on impossible stuff to get hold of. With one exception: he had no bananas! So I decided to do that song if required, as I was sure the pianist would know it and I could read it from the script. I could get some laughs out of it too. Anything to relieve this depression I was in!

The First Rule of Comedy..!

I was called in and I was trying my very best to hide the fact that I didn't want to be there. What was I thinking? Still, the moment I stepped into the auditorium the adrenalin started to kick in, as it always does at auditions. Just then, Roger introduced me to Jimmy Perry and David Croft. Eyes and teeth were the order of the day and I did my utmost to overcome my torpor.

It was David who then asked me to read a couple of scenes as Private Pike. I didn't realise till a little later that they were looking for understudies too. I read the scenes with the Company Manager reading Sergeant Wilson's lines. Let's just say that John Le Mesurier had nothing to worry about! This Company Manager, as they often are, was such a bad actor that he made me look brilliant. I was feeling better already! David and Jimmy then asked me to read a silly little scene as a mad German inventor. This was sight-reading on the spot, but it was such a delightfully dotty character that I lapsed into a strangled German accent. A bit like Peter Sellers as Doctor Strangelove and, now I come to think of it, very much like the voice Sam Kelly adopted for *'Allo 'Allo!* several years later. Maybe David made a mental note and remembered. Regardless of that, at that Mermaid Theatre audition for *Dad's Army*, my comic German characterisation made Jimmy and David roar with laughter!

Next came the question, 'What about a song?'

Well, by now my mood had shifted considerably and I was feeling much happier with the way things were going. So I said, 'Well, I found this in the script' and pointed out the aforementioned 'bananas' song. I said, 'Do you mind if I do this for you with the book in my hand?'

They said that they didn't, so the pianist and I fixed a key and off I went into my full Private Walker performance. It was a very funny song and they both fell about laughing. By now, of course, I was quite elated and getting rather cocky too, and I said to them, 'You enjoyed that, didn't you?'

They said, 'Yes, we did!'

You Must Have Integrity

Then I said, 'But you wrote it!' to which David replied, 'Yes we did. We wrote it down in long hand, handed it to the typist but we haven't seen it since!'

Well, suffice it to say that against all the odds I got the job. I was asked to be a part of the ensemble, and all the boys and girls in the chorus were dressed in the Reserved Occupation attire – like a Land Girl, a bus conductress, a Bevin boy, a nurse, etc. I was a fireman! I was also asked to understudy Privates Pike and Walker, so I must have got something right! We did six months at London's Shaftesbury Theatre with all the TV cast except John Laurie – he didn't want to do it for personal reasons, so they got a lookalike to play Frazer, a heavily eyebrowed Scott called Hamish Roughead. Private Walker was played by Cockney actor John Bardon, who later went on to fame as Jim Branning in *EastEnders* and married Dot Cotton! James Beck had died two years earlier, but Croft and Perry wanted to put the character of Walker back in as a comedy foil to Captain Mainwaring in several scenes.

After the massively successful six-month run at the Shaftesbury, we were to do a national tour in the spring of 1976, but John Bardon didn't want to do it as he had other things planned. So I got a call from Jimmy Perry asking me if I would like to play Walker myself. I was amazed and totally thrilled! The fact was, I already knew the role as the understudy so that saved them extra rehearsal time and the producers saved a salary. I had the time of my life. When we opened that spring at the Theatre Royal in Nottingham, there I was with my rifle at the ready, a member of Captain Mainwaring's platoon, with tears of pride rolling down my cheeks!

We had originally opened on 4 September 1975 at the Forum Theatre in Billingham, to run it in for a week before our London opening at the Shaftesbury, and we closed the tour on 4 September 1976 at the Theatre Royal in Bath. Exactly one whole year, and I spent that year in one of the finest shows it has ever been my privilege to be involved in. Talk about being in the right place at the right time – and not bad for a lad who didn't want to go to an audition on a day that was to change his life forever!

Joining the Croft Rep

You know, people lucky enough to have been employed by David Croft – and I am luckier than most – always used to call him 'The Guv'nor', myself included. He was also the star-maker of British TV comedy. Honestly. Just stop and think for a moment of those familiar faces that became huge, huge stars because of a regular role in a series David was writing, producing and directing. I'll start you off with Simon Cadell, Windsor Davies, John Inman, Su Pollard ... There's four big hitters for you. And there are more. Many more.

Following my gleeful experiences with the *Dad's Army* stage show, something must have struck David and Jimmy about me, and I was invited to take part in the actual TV series of *Dad's Army*. Can you imagine the excitement in the Holland household? As fate would have it, it was the very last series. David and Jimmy were wrapping it up because, with actor James Beck in the guise of Private Walker long gone, the others – much older than him in the first place – were really beginning to show their age. Besides, David had other shows he was working on, and another one in the very early stages of pre-production ... a little thing about a holiday camp in the 1950s!

Anyway, I digress. I told you before that I do that sometimes.

It seemed almost impossible that *Dad's Army* was coming to an end, but the time had come. I got the call to ask if I would like to go up to the location filming in Thetford to play the tiny role of a disgruntled army truck driver. Of course, I would. What joy! The episode was 'Wake Up, Walmington!', in which Captain Mainwaring and his Home Guard platoon try to warn the local, rather lackadaisical community that an attack from the enemy is imminent. I'm as lackadaisical as the rest of them, if not downright aggressive! I'm actually driving that truck in the scene ... and there they were. All of them. Mainwaring. Wilson. Pike. Frazer. Godfrey. Jonesy. Ah, Jonesy, as played by the impeccable Clive Dunn. I have to admit that I nearly ran poor old Clive over with that truck, but I didn't, thank heavens! And that final moment, when I drive off and splash mud all over poor old Arthur Lowe as Mainwaring. It's all slapstick, it's all Laurel and Hardy, it's all big boys playing in mud. That's the eternal secret of *Dad's Army*. It's a comedy of manners and set safely in the past, so it can never date. Those characters will always be with us, part of the DNA of our nation, and I am very proud to have been even a very small part of it!

Now, one of those other shows that David and Jimmy were keen to concentrate upon, once *Dad's Army* had been put out to pasture, was another wartime situation comedy, *It Ain't Half Hot Mum*. For Jimmy Perry, Private Pike in *Dad's Army* had represented his own experiences in the Home Guard when he was 16 years old in Watford, prior to being called up to active service. As it turned out, Gunner Parkin in *It Ain't Half Hot Mum* represented Jimmy's memories of performing in a concert party in India after he had joined up into the Royal Artillery. Jimmy actually ran that concert party in Deolali.

The series had been on air since 1974 so was happily running concurrently with *Dad's Army*, and I was called up to serve in the role of a Royal Air Force serviceman in an episode called 'Flight to Jawani'. It was sort of a cough and a spit really, but he was in and out for most of the programme and I was game to do any bit on TV in those days. I also hoped my willingness would prove to David that I was a team player. He liked a team player and it obviously did impress both of them because, sure enough, I was asked back to play a different character on the show in the following series.

This time it was a very starry guest appearance. The episode was called 'The Superstar', and I was the superstar. My character was

The First Rule of Comedy..!

Aircraftsman Ormanroyd, who, frankly, I can only describe as a bit of a gormless twit! Mind you, he was a very funny gormless twit and, as it happens, a very talented one. I had a brilliant scene in which this shy, monosyllabic idiot auditions to join the established members of the Royal Artillery concert party. Melvyn Hayes, absolutely brilliant as the camp female impersonator 'Gloria', is the one who has to decide whether I'm good enough. He is in his usual listless, pursed-lips, disinterested state as he asks me to start. The joke is that, once I get going, I can do the lot! Classical piano like a virtuoso, wonderful opera baritone voice, soft-shoe shuffle and tap-dancer, ventriloquist with a little RAF dummy, and even a fantastic jazz trumpet-player – at the same time as voicing the dummy! As the wonderful Donald Hewlett, Colonel Reynolds, says: 'Where on earth is that voice coming from?'

Windsor Davies, as the forever-yelling Sergeant-Major Williams, mutters, 'I shudder to think, sir!' Brilliant!

I have to admit for the first time, dear reader, that although those dancing feet were yours truly's, the tap-dancing sounds were provided by choreographer Miki Lavender (wife of Ian), the baritone voice was borrowed from an opera singer whose name eludes me, the Grieg piano concerto was played by a brilliant pianist in the studio, out of sight – his hands had a close-up for a wonderful moment which I took all the credit for – and, although I pre-recorded the voice of the dummy myself beforehand, I have never been able to play the trumpet. Sorry! I did, however, have the ultimate back-up from none other than internationally acclaimed big-band jazz virtuoso Kenny Baker, who played 'The Flight of the Bumblebee' while I mimed to it. How thrilled I was!

The final pay-off line belongs to Melvyn Hayes, though. After this utter orgy of 'borrowed' talent, he rather reluctantly asks, 'You can't do anything else, can you?' Huge laugh! But it's only so huge because Melvyn waits and waits and waits for the studio audience to stop reacting to my big spot. Honestly, you could drive a bus through the pause that Melvyn leaves between the end of my act and his line – but it works. A lesser actor would have bottled it and come in just a second or two earlier and got a much more muted reaction. Congratulations Melvyn, and respect, my friend. You are a brilliant master of timing! And, you know, something tells me that the ability I displayed there – that quick-change, try-anything-for-a-laugh attitude that I had – convinced David and Jimmy that I would be right for Spike in *Hi-de-Hi!* when it eventually came along. So not only respect, Melvyn, but many, many thanks. What a performance!

Although I had never wanted to be a 'star' as such, I certainly became known. And *Hi-de-Hi!* made me known by a lot of people. The great thing about that, quite usefully for comedy, was the timing of it. I had been an actor for fourteen years by the time *Hi-de-Hi!* arrived, so I knew how the business worked and where my place in the business was. You don't rock the boat; you just get on with it. I could cope with that level of attention.

Another team player for David Croft was Ian Lavender, who went straight into *Dad's Army* at the age of 22 having done little else – just a telly play or two. Suddenly – whoosh, you are a megastar! That's not easy to deal with. In actual fact, Ian is the only actor I've ever really got angry with in the theatre. We became great mates later on and couldn't have been closer, so he wouldn't have minded me saying this, but during the *Dad's Army* stage show, when I was playing the Spiv Walker, Ian, as Pike, accused me of standing in Arthur Lowe's eyeline deliberately. As if I would do that on stage – during a performance – with an audience out front! It was an unforgivable accusation! Although I did forgive him later, of course. Poor old Arnold Ridley, playing Godfrey, was sharing a dressing room with Ian, and had to sit and awkwardly listen to my ranting at Ian about it. It blew over, though. It was just Ian's inexperience showing.

When you go through rep and all the other bits and bobs of theatre and TV life, you just learn your craft. And you learn not to say certain things, especially on stage, even if you think them.

The First Rule of Comedy..!

Simple. It's why I despair when I hear people saying they want to be famous. I think, 'Famous for what?' They have no idea. They are simply in love with the idea of being well known. I wanted to be an actor, and the fact that my ten or fifteen years of hard graft brought me to a role that made me well known was a welcome fringe benefit of being an actor with, I believe, the wherewithal to deal with it.

I can honestly say that nothing unpleasant ever resulted from becoming a face on TV. Some fans don't know how to respect your personal space, though, or when to stop talking. Sometimes you sign an autograph and the person thinks it's an invitation to join your group! But you find coping mechanisms for that over the years. The only thing I really didn't like was when I got roped into things like charity football matches. Paul Shane used to get me involved in stuff like that. He was wicked! I remember once, we were in Blackpool for the summer season with the *Hi-de-Hi!* show. A charity football match came up against the 999 Boys – the three services, Fire, Ambulance and Police. Shaney and I were recruited to go along and play in this match. Now, I don't like football. I never have. I can't do it. I've never been any good at it, at all. I just don't enjoy anything about it. But anyway, Shaney and I got on the pitch and it was all 'Hey, here we go! Hi-de-Hi! Ho-de-Ho ...' All that lovely stuff was going on from the crowd. That was fine. Very nice. It was the pain of the football itself that I didn't like or relish. I didn't know what position I was supposed to be playing, and even if I had, I wouldn't have known what to do. I just tried to kick the damned ball if it came anywhere near me, which, thankfully, it didn't very often!

But the big pay-off on this story is that about a minute – maybe less than that – into the match, Paul Shane faked an injury and got stretchered off, leaving me on the field alone with no discernible talent for the game at all. I'll never forget the look on Shaney's face as he was being carried off on that stretcher. He just looked at me and went, 'He he he he!' ... He just cackled at me, the little devil!

I didn't enjoy that, but, still, you can't complain. I was only there because they knew who I was. Which was lovely. And they were lovely. It was Shaney, seeing an opportunity for a bit of, well, what he thought was fun!

This may be the right moment to give voice to the opportunity that running a repertory theatre afforded Jimmy Perry when it came to casting his many TV shows later on.

Jimmy and his wife Gilda ran the Palace Theatre in Watford for several years in the mid-1950s as a weekly rep venue. Doing a play a week was an unbelievable undertaking, but it was the backbone of the British repertory system for many years and gave thousands of actors their start in showbusiness. Many said, if you can do weekly rep, you can do anything! Jimmy and Gilda both played roles in the plays they produced as well as directing and organising everything else.

The many actors they recruited were to come in very handy later when the TV shows came along. Among the many useful types they used were Michael Knowles, whom Jimmy adored and loved to cast as what he described as 'a silly ass', perhaps best pronounced 'ahss'. It was a character that Michael was able to utilise in many roles, most notably as Captain Ashwood in *It Ain't Half Hot Mum* and later as the Honourable Teddy Meldrum in *You Rang, M'Lord?* I wish I could have seen him play Bertie Wooster – he would have been perfect!

Another couple, literally, were John Clegg and Mavis Pugh. They both worked at Watford many times and were married. I had the pleasure of working with John quite a few times at The Belgrade in Coventry during my rep days. He came along and did quite a lot of productions there with me. I remember that, as he was quite bald, with a fringe of hair all the way round the sides and back, he had a very effective toupee that he used when the occasion arose, which had a very clever little clip on either side that he attached to his own hair very discreetly, so you would never know. I asked him about this many years later when he guested in an episode of *You Rang, M'Lord?* and he said he had to abandon it as what was left of his own hair had receded too far. Shame!

Whenever John appeared with me at Coventry he was visited on every occasion by Mavis, whom I was always delighted to see. I found her utterly charming with the most amazing face – she looked as if she had stepped straight out of the 1920s! I never worked with her in Coventry, but that was made up for when she joined the cast of *Hi-de-Hi!* as David Griffin's aunt and later when she played the unforgettable Lady Lavender in *You Rang, M'Lord?*, where that perfect face came into its own. John Clegg, of course, was cast as 'Mr La-de-Da' Gunner Graham, the piano player – or in John's case, as in mine, mimer! – in *It Ain't Half Hot Mum*. He never did learn to play piano but managed to get away with it all those years. I also did a tour with him in 1986 of a play called *Look No Hans!* by Michael Pertwee, brother of Jon.

Another of Jimmy's regulars at Watford was the lovely Frank Williams. He did many things for them at Watford and was also an accomplished playwright. When Jimmy and David were casting *Dad's Army* there were no immediate plans for a vicar, but Jimmy said he always knew that if there was ever a vicar in Walmington-on-Sea, he would definitely be played by Frank Williams! It came to pass, of course, and not only did Frank also play a vicar for us in *Hi-de-Hi!* when officiating at Gladys and Clive's wedding in the penultimate episode, but he was promoted to bishop later in *You Rang, M'Lord?*. He was also given the ultimate accolade of recreating the Rev. Timothy Farthing in the 2016 movie remake of *Dad's Army*.

Another find for Jimmy was the young Ruth Llewellyn Baker, who later was to marry Philip Madoc ('Don't tell him, Pike!') and, after divorcing him, kept the name Ruth Madoc. She had quite a busy career in the musical theatre, being the possessor of a wonderful soprano voice, and worked for several years with George Mitchell's Minstrel Show before Jimmy recruited her once more to play the unforgettable Gladys Pugh in *Hi-de-Hi!*

What else can I say about *Hi-de-Hi!* What a success it turned out to be! With those two writers and that cast, how could it fail? I'm often asked if we had any idea when we were starting out on it if we thought it would be as big a hit as it became. The simple answer is, we hoped so. It isn't really a fair question to compare it with *It Ain't Half Hot Mum* and the incomparable *Dad's Army*. But we all realised that it had the same great pedigree and captivating characters, all failures in their chosen professions, forced to work together as entertainment staff and in the very colourful setting of the holiday camp environment, which gave us a good head start. We all had our fingers crossed and, as it turned out, would not be disappointed.

What a mix of characters! Gladys Pugh, the all-round sports organiser, was brilliantly played by the incomparable, aforementioned Ruth Madoc. Ted Bovis, the camp host and all-round 'good egg', was forever on every fiddle going behind the campers' backs, and with Spike Dixon in tow as his protégé comedian without a hope in Hades of becoming a successful comic but, like Jimmy Perry himself, with all the enthusiasm in the world. Then there was Fred Quilley, the bent jockey, who had lost his licence by pulling a race, in charge of the horses and donkeys and forever looking over his shoulder in case someone was coming after him. Fred was played by the wonderful Felix Bowness who, in addition to his role as the ex-jockey, did all the audience warm-ups for the studio recordings. He had been doing warm-ups for many years and had kept all the scripts for all the shows he had warmed up. He told us he had almost 4,000 of them piled up against the wall of his garage! A fabulous coup happened when, doing the warm-up for an episode of *This Is Your Life*, Eamonn Andrews came on early and asked Felix to remove the cover from the name hidden on the sleeve of the 'red book', which he did, only to discover that the name was his! It was 'Felix Bowness, This Is Your Life'. What an evening that was with all of us cast members in attendance!

Felix had an inexhaustible supply of energy and sat on top of the safety rail in front of the studio audience throughout the recording of *Hi-de-Hi!*, geeing the audience into a frenzy of hilarity for which we were all eternally grateful.

Mr Partridge, the Punch and Judy man who hated children, was another genuine character whom Jimmy and David had come across during their days at Butlin's. This was an inspired piece of casting that went to veteran British film actor Leslie Dwyer. This was a man I had admired at the cinema for most of my life. Leslie appeared in innumerable films over the years, including the unforgettable *In Which We Serve*, starring Noël Coward and based on a true story in the wartime career of Lord Louis Mountbatten.

I got to know Leslie very well in the comparatively short time he was with us in the series. He came to stay with us as a house guest a few times when in London for the show and became rather partial to my mother-in-law's homemade elderberry wine. He lived with his wife Gwen in North Wales at the time and was glad of the break from his digs. I remember taking him for a pint at a local pub once in the nearby Hertfordshire village of Chipperfield, and he remarked that he remembered shooting a movie there on the village cricket ground and drinking in that very pub back in 1935. He said to the manager, 'Chap who ran it then was a big man with a huge moustache. Is he still here?' This was 1981! Needless to say, he had a long memory. He stayed with us until the start of series 6 in 1984, as ill health prevented him from continuing after he had a pacemaker fitted. He retired gracefully and died a couple of years later.

Then there were Barry and Yvonne Stuart-Hargreaves, the ballroom-dancing couple who hadn't won a cup since 1943. The character of Yvonne was expertly drawn by Diane (pronounced 'dee-ann') Holland — no relation! — who was actually the sister of Jimmy's wife Gilda, so Jimmy already knew how perfect she would be. She had been a member of an adagio act in variety many years before and, because she was so slight of build, was ideal to be thrown around the stage by the two burly dancers in their act. It took its toll, however, and Dee suffered with arthritis for the whole time she was with us, but she managed to cover it up while working and you would never have known. She had a slight limp off stage but that was the only giveaway. A true 'pro'!

Barry Howard was cast because David remembered him when he was partnered with John Inman in pantomime in the 1970s, when they were known as the best 'Ugly Sisters' in the business. Barry and Diane danced together impeccably and he was perfect for playing his own namesake in the show. He was also famous for some of the best acid-lipped snide comments and tongue-in-cheek remarks ever! I enjoyed Barry's company enormously over the years and we also did several pantos together. He was a very funny man! We worked together until he left *Hi-de-Hi!* under something of a cloud. He suffered from alcohol addiction and was very open and honest about it later in many interviews, so I'm not telling tales out of school here. He was warned on several occasions but was beyond redemption at that time. He went into recovery and by the time he died he had been dry for well over thirty years – nearer forty, I would say.

All these wonderful personae, all based on real people who Jimmy and David had come across in the 1950s. All real! And then, to cap it all, the new recruit: the new Entertainments Manager Jeffrey Fairbrother, a Cambridge University professor of archaeology who was in a rut and wanted a change of scenery. Well, he certainly got that! How blessed we were to get Simon Cadell to play the part. He was magnificent! His ability to underplay and his subtle, even minuscule, facial expressions were worth their weight in gold. The magical mix of flirty Gladys and shy Jeffrey as she continuously 'came on' to him was utterly priceless. Those scenes will go down in TV history as prime examples of how to play comedy.

I was not neglected myself, though, in comic opportunity as the writers decided that Spike should be forever trying to 'be funny' with a succession of 'funny costumes'. The stuff I was seconded to wear was, by turns, very funny and not so funny! One of my personal favourites was the 'Funny Bertie Bassett' costume, based on the famous Liquorice Allsorts logo. It was brilliantly made, true

The First Rule of Comedy..!

to the design, and when I ducked down and entered the chalet wearing it, it stopped the show. I must have been about 8 feet tall! I managed to get a round of applause for the lady who made it, who was in the audience that night, which I was very pleased about. Full credit to her. I forget her name, but if you're reading this, then well done you!

One of the quirkiest and unquestionably unfunniest costumes – although by that very token a huge hit – was Spike's 'Funny Fireplace'. As I walked into the chalet to meet Ted, I was encased in this rectangular creation with a hearth, a painted-on fire, a cat curled up on the hearth and my face encased in a clock on the mantelpiece. I had a black ping-pong ball on my nose with two clock fingers sprouting from it and a set of clock numerals painted around my face! I stood quite still when I entered the set to let the audience take it in, and as Ted did the same, he was moved to ask, 'What's that Spike?' to which I replied, 'It's me Funny Fireplace!' There was a big laugh from the audience, and as the camera cut to Ted, he said, 'Correct me if I'm wrong, Spike, but what's funny about a fireplace? Tell me. I might learn something!' There ensued a grumbly conversation about Ted never appreciating Spike's efforts – it was a very funny scene which the audience loved. The thing about it was, though, that the following week, when we were in rehearsals for the next episode, David came over to Paul and me to explain that last week's show had overrun and, as the fireplace scene was free-standing and self-contained, he had decided to cut it for now, but he told us that he would keep the prop and the scene would be reshot and included in next year's series. That fireplace stood against the wall in David Croft's office on the fourth floor in Television Centre for a whole year and everyone said 'hello' to the cat as they came in! It was used again and was as big a hit, if not bigger, the following year. Waste not, want not!

Hi-de-Hi! was an enormous success and, it's fair to say, still is, with many, many supporters still avidly glued to the DVDs and its repeats. The antics of the Yellowcoats and other characters continued to astonish and entertain. Not least of these was the immediate development of Su Pollard's character of Peggy, the chalet maid. Right from the off it became apparent that Peggy was going to be a firm favourite with the viewing audience even after only having one notably small scene in the pilot with Simon Cadell. Peggy was always there at the back of the staff room at meetings, although she wasn't a member of the entertainment staff, and was always making it clear that 'One day I'm going to be a Yellowcoat!', for which she was incessantly berated by Gladys and told to get on with her work. She was the underdog and the British public love an underdog. She couldn't fail and went on to become one of the biggest stars of the series. We all knew really that, if Peggy were ever to get her yellow coat, it would have to be in the very last episode – and we weren't wrong!

One of the questions I get asked most frequently is 'What is Su Pollard really like?' Well, I can tell you. What you see is what you get! Su is one of the most honest and open personalities you will ever meet. She is wonderful with people and seems to make a friend for life every time she meets someone new! I have to tell you, though, I felt very differently towards her when I first encountered her. I was rather shy and retiring in the early days (I'm better now!) and when I arrived at the North Acton rehearsal rooms for that first day on *Hi-de-Hi!* I was petrified. When Su bounded over, I thought, 'Who is this lunatic and what is she doing in a Perry and Croft sitcom?' Knowing her now as well as I do, I know that Su was just being Su, but she had turned up wearing a floor-length gentleman's double-breasted brown tweed overcoat and a bowler hat that was clearly three sizes too large for her head!

We were all quite nervous that first day, but Su wasn't just speaking – she was shouting about 10 decibels louder than everyone else! Jimmy and David, I recall, were laughing away at all this, having already met Su at her audition at Jimmy's flat in London. On that occasion Su had arrived and knocked at Jimmy's door wearing a not dissimilar outfit to the one she was wearing when I first met her. Jimmy's reply to this vision on his doorstep was, 'No, we don't want any pegs today, thank you!'

I know both David and Jimmy were totally taken by Su and thought, quite rightly, that she was perfect for Peggy, the chalet maid. As I say, there wasn't much for her to do in the pilot episode, though, just that one lovely scene with Simon Cadell in which her reply to his requests for absolutely everything he needed was: 'You'll get it on Thursday!' Her potential became immediately obvious and the studio audience adored her. Soon Su's maid became a heavily featured character, always the underdog but ironically an absolute winner.

I soon got to know Su very well, and we developed a lovely close friendship over the years. I'm delighted to say that that friendship has become even stronger as the years have gone on. I adore Su and she really does have a unique way with people, no matter what their status. I will never forget in the mid-1990s, when we were doing *Oh, Doctor Beeching!*, we were all invited to a Buckingham Palace garden party on behalf of the 'Not Forgotten Society', a charity for ex-servicemen and women. Su was dressed quite conservatively for her, as Mary Husband, our costume designer, had supervised her apparel for the occasion. Even so, Su was wearing a somewhat eccentric hat that she had worn in the series. His Royal Highness Prince Andrew, the Duke of York, was officiating on behalf of the military. The Duke stumbled upon Su in one of the refreshment tents and, typically, she was not at all fazed by his presence. He had no idea who she was but made the mistake of asking her what she did, to which Su, in her own unique way said, 'Oh, I'm a hooker!' I'll never forget the look on his face as he turned to share a raised eyebrow with one of his equerries and swiftly moved away. Considering recent revelations, it may have been more panic than shock!

Talking regally, I was sitting at home with my wife Judy, watching the wonderful parade of 'National Treasures' to celebrate Her Late Majesty the Queen's seventy-year reign, the Platinum Jubilee. What an incredible weekend! As the commentator started reeling off the list of impressive names in the 1980s bus, including Gary Lineker and Timmy Mallett (oh yes, really!), I turned to Judy and said, 'Where's Su?' Honestly! Although she played a character from the late 1950s and early 1960s, Su as Peggy Ollerenshaw in *Hi-de-Hi!* was a comedy icon of the 1980s if anybody was. As for 'National Treasure', boy, oh boy, Su has done the lot!

I was particularly glad to share what became my final pantomime appearance with Su at the Grand Theatre, Wolverhampton, in 2019/20. We meet fairly frequently, mostly at charity functions these days, and speak regularly on the phone. Love her!

It wouldn't be fair at this point to talk about the show and not mention the assistance and support we got from the Yellowcoats, both boys and girls! The Yellowcoat girls were always a fairly flexible commodity on the show, if I can put it that way! The mainstays of the group were Nikki Kelly as Sylvia and Ricky Howard as Betty. In the first series we had Penny Irving, but she left us to go elsewhere, having already become established as Young Mr Grace's 'secretary' in *Are You Being Served?* There really wasn't much for them to do in the show as most of the air time was given over to the principal characters and their tasks were often confined to crowd scenes around the pool and in the ballroom looking after and/or dancing with the campers.

Nikki Kelly's Sylvia was a great foil for Ruth Madoc's Gladys, whom she regarded as a serious threat to her relationship with either Jeffrey Fairbrother or, later on, Clive Dempster. Ricky was a great friend of Nikki and it suited them both to stay on the show while others came and went. Gail Harrison joined us for the second series as Val, but she moved on to better things when she got cast in a wonderful series called *Brass* starring Timothy West. She was replaced by Susan Beagley, who stayed for two series, and then in 1984 three new girls were brought in: Linda Regan, who was to link up with me as Spike's girlfriend April; Julie Christian-Young as Babs, who, like some of the others, only stayed for one series; and Laura Jackson as Dawn, who stayed until the finish and ended up marrying our sound engineer Mike Spencer. Su had a lovely moment with me in a scene in which the new girls were introduced to the staff, and she said rather sadly, 'They're ever so pretty, Spike! What chance have I got of becoming a Yellowcoat now?' It bears repeating that all of us assumed that, if Peggy were ever to get her yellow coat, it would have to be in the very last episode – and we were right!

The Yellowcoat boys were a solid presence too, having been recruited initially for the sole purpose of throwing me into the pool! David and Tony Webb were identical twins and they added a unique quality to the show alongside, originally, Terence Creasey, an Australian lad who again only stayed for the first series and then went back to Australia, where he is now a very successful businessman. He was replaced by Chris Andrews, who stayed with us to the end. Chris was a pro boxer and was still fighting when he joined us. Paul Shane used to go and see his bouts and loved them. Again, Chris was quite powerfully built and came in very handy around the pool! He has since gone on to be a bodyguard in the pop music world, where he has spent many years looking after Chris de Burgh. The Webb Twins, as they were billed, were a cabaret singing act for many years and have always been very close friends of mine. Whenever possible we meet up at Harwich and appear at *Hi-de-Hi!* events at the Harwich Museum, where they have a huge room with memorabilia from the series. It's well worth a visit!

The series survived the departure of Simon Cadell, who went on to pastures new. In 1984 David Griffin joined us as the new Entertainments Manager, Clive Dempster, DFC. His character, being an outrageous flirt, turned the Gladys relationship on its head, which Ruth handled brilliantly. She ended up fending off *his* advances instead of the other way around! We went on for four more years, at the end of which Peggy *was* finally made a Yellowcoat. It was very short-lived, though, as she ended up in hospital with nervous exhaustion due to overenthusiasm – and then the camp got closed and that was the end of that!

You Must Have Integrity

The Hurricane of 1987

All good things must come to an end, and in 1987 the end was indeed coming for *Hi-de-Hi!* David Croft was held in such high esteem at the BBC that the old corporation had always given him and Jimmy Perry the opportunity to call the shots as to when a particular series had reached its sell-by date. As a result, David and Jimmy were afforded the pleasure of writing some particularly moving final episodes. Who can forget Captain Mainwaring and his comrades raising a glass to the heroes of the Home Guard at the very end of *Dad's Army*? Or, in *It Ain't Half Hot Mum*, gauche Gunner Parkin inviting that loud-mouthed and ultimately lonely Sergeant Major Williams back home to live with him and his mum?

So it was with *Hi-de-Hi!*

The show did not go quietly into that good night, however, for during the location filming for that last series, on the night of 14 October 1987, I was fast asleep in my bedroom at the Cliff Hotel, Dovercourt. All of a sudden, at around three o'clock in the morning, I was startled awake by the most almighty crashing of the wind on my window. 'What the …?' I asked the heavens, with a few more expletives thrown in! The clamour was so severe that I pulled on my clothes and went downstairs to the public area to find several of my colleagues foregathered there in a terrified state. Apparently the bedroom window of the room allocated to Ruth Madoc had been blown in completely! The nightwatchman on duty had heard the commotion and, no doubt, poor Ruth's cries of concern, and immediately summoned John Wade, the assistant manager, from his peaceful slumber. Luckily, John, who lived locally, arrived swiftly and attempted to take charge and calm everyone down – not an easy job. Still, we all soon realised that there wasn't anything anyone could do but take cover and hope for the best!

One by one, more of our team appeared, bleary-eyed, in the hotel lounge, all in scared mode. It was an unprecedented situation for all of us. I seem to remember that tea and coffee were made and

The First Rule of Comedy..!

sent round – and very welcome they were too – but none of us had had much sleep. What's more, we were all on situation-comedy duty, due up at the holiday camp location for our 8 a.m. call ... with a full day's filming ahead of us. Speaking for myself, I wasn't feeling very funny at that particular moment. Worse was to come, for little did we know what we would find when we got there: the vicious winds continued to devastate everything in their paths and it soon became clear that not much *Hi-de-Hi!* filming was going to get done that morning!

I recall that, at seven o'clock in the morning, I offered to help John Wade start breakfast off in the kitchen. So I started laying out strips of bacon on the grill. John came and took over eventually, but at the time I just felt like I had to do something, not only to help out my anxious comedy colleagues but also to occupy my mind. On a mission to put all our minds at peace, our brave and intrepid production manager Roy Gould set off to recce the situation up at the holiday camp. Decisions were soon reached about what was, or what was not, going to be possible for the day ahead. As all this was going on, at exactly 8.30 a.m., as was the norm, dear Paul Shane appeared at the foot of the stairs. Typically, he had slept through the entire thing! Several pints the night before had helped, of course. A little bewildered, but fully rested, from out of Paul's disgruntled mouth came the unforgettable question, 'What's goin' off?' He had been blissfully unaware of anything unusual, safely in the arms of Morpheus all night!

As the morning wore on, it became clear that the situation up at the camp was pretty devastating. The whole place, including the lines of chalets, was surrounded by trees, mostly poplars, and fifty-eight of them had been blown down! The generator wagon had been hit by a fallen tree and it was some time before they knew if it would provide the necessary power for any work to be done.

However, the scariest scenario was a potentially fatal one. In order to save on their expenses, many of the technical crew had opted to take accommodation in the chalets at the camp for the duration of the filming. The chalets, of course, were not 'en suite' and the toilets were down at the end of the line. During the clamour that ensued, one of the crew got up and decided he needed to relieve himself, so made his way down to the facilities. Well, to his astonishment, when he got back to his chalet, it was no longer there. One of the poplar trees had come down and crushed his chalet like a matchbox! Someone was looking down on him that night because, if he had remained in the confines of the chalet, he would almost certainly have been killed.

One of our supporting artists was less lucky. He was safe, thank heavens, but he had recently changed his car insurance from fully comprehensive to third party, fire and theft ... and there was his car, squished with a tree right across it. That was very bad luck!

Eventually it was decided that it was indeed impossible to do any work in and around the outside areas of the camp that day. We did have a stand-by day available, so luckily, as the generator was able to function after all, it was decided that the final scene of the shoot could go ahead, with a little thinking outside of the box ... or the camp. As scripted, the scene was supposed to be around the pool, but David Croft made the executive decision to move the action into the ballroom, where it was safe and dry. It was a true realisation of that classic old holiday camp maxim, 'If wet, in the ballroom'!

However, it was definitely a traumatic situation. Some might say it was God's way of saying *Hi-de-Hi!* was over. The episode was called 'The Wind of Change'. And it was!

From *Hi-de-Hi!* to *You Rang, M'Lord?*

Thankfully for some of us, the occasion had been prepared for.

As with those emotive finales for *Dad's Army* and *It Ain't Half Hot Mum*, David and Jimmy had written the most beautiful last scenes for *Hi-de-Hi!* During the filming of that 'Good Night Campers!'

The First Rule of Comedy..!

scene there wasn't a dry eye in the place. Even David and Jimmy were in floods of tears. Paul Shane was in bits! He really didn't want it to end. That last moment with myself and Shaney, sitting with our suitcases by the pool, was heart-breaking. You can hear Paul's voice beginning to break on that lovely line of dialogue about the leaves in the pool. Believe you me, there was absolutely no acting required for that very touching farewell to Maplin's! And to give Su Pollard, as Peggy, the very last moment was an inspired idea. Poor Peggy – after eight years of longing to be a Yellowcoat, she had finally achieved her ambition ... only for it to be snatched away from her with the enforced closure of the camp.

That tracking shot as Su walks dejectedly, alone, across the camp for the very last time took forever and a day to set up, but it was well worth it. It's what is known as a 'crane shot', which tracks Su as she waves the coach off and then walks away. It starts high in the air, closes down into Su's face as she whispers a sad 'Hi-de-Hi' to herself after the coach has gone, then pulls back and goes high again for the final shot. Su's last gleeful scream of 'Hi-de-Hi!' is the perfect antidote to the sentimental scenes that precede it. That frozen image, Su having leapt into the air, is literally uplifting and pure fun! It's a happy/sad scene which took twenty-eight takes to get right. That's showbiz – but so worth it!

The clever production team cunningly placed the filming of that sequence right in the middle of our three-week filming schedule, so there wouldn't be a heavy 'this is the end' feeling about it. It was just another day's shoot on the second Wednesday of three and, having got it in the can – eventually – we moved on to other stuff. A very clever move, it has to be said, because the final episode ended with fifteen minutes of film on location, culminating with Peggy's big 'Hi-de-Hi!', which was played for the studio audience to watch on their monitor screens. The first fifteen minutes was live in the studio and, just before they switched over to the film, someone said, 'Oh, we're just going to record the closing credits now before we move on.' So we set it up quickly and all did our final goodbye waves to the camera for the last time. That in itself was quite moving for everyone, but when the final sequence was played in, there wasn't a dry eye to be seen anywhere. Everyone was sobbing their hearts out and mascara was running down all of the girls' and some of the men's cheeks! The production team knew what we were like and saved a huge amount of time in not having to give everyone fresh make-up. They were the best!

Mind you, we three – we happy three – were already privy to the next comedy move by Croft and Perry. Thankfully! Or else our emotions would have been run even more ragged.

It was towards the end of the studio recordings of the penultimate series of *Hi-de-Hi!* in late 1986 that the plan was mapped out for us. At the end of rehearsals one day, Jimmy and David asked if Paul, Su and I would mind staying behind after we had finished, as they wanted to have a word with us. Well, we looked at each other. Oh, dear! What had we done? Were we in trouble? Were we going to be sacked? We didn't know what to think!

As it turned out, it was quite the opposite. They told us that after this series, the next one in 1987 would be the last series of *Hi-de-Hi!* This was something of a shock, of course. I thought Paul would burst into tears. He was devastated! It was heavy news, for sure, and Su and I were pretty dumbstruck too. We knew the end had to come at some point, but actors, being actors, start worrying immediately about where the next job is going to come from. We need not have worried, though, because the bombshell of the ending of *Hi-de-Hi!* was softened by some brilliant news.

Jimmy and David told us that they had written a new outline for the pilot of a series called *You Rang, M'Lord?* It was to be set in a grand house during the abdication years of the mid-1930s. Su, Shaney and myself were to be retained as the principal members of the cast, playing the servants below stairs who would serve the aristocracy above stairs. In other words, it was a comedy spoof of the popular *Upstairs, Downstairs* series, which, although it had been made a decade or so earlier, was still being repeated all over the world. More than that, *Upstairs, Downstairs* was a TV drama classic. The codes and conventions were well known and ripe for a situation comedy to affectionately take the rise!

That was their original concept anyway. However, Mary Husband, who had been the costume designer on all of David and Jimmy's shows and had already set to work on the new series, persuaded them to change their minds. Never an easy thing to do. But Mary explained her reasoning. She said it would be much better if, instead of the 1930s, they took it back a little more, to the 1920s. This was for the simple reason that the costumes for the ladies, in particular, would be so much more sumptuous and attractive from that period. For the men too, it has to be said. How right she was!

The opening scenes of the pilot episode of *You Rang, M'Lord?* were set in the trenches during the First World War and involved a lot of explosions for dramatic effect. The FX team were brilliant, as always, and as Paul Shane and I staggered across this battlefield, rifles in hand, we were surrounded by explosive charges going off all around us. We were given a strict route to follow as we made our way over to the next part of the site for another scene. We were told about where and when the explosions would be, so in theory we would be safe. There was going to be one particular big bang that was not far from where I was walking, so I was aware of it. David Croft was watching all this going on from a safe distance, along with his assistant Roy Gould, and as I walked across that part of the battlefield the huge explosion went off and it was a cracker! An enormous bucket of cork bits was detonated in front of me, and although I was well away from it, from where David and Roy were it looked as if I had been blown to kingdom come! Roy turned to David and quietly murmured, 'See you in court!' As the smoke cleared, however, they could see I was safe and all was well. It's worth a look at that scene as it really does look as if I copped it!

Talk about explosive …

The pilot was made under extreme duress because on the day of recording there was a union go-slow at Television Centre. As a result, when we were trying to record one scene, another was being assembled next to it. The reason for this was that they hadn't been able to get it all set up overnight, as was their usual practice. The hammering was unbearable! David Croft had to get them to stop for a few minutes while we were recording one scene before we could move on to the next one. In fact, David told us later that he got close to actually pulling the plug on the whole thing but realised that if we hadn't completed our work that day it might never have got made at all. How wise he was to stick it out!

The first series was commissioned, and we moved to Elstree Studios, where *EastEnders* was filmed. This was a brilliant move because we were then able to leave the set up permanently for the duration of the recording. Not only did this save an awful lot of time, but it gave us cast members a real sense of stability and permanency. Like *Upstairs, Downstairs*, our programme was made up of a series of fifty-minute episodes – revolutionary for situation comedy! Each episode took two weeks to record. We were based in what they called the 'Tom Jones Studio'. It was where 'Jones the Voice' had recorded all his shows previously, including his hugely successful *This Is Tom Jones* series. So, not only had the mighty Welshman sung his heart out there, but so had his amazing array of international guest artistes, including Shirley Bassey, Janis Joplin, Liza Minnelli, Little Richard, Stevie Wonder and The Who! His comedy guests had been equally impressive, ranging from Bob Hope to Peter Sellers – more of whom later! Both Hope and Sellers were special guest stars on *The Muppet Show* too, and that had also been filmed in the very Elstree studio that we had been allocated! They hadn't even dismantled all the scenery, for the theatre box from which those grumpy ex-music-hall comedians and acidic critics Waldorf and Statler heckled was still on the wall. If only those studio walls could speak … I might have got a few outrageous unwanted comments on my performance from that old box on the wall!

The set for *You Rang, M'Lord?* was incredible. And very, very expensive! It was like a permanent three-dimensional house with some of the sets behind the others. This enabled us to record all the scenes that were out of sight of the studio audience in the first week. Then we would have an audience in for the second week of recording. The audience seating was in front of all the sets they could see, namely the kitchen, the dining room and the study. The difficulty we actors had was leaving what we hoped was enough of a gap for the audience to laugh when they weren't there for a funny line! We mostly got it right, thanks to David's skill and the experience we had all gleaned over many years of working with him. So, when the whole programme was cut together, combining scenes shot both with and without an audience, the laughs were all there, all the time, I'm proud to say!

THE FIRST RULE OF COMEDY...
YOU MUST HAVE REALITY

The Early Years

Let us, however, begin again – this time at the beginning!

I was born Jeffrey Michael Parkes and made my grand entrance, as it were, on 17 July 1946 at the Garth House Nursing Home, 17 Mellish Road, Walsall, at a time when Walsall was still classed as Staffordshire. They later insisted on moving it to the West Midlands. Apparently, I was overdue by a couple of weeks or so and had to be induced. I'm happy to say it remains the only time I have ever been late on cue! Alas, my long and winding career on stage and screen cannot be honoured with a blue plaque on the place of my birth, for that sadly was pulled down and another nursing home built over it. In fact, it was directly opposite where I went to school when I was 11, so I was born where I was meant to be ... but I'm digressing, again!

My earliest years:

My mother, or 'mom' as we Black Country folks would say, found my impending arrival quite a traumatic event and claimed to have screamed the place down until she was hoarse. Things didn't improve much after I arrived, either, leaving her needing stitches and with the added indignity of the inability to spend the proverbial penny!

Obviously, the latter proved to be quite a serious problem and one which needed urgent attention. The powers that be initially decided the best remedy to said problem would be for her to stand and watch the pouring rain as it ran down the windowpane, thus encouraging the desired effect. When this didn't work, they had to resort to drawing the fluid off by more drastic means – a far more painful process. Thankfully medical science has moved on in leaps and bounds since those days!

Despite all this, I'm happy to say my parents were both delighted to welcome their new baby son into the family and gave me the names Jeffrey Michael.

My mom, like my father, was born and bred in Walsall. She came into the world just eleven days after the signing of the First World War armistice on 22 November 1918 and was named Doris Maud Harrison. It was a harsh winter and, according to Mom's memoirs, my grandfather paced the garden in deep snow waiting for her to arrive!

Not long after, my maternal grandparents moved to No. 19 Walsingham Street in the Chuckery area of Walsall, next door to a family by the name of Parkes. The Parkes household included two children, Emily and Samuel. Samuel was the younger of the two children but older than my mom by eight years. He would only have been about 12 when he announced to my grandmother that he was going to marry her daughter Doris – or Dot as he always called her – one day. More about that later!

It was to be eleven years before Mom was joined by a baby sister, Betty, who arrived in 1930 during the great slump. Times were hard and there was little work to be had anywhere. Everyone was struggling to make ends meet. A little before that, in 1929, Sam Parkes next door had reached the age of 19 and, wishing to avoid the dole queue, resolved his unemployment problem by enlisting into the regular army. He joined the North Staffordshire Regiment and was stationed at Whittington Barracks near Lichfield, where he completed his basic training before being drafted to Gibraltar and then India, where he remained for many years before the war started. During his years in India, he travelled the country, rising through the ranks to lance sergeant (a rank which no longer exists) and, later, warrant officer. By all accounts he enjoyed quite a good life, billeted in a bungalow with servants to wait on him!

In 1935 Sam came home to England on leave and paid a visit to my grandparents. It was at this point that he was reunited with his childhood sweetheart, Doris (Dot), then aged 16. Despite him wooing her with trips to 'the pictures' and such like, my mother showed little interest in his attentions but promised to write to him when he went back to India. True to her word, she kept in touch with regular letters and sent him magazines, mostly about films. This perhaps is not surprising, since one of her jobs had been as a cinema usherette during the ensuing years.

Life continued in this routine manner until one Sunday, on 3 September 1939, Mom came home from church (she was brought up a devout Catholic) to hear Prime Minister Neville Chamberlain declaring war on Germany in that fateful speech.

Like many women of the day, Mom, who had been enjoying life working in the local library, found herself called up to war work in an aircraft repair factory. The firm Wallows, known as The Wallers locally, repaired Spitfire wings, and Mom's excellent clerical skills were put to good use in the stores, from where she issued screws and other spare parts. The job was quite a change from others she had been used to, especially for a shy, innocent Catholic girl! The factory environment was pretty much male dominated and she was often the recipient of a great deal of teasing, but she claimed to have enjoyed the work nonetheless and was proud to be 'doing her bit'.

As the war progressed, life in the Midlands worsened greatly. The air raids were horrific. Anderson shelters were distributed to families and erected in back gardens. Conditions inside were far from ideal and Mom would often refuse to go down to the shelter with her parents when the sirens wailed. Stubborn to the last, she was apparently often heard to pronounce, 'If I'm going to die, I'd rather die in my own bed!'

Meanwhile, Mom was still writing regularly to Sam Parkes in India, who informed her he was coming back to England to retrain. Little did anyone realise it at the time, but it was in preparation for the D-Day landings in June 1944. My dad was caught up in D-Day Plus One. Terrifying, heroic times. The thought of his homecoming gave rise to a certain amount of trepidation and excitement for Mom as it had been so long since their last meeting. Then, suddenly, there he was, standing in her kitchen one afternoon when she came home from work! She knew the moment she saw him that he was the man for her and so it was. Plans were made for the wedding that April.

Sam returned to camp, Mom would telephone him regularly to keep him informed of the preparations and all went swimmingly until one day, shortly before the wedding, Sam had some devastating news to impart. All leave had been cancelled with immediate effect. Despite this, he reassured Mom he would be at the wedding (although she had no idea how) and she should carry on with the arrangements. He would meet her at the altar. And sure enough, he did. Not to put too fine a point on it, he went AWOL – that's Absent Without Leave, folks. He ran away from his barracks the night before! There's a lovely wedding photograph that I treasure: my dad is wearing his uniform as a lance sergeant. Soldiers would joke that the army was clutching at straws for ranks, but there you are: a lance sergeant. He was more than a corporal but he wasn't quite a sergeant. He wore three stripes, so I suppose as far as everybody was concerned he was a sergeant ... but not quite. Anyway, there he is. In his dashing uniform.

My parents were married at St Mary's the Mount church in a brief and simple ceremony, with Mom's sister Betty and Dad's niece Clara in attendance as bridesmaids. Dad returned to his barracks the following day and was stuck in the Glass House for seven days ... and promptly demoted to corporal for his misdemeanour! It wasn't long, however, until he regained his rank of sergeant (sort of).

It was another month before the happy couple saw each other again, honeymooning in Stratford-upon-Avon. Then it was back to normal. Well, as normal as it could be when there was a war on.

Then came the sickening news that everyone dreaded. Dad had been injured in action. He'd joined his unit in France for the second wave following the D-Day landings, pushing the Germans back as the Allies advanced.

Mom received a telegram which simply read: '... your husband badly wounded and in hospital in Swansea, South Wales. Suggest you visit at once.'

Of course, what it didn't say was how badly wounded he was.

The journey to the hospital was emotional, to say the least. Accompanied by Dad's mother, Mom travelled to Swansea, from Walsall, in a packed steam train, full of soldiers – having to stand all the way, and change at Birmingham – not knowing what to expect. Had Dad lost a limb? Was he blinded or disfigured in some other way? It later transpired that Dad had come under heavy artillery fire on the Caen beaches and had been hit by shrapnel from an exploding shell.

It was sometime later before Mom was informed of the whole story. Probably just as well! A lot of men had been killed in the attack and Dad was passed over as dead by stretcher bearers several times before he was eventually found and brought back from France to England.

Anyway, after a long and arduous train journey, my mom got to the hospital where my dad was recovering and she was told which ward to go to. She looked into this ward and saw him, in a bed right at the far end of the ward, and the first thing she did was to check that he still had two arms and two legs – thank God, he had!

His recovery took months and there were many visits to hospital before he was eventually allowed home. Among other minor injuries, he'd sustained major trauma to his ribs and lungs, leaving him with a great chunk of shrapnel and a substantial scar in his side, just below his ribcage. It was horrendous. The size of a man's fist!

I remember as a child on rare family holidays, it was something he always tried to hide while playing with us children on the beach. I vividly recall seeing it, but for some reason he seemed ashamed of that scar. Although he had been in the army, a peacetime soldier and a man at war are two very different things. My dad was embarrassed by the scar, even though my mother always told him it was something he should be proud of, having received it while fighting for King and country. I can hear her saying it: 'You should be proud of that. It's a war wound!' And it was. But he could never be persuaded. I'm certainly proud of it, on my father's behalf, and I'm glad he survived.

Like a lot of people from that generation, Dad didn't want to talk about his wartime experience. I remember one day, as a small boy, blurting out *the* question: 'Dad! Dad! How many Germans did you kill in the war?'

It was stupid, but he just got a little gruff and, with a weary shake of the head, muttered: 'Oh, oh … I don't know. About four!' He just brushed it aside. He didn't want to discuss it … but I got my answer. Years and years after his death, when I think back to asking that question, I try to put myself in his position. He was a young man, commanded to master and carry a rifle and to shoot and kill other young men with rifles. It was a case of shoot or be shot. Kill or be killed. Dreadful. Bless him. He's a hero to me.

That first year of marriage was particularly tough for Mom. No sooner had she received the news about Dad than she learnt that his father had been diagnosed with lung cancer.

With Dad still in hospital, the thought of attending his father's funeral proved too much for her. Perhaps not surprisingly, there was some backlash from certain family members over it, but Mom simply wasn't up to it and that was an end to it.

Following Dad's release from hospital, he had to stand before a Medical Board for assessment. They determined he was unfit to return to active duty and so he found himself pensioned out of the army and on 'Civvy Street'.

As for so many long-term ex-servicemen, this meant a period of adjustment. Facing the fact that his army career was over didn't come easy to Dad. In those days there was only your family for support, and Mom and Dad found themselves living in one room of my grandparents' house, in Willows Road, while Dad looked for suitable work.

By the end of 1945, with the war finally over, Mom discovered she was expecting me. This put a whole new light on the situation and they realised they needed to find a place of their own to live.

The solution to that problem came in the form of a small bungalow known as a prefab. Over 156,000 were built after the Second World War as a fast and efficient way of solving the housing problem for servicemen and those who had lost their homes in the Blitz. Prefabs were first designed in the early 1940s and were quick to erect. Some were better than others, but basically they were a far cry from the eco-friendly prefabricated buildings available today. In any case, considered adequate, they were only meant to be used as temporary accommodation. To that end, they were stable but very basic. The truth of the matter is, some were still in use over thirty years later and beyond!

And so it was, Mom brought me home from the nursing home to our little prefab bungalow at No. 11 Bell Wharf Place – a little home for the three of us – just off the main Birmingham Road. Often built from blocks of concrete, our prefab was constructed of corrugated asbestos panels. I know exactly what you are thinking! Health and safety would have something to say about that these days. If anybody had any idea of the dangers of asbestos back in the 1940s, they certainly weren't telling the people living in these places anything about it. Besides the risk, it was also, by all accounts, extremely draughty and cold in the winter. Of course, in those days there was no such thing as central heating and years later Mom told me she would turn the gas cooker on and sit next to it with me in the pram, with the cooker door open to keep me warm. This was with clothes on – both Mom and me! When she gave me a bath, I can only imagine she pulled me – and the bath – a little nearer to that open door of the gas cooker and its meagre bit of heat. The winter of 1946–47 was particularly cold – one of the coldest on record – and if things weren't bad enough, there was a coal strike on.

All this stress and hardship must have taken its toll on Mom, especially coupled with the fact that she was suffering from post-natal depression – again something no one really talked about at that time. Mom was a homemaker, of course, doing all the home chores: cooking, ironing, cleaning the house, washing the clothes ... and all done by hand in those days. She had a tub with what we called a 'posher' in it. You know, the thing you push down into the water to clean the clothes. That was the noise it made: posh! posh! posh! My grandma had one too, although she called hers a 'maid'. Whatever you called it, it was hard work! Mom spent a lot of her day in tears while my Dad was at work, doing rough-and-ready office jobs, which he hated. So neither was very happy at the time. In later life, Mom would tell me about these particularly harsh times. She would freely admit to finding them challenging, but like everyone else she exclaimed, 'We just had to get on with it!' What a generation!

Still, that awful winter of 1946–47 was the final straw. After that, my parents decided to try to find somewhere warmer for us to live. By the spring of 1947 they had found someone willing to exchange their little terraced house for our prefab. Heaven alone knows how they persuaded them. Maybe they took pity on them because they had a little one, me, not yet 2 years old, in tow. My need for warmth perhaps melted this person's heart. Whatever the reason, we moved into a little two up, two down terraced house – with an outside loo, oh yes – at No. 56 Thorpe Road. This was in the Caldmore area of Walsall. A rented home. My parents never owned a home of their own. In fact, my mother rented all her life. Owning houses was something posh people did, and we were never very posh. In more recent years, the Caldmore area gained a reputation for being very disreputable – red light, in fact – but at the time we moved there it was a cosy little village!

My mother's recollections of living there were much rosier than mine, which can only serve to reinforce just how basic the prefab had been. Again it was pretty small with, as I say, an outside loo. To me, its only saving grace was a tiny back garden where I could play. Talking of play, in 1949 they found enough money to take us on an albeit cheapie holiday to Butlin's at Clacton, where, at some cosy time during that week, my brother was conceived. Then it was all change again. Mom found herself pregnant once more. I well remember the doctor calling quite regularly to see my mom before the birth – do they still do that? I don't think so. We really did have it better, you know! Anyway, the doctor would be escorted to the door to the upstairs, which was in the corner of the sitting room. Once I noticed that he carried a small medical bag with him and I remember asking my dad, 'Is the baby in the bag?' Bless!

The baby wasn't in the bag, of course, but he did appear without a hitch. Steven John was born, at home, some three and a half years after me, on 16 February 1950, and gave my mother a much easier time of things than I had on my way into the world.

At the time of the blessed event, I had been taken to stay with my Grandma Parkes, Dad's mom, for a few days while Mom had the baby at home ... maybe because I had asked such delightfully silly questions! Whatever the reason, I remember Grandma Parkes spoiled me rotten. She was a very kind lady, but I have very little memory of her, other than that occasion when Steven was born. Sadly she died not long after.

So, now I was 4. And that wonderful garden became the playground for both myself and Steven. There was a little more money about at the time – luckily, as my parents had another mouth to feed – for my dad had a regular job then, and it was a job he enjoyed. He was an agent with the Britannic Assurance Company. He had found his niche in life, at last, and he threw himself into the role with relish – even though he had to do his rounds on his bicycle, collecting twopence here and twopence there from folk on their post-war life policies. The car he'd once owned, a little Austin 7, which would have been a great help in his career, had had to be sold in order to buy me a pram! They did, however, manage to find enough cash for two more Butlin's holidays: Skegness in 1952 and Pwllheli in 1953.

Towards the end of her life my mother would often recall to me that we'd had some very happy times in that 'little house', as she called it. Well, she might have had some happy times there, but from my perspective it was quite tough growing up with such strict parents. My dad was of the old school and, if you stepped out of line, you got a clip round the ear. Of course, you can't do that now! Moreover, my mom was an avid, devout and staunch Catholic. Steve and I were both brought up as Catholics too. My dad, strict though he was, was not Catholic. He wasn't really religious at all, but when he married my mom he had to sign an agreement that any children who resulted from their union would be brought up in the Catholic Church. We had no say in the matter. That was the way the Catholic Church ruled the roost in those days. It's something that really rubbed me up the wrong way.

But it obviously was altogether a happier time for my parents.

It's fair to say a lot of families experience sibling rivalry and ours was no exception. It's even fairer to say that, in our case, it was somewhat one-sided! As the older 'big brother', I suppose you could say I was the more confident of us. The fact of the matter was, I had been an only child for almost four years and Steve's arrival had put my nose right out of joint! Suddenly, there was someone else vying for my parents' attention and I didn't particularly like it. As children, my brother and I had very different personalities and there was little common ground between us. We weren't close then, but happily our relationship did improve greatly in our adult years. Steve was certainly the more academic of us and went on to carve himself a successful career as a graphic designer. He's a brilliant artist!

And so the months and years passed until my first day at school loomed large. Having been brought up as Catholics, it followed that my brother and I would go to the local Catholic primary school, St Mary's the Mount Infants School, not a long step away from where we lived. I remember on my first day, when the lunch hour came, I didn't want to stay for school dinner so I made good my escape and walked home to my mom! I'll never forget her face when I got there. 'What are you doing here?' she cried. 'You're supposed to have your dinner at school!'

'I didn't want it,' I think I said, but she grabbed hold of my hand and marched me off back to school pronto! They said they would make me 'table monitor', as if that made any difference, but I got the message and stayed from then on.

After that, I began to really rather enjoy school life.

It was during that first year when I was 4 that I met my best and oldest friend Peter Smith. He and I were put together in a double desk at the back of the room, as we were the two tallest boys in the class. It was the joining of two like souls, and Peter and I are still the best of friends today, as we were then, over seventy years ago!

It was at this school, at Christmas in 1953, that I made my performance debut as an actor. We were in Miss Donnellan's class and I was 7 and she had us doing a short play for Christmas. I don't think it was a traditional nativity play, as I was given the part of Good King Wenceslas! A boy called Paul Sadler was my page, and I, dressed in a reversed dressing gown for my 'robe' and a pair of wellies as my boots, topped off with a gold cardboard crown on my head, entered from the classroom doorway, followed by my 'page', and declaimed, 'How peaceful it is!' I have absolutely no memory of anything other than that opening line!

The First Rule of Comedy..!

I know that I was showing early signs of being a performer of sorts. One day, when I was throwing myself on to the floor and getting laughs from my contemporaries, which I apparently did quite frequently, another mother who had joined my mom in conversation while waiting to take their offspring home, said, 'Mrs Parkes, I think your son is going to become a comedian one day.' The writing must have been on the wall!

I got a Saturday job at Fletcher's the baker. I was the Saturday boy there. The man who ran it liked me very much, and when I became known on *Hi-de-Hi!*, he put up a photograph of me in the main shop in Walsall, with the heading: '*Hi-de-Hi!*'s Jeffrey Holland. Our one-time Saturday Boy!' I thought that was lovely! He was very proud of me because I worked for him. It was a great memory for him. And it was grounding for me. I've been in showbusiness most of my life, but I did do these odd jobs when I was younger, and got to meet people and learned how to deal with them. I'm still very much a people person. I'm not one of those actors who shies away from signing autographs at the stage door after a show. I see it as part of the job and I enjoy it. I enjoy talking to people!

While I was finding my feet at school, my brother Steve took a leaf out of my old school book. He didn't fare too well either and also walked out on several occasions. As you can imagine, this became something of a source for concern to my parents until he finally settled down. By the time Steve was old enough to start school, I was already moving into the junior classes, aptly named the Mount Juniors.

At the age of 11, Steve and I both sat an exam, known then as the 11+, and passed. This meant a transfer to grammar school. Queen Mary's Grammar School, Walsall, to be precise – the most elite of Walsall's secondary schools. Not only were the students all boys, but the teachers were all male as well. In actual fact, the school is still going strong today and, much to my surprise, they follow my career with great interest on Twitter – or X, as they insist on calling it now. Of course, our parents were extremely proud to have both sons pass the 11+. This educational prowess gave them a great deal of pleasure and pride!

As for my educational progress there, well I'm not sure the subjects I did well in were conducive to a life in the theatre, but I seemed to excel in languages: English, French and German.

My parents were very proud of me, as getting into 'QM', as it was known then, was considered no mean feat! The big coincidence was that I started my grammar school days in the junior section of the school, which was called Moss Close, and it was found right opposite No. 17 Mellish Road in Walsall, where I had been born eleven years earlier. I spent the first two years of my 'QM' time there and then moved to the big school down the road. I was there for five years altogether, as circumstances for our family changed dramatically.

The Day My Father Died

Tuesday, 20 June 1961 is a date that will live with me forever. It is the day my father died.

He was taken ill a week before that with pains in his upper arms and he was feeling dreadful. He was confined to bed while the doctor came to visit, and my brother and I were told that Dad was not feeling too well at the moment but the doctor was looking after him. Nothing could have been further from the truth! The doctor apparently knew full well what was wrong but was powerless to help.

This went on for almost a week while my brother and I carried on going to and from school as normal. On the Monday the 19th, as I was on my way home from school on my bike, I had an altercation with a grizzled little man driving a small truck near the street where we lived. He took umbrage at me as he claimed I was

The First Rule of Comedy..!

cutting him up as he crossed a white line. The general gist of his shouted retorts to me were: 'What do you think you're doing?', although his actual words were far more colourful! He carried on with a threat, yelling: 'I know which school you go to!', as he clearly recognised my colourful school cap and tie. I made my way home hoping he wouldn't know my name and report me. How could he? I'd never seen him before in my life!

The following morning we dressed for school as normal, exactly the same as every school day, and went off at the usual time. My father had decided he felt well enough to go to work himself. So, he set off to walk up our street to collect his car from the small lock-up garage he rented behind a row of shops along from the top of our road. He never got there.

Later that morning I was in my classroom getting on with things as usual when a boy knocked at the door with a message for the teacher in charge: 'Would Jeffrey Parkes report to the headmaster's study.' Well you can imagine the whooping that went on from my pals in the room!

'That will do! Settle down!' said the teacher as I left the room, quaking in my boots. Had that crabby little man in that old truck reported me after all? How could he? He didn't know my name.

I got to the headmaster's office and knocked on the door.

'Come in,' said the head.

So in I went. I could see from his demeanour that something was up but he was trying to smile. He composed himself and addressed me with the words I will never forget: 'I'm afraid your father has had a seizure and has passed on.'

I couldn't take it in at first. Everything seemed to slow down and I tried to speak, but I think all that came out was 'Oh no!' I remember choking as the tears came and I was sent into the room next door to digest the devastating news in my own time.

Eventually the headmaster came in to see how I was and to tell me that there were two policemen who were going to take me home in their police car. They had obviously called to tell him the bad news so that he could break it to me. They drove me home and were very sympathetic. I remember one of them asking me how old my mom was. I told him she was 42 and he replied, 'Oh, she's still a young woman then.' I know what he meant now, but at the time it puzzled me! My mom was a mess when I got in, but the next-door neighbour was with her, being very kind and making all the right noises, like you do.

I think my gran was there too, although my memory is quite hazy and muddled and sort of out of order. I clearly wasn't thinking straight. Gran may well have come over later, when I got back from school at teatime. It's all a bit of a blur, as you can imagine, but when I saw my younger brother arrive at the back gate for his lunch break, I couldn't bear it and said, 'I think I'll get back to school!' I couldn't think of what else to do, so I set off on foot. You see, my bike was still at the school — me having been ferried home by the police.

Apparently my father had been found by one of the shopkeepers who was walking his dog behind where the garages were. He lost sight of the dog and then found him standing over my father's body just a few yards from his garage door. He had apparently had a massive coronary and died almost instantly. The post-mortem revealed his heart was almost completely clogged with fat — just like the health-warning picture they put on cigarette packets — which accounted for the pain he was in. As I surmised, much later, this is why I now know the doctor knew what the problem was. He was simply unable to do anything to help — it was long before bypass surgery was with us. My dad was heavily overweight. He also smoked untipped cigarettes, and had all his life. At the time of his death he was just 50 years old.

The last word on the Catholic Church. They did 'allow' my father to be buried in the Catholic section of Walsall Cemetery. That was one thing they did allow. 'Because he had been a good Christian man all his life,' they said. And now my mom is buried with him. She is there in the same grave. That is what they wanted, so that is what we made sure they got. Despite the fact that she did remarry. In fact, she remarried twice!

Much, much later in my life – but it's relevant here – when I was 17, my mom met another man and wanted to marry him. They naturally wanted to get married in a Catholic church, but when the priest heard about it, things turned very unpleasant. The man in question was not only Church of England, but also a divorcee! As a result, he did not exist as far as the Catholic Church was concerned. A divorcee was simply unacceptable. All that business about being married in the eyes of God, and only death can pull you both asunder. Right. So Mom was free to marry. She just wasn't free to marry him! The priest came round to the house, and my brother was there. That evening and that conversation with the priest broke my mother's heart.

And that was what finished me completely with the Catholic Church. It was inhumane and wrong and immoral. Mom had been a devout Catholic, trying to live a good life, all her life, and that wretched priest came into our house that night and broke her heart. He excommunicated her from the Church, which she loved. So she did the only thing she could and she turned her back on it. She enrolled in the Church of England because she believed in God. In her world, God existed and she believed it, whatever label you might otherwise put on it. One would have hoped that the Catholic Church would have supported her in her next chapter, but no. It turned its back on her and condemned her. For me it showed its true colours then, so I walked away too. I've never had anything else to do with the Church from that moment on. I never have and I never will.

My stepfather was Joe Smith – now there's a name and a half! It was Joe Smith she married, and he lived until the mid-1980s. She was on her own for several years after Joe died and then, while my wife Judy and I were in Hong Kong for Derek Nimmo in 1995 (of which more later), she married a man my brother and I and the rest of the family used to call 'The Old Git'. As soon as he got his feet under Mom's table, he started treating her like a doormat, and she eventually walked out on him. She walked out of her third marriage, at the age of 80. I was so proud of her. What courage! She went down to live near my brother in Somerset. We all shouted, 'Wha hey! Good old Mom! Good on you! He was a real old grump!'

That was the one problem with Mom. She was strictly marriage orientated. She would not live with a man unless she was married to him. She still thought of it as a 'sin'. She wanted a partnership and she wanted company, but she made some very bad choices. My stepfather was a bad choice too, and he didn't make her all that happy either, but she wanted somebody in her life and in her home and that's naturally quite understandable.

One of my jobs between school and acting was working for a wine company, which I absolutely loved! I love wine to this day, but I was fascinated by it as well. There was a wine and spirit company in Walsall and at Christmas time they used to employ lads from the grammar school that I attended. They had branches all over the town – outlets for their wine and spirits. Obviously their trade had a boom at Christmas time. They had a lot of corporate gifts to wrap and distribute. You know the sort of thing – a bottle of whisky to a valued client by post. So they got lots of lads to come in and do that job: packing the bottles and wrapping the parcels and getting them ready for the post.

I knew a lot of my friends had been doing this. So when I left school, in July 1962, I applied to them for a job. I was interviewed and taken on. They told me that they were going to train me up in advance for the Christmas trade, which I thought was rather marvellous: I would be getting at least five or six months' work here. So they put me to work, just stacking shelves with wine and spirits, but I learnt an awful lot about the business in general and wine in particular. I mean, I couldn't drink the wine. I was only 16, so I wasn't old enough. I certainly wasn't drinking in those days, although I've made up for it over the years! The elderly man who ran the company, and his son who was his assistant, were just lovely to me. The old man once said to me, 'I'm in my seventies now and

I'm still learning.' I could well believe it. He was very forward thinking and had just got some wines in from Russia: a riesling and a bordeaux. I had no idea Russia made wines, but this man was just finding out about this new region, this new country. A whole new avenue had opened up to him. I found it as fascinating as he did!

There was so much to learn – I found it absolutely enthralling. I still do. I honestly believe, if I hadn't made it as an actor, that's what I would love to have done: become experienced in the wine trade – and I would still be learning now, even at my time of life!

How I Got into Acting

It is the eternal question for any actor – whatever their status in the business is – what first attracted you to a life on the stage? And how did you get started? It's not just curious journalists interviewing you about your latest stage or screen role. Invariably it's wonderful young hopefuls who dream of the roar of the crowd and the smell of the greasepaint.

For me, I have to look back to 1962 – gracious, over sixty years ago! I was 16 years of age and, together with my good friend Peter Smith, I was desperately trying to relieve the boredom of the weekends by attending the church youth club. It didn't help a great deal. That place was boring too!

Peter surprised me on one particular evening by saying that he had discovered an amateur dramatic society for under-21s. This was run by the Co-op in Walsall, where we both lived. Did I want to go with him next Friday?

My response was somewhat less than enthusiastic. In actual fact, I blurted out, 'What are you talking about? What do you mean "amateur dramatic" …? What do they do?'

He said that they did play readings and put on shows and that sort of thing.

I can see myself now, a look of something between bewilderment and incongruity. 'What do you mean? Act?'

You have to understand that at this time in my life I was as tall as I am now. Not only that, but I had a spotty acne-face with big teeth, Buddy Holly-style bottle-end glasses and no self-confidence at all. The last thing on God's earth I ever thought I would be doing was making an exhibition of myself on a stage in front of people! It was anathema to me.

Peter then said those few words that changed my life: 'Some of the girls are very pretty!'

So I said, 'What time do you want me?' I was in!

So, if you're a reporter or a youngster with aspirations of the stage, the immediate answer I always give is that I came into acting as a result of my raging hormones!

I was an enthusiastic amateur actor for a couple of years, and while some of the girls were actually very pretty, I also found that I rather enjoyed it. And I knew I was good at it. The time came when I eventually decided that I wanted to become a professional actor.

My mother hadn't remarried at this time, so there she was, a young widow. Well, when I told her what I wanted to do – it was an actor's life for me – she went absolutely mental! She knew nothing about the acting profession. The only thing she did know – or thought she knew – was that it was such a precarious profession that most actors were out of work most of the time. That was a well-known fact. (It still is!) As a result, Mom was scared to death for me. She hit the roof! She was dead against the idea, and she was going to lay down the law about why I should not become an actor.

I was just 17 then and, at that time, there had been a member of our local amateur dramatic society who *had* just gone on to drama school and *did*, eventually, make a life on the stage. So, I thought, it *could* be done. What I didn't know at the time was that this chap was gay and he went into the musical theatre side of the business – as well as being, if you'll pardon the expression, a straight actor!

Anyway, because of Mom's advice I waited and waited and waited. I had decided that I wanted to go professional because acting was the only thing I actually enjoyed doing. And the only thing I felt I was any good at. I had been acting with the amateur groups and I thought, 'Yes, I can do this.' It was something I really felt I had an ability for. Funnily enough, or not as the case may be, I hadn't really got into comedy at this stage. Comedy came later. Still, I had been mentored by one or two of my amateur contemporaries – in particular, two of the ladies. Firstly, June Mellor, who had been my first director when I joined the Co-op group, and later Celia Gravely, at the amateur group I subsequently joined – the Minster Players at the Grange Playhouse in Walsall, of which I am now very proud to be the patron. That's a lovely thing, that I'm now the patron of the Grange. What a turn-up for the books! Celia was a brilliant actress, and so supportive. As was her husband John, who was on the technical side. He was a wizard on the sound and lighting. Celia was so good and looked absolutely beautiful. She was very supportive and she would keep on saying to me, 'Well, if you don't try, you'll never know!' That was what really clinched it for me.

But I waited and waited ... until Mom remarried. Then when Joe came along, I thought, 'Right! She's secure now ... and I'm free to pursue what I want to do.' So I did!

What I actually did was sit them both down one evening, take my guts in my hand and say, 'I've decided that what I want to do is to go into the professional theatre.' I told them why – because I loved it and because I felt it was the only thing that I really wanted to do. So I told them that I was going to apply to go to drama school. In fact, I had already started sending off letters to drama schools. I was that determined! I had actually got one reply come back to me. It was in a plain brown envelope. Thankfully, it didn't have a logo on the top of the envelope, or else I would have been rumbled before I made my big announcement ... so I came clean. I thought, 'This is the time to tell them, before any other letters come through the door!'

So, I told them, and they looked at each other and they looked at me, and I thought, 'Uh-oh, here it comes …' and my mother just looked me in the eye and said, 'Well, if you don't try, you'll never know!'

Wow! I was totally gob-smacked, but I got their support. Mom was in a different world now. She'd got a husband and was happy. And she knew I had to go out and get some work. I had left school at the age of 16. I didn't stay on for sixth form, I just left school to earn some money to help with the income because Mom was doing a part-time job trying to bring me and my brother up. That was why I had worked for three years before finally applying for drama school, and thank God I had because by that time, in 1965, you could apply for a grant from the Education Authority. So I applied for one and, because I had worked for three years, I qualified to be what they called a 'mature student'. So I got a full grant – of £380 a term, which was an absolute fortune in those days. And my fees were paid. I thought, 'This is marvellous and amazing!' Both of those things! I had secured financial support to go to drama school for three years.

I got into the one in Birmingham, in Edgbaston, and I was away. That place really suited me because I didn't have to leave home straight away either. I stayed at home, in Walsall, and commuted by train. It was only 10 miles down the track, by train and bus, so that's what I did for the first year. Then I wanted to move away and be independent and grow up … which I did. That was when I was 20 years of age, so I wanted a bit of a life. And I got it! I teamed up with one of the boys in my year, Stephen Thompson, and we shared a flat together at the top of a house in Acocks Green in Birmingham, a short bus ride from the college. We lived there for the next two years of our stay at college. The landlord – a very camp man who would have no truck with visitors of any kind – gave us the flat for a peppercorn rent during the summer break between our second and final years, so that we wouldn't have to move out in between and he wouldn't have to relet the flat in the meantime.

It was a fantastic time in my life and I made some really close friends at that college, friendships which have lasted all my life. A few of us still meet up at least once a year, if not more, and we call ourselves the 'Chappies' after the nickname of our principal, Pamela Chapman, who ran the school back then. The college was known as 'Chappie's' and the name stuck! I had a wonderful three years there and learned a lot. No one can teach you to act – that is a gift – but they can teach you techniques, which are invaluable. One thing that we were taught there in great depth was the art of voice production – the ability to project the voice to fill a theatre without any amplification. Sadly, no one seems to teach this any more and all that people rely on to reach the back of the 'gods' is a throat mic! It really irks me when I go to the theatre and from about the third row back I can't hear what's being said. That's unforgivable. I thank Thespis for the training I had. Nobody sleeps while I'm on!

Going to Coventry

Having completed my three years at Chappie's drama school in mid-1968, I was back at home in Walsall writing letters off to repertory theatres, of which there were many, for potential employment. Earlier though, in 1967, Jeffrey Parkes had become Jeffrey Holland, my new stage name. Legally, I am still Jeffrey Parkes, of course. That's the name my bank manager knows me by. That's the name on my birth certificate, my passport and my marriage certificate – and on invoices when I'm claiming a fee! But, professionally, I have always been Jeffrey Holland.

It all came about in 1967, because Equity wouldn't allow me to use Parkes. When I joined our esteemed union, I was told that I could not be Jeffrey Parkes because they had a member with a similar name, if not the exact same name. Whether Jeffrey Parkes as an actor existed or still exists, I don't know. Maybe it was Jeffrey Parker or Jeffrey Parkinson. Whatever it was, I couldn't use Jeffrey Parkes. So, knowing I had to change my name, I decided to keep 'Jeffrey' because everyone calls me that, but the surname had to go! I chose 'Holland' because it was my grandmother's maiden name. It was as simple as that. She was Miss Holland, so I kept it in the family deliberately, and I liked the sound of Jeffrey Holland – it suited me. So I adopted the name with alacrity and it has been very good to me ever since. But I do answer to both! I can just as easily sign either signature, but I do sometimes have to think, 'Which one am I today?' I certainly find it hard to get my head around actors who decide to change their first names as well. I was always Jeffrey, called Jeff by everybody, but to get used to being called another first name, by friends, must be so weird!

Anyway, things started happening for me while I was still at drama school. They wanted a couple of lads to help as dressers and to play small parts in a new production at the Alexandra Theatre – 'The Alex', as we knew it – in Birmingham. It was a courtroom drama and they needed a couple of jurors, and they asked me to play the Judge's Clerk on stage. Backstage I was dresser to the actor playing the Judge – seasoned British stage and screen actor Walter Fitzgerald – so it was a good dual role for me, backstage and on stage too.

Having joined Equity, this was my debut in the professional theatre. There I was with all the grey powder in my hair and the tramlines make-up to age me up. Proper greasepaint and proper rep-company acting, and I absolutely loved it! The play was called *No Fear Nor Favour* – which is part of the judge's vow – and was a follow-up to playwright Henry Cecil's previous West End hit *Alibi for a Judge*. The star of the show was none other than Richard Greene, best known at the time as TV's Robin Hood, playing the self-defending accused.

No Fear Nor Favour opened at The Alex on my 21st birthday. I thought, 'Well, there's an omen for you – my 21st!' Opening

The First Rule of Comedy..!

night was 17 July 1967 and I bought the cast a round of drinks in the bar after the show because it was my birthday. My shout. Everybody came into the bar to toast my birthday. And do you know how much that round of drinks cost? No? Seventeen shillings and thruppence. Which is about 75 pence in today's money. A good eight or nine drinks for less than a pound! The funny thing is that I didn't have enough cash on me because I was only a student at the time, so I had to write a cheque. I wrote a cheque for 17 shillings and thruppence! Oh, dear. It was quite a chunk of my pocket money too, because I was smoking at the time, so you could easily get through £4 or £5 a week on fun stuff!

I didn't have a theatrical agent at that time, and even after I left drama school I was, by necessity, fairly independent. This was in 1968, and I had no job to go on to. In those days, as I have said, you used to have to write to all the rep theatres in the country, and there were lots and lots of those. So that's what I did. I got writer's cramp, sending out my letters to rep companies. I wrote up all my – admittedly limited – theatre credits, I got all my photographs taken, and I wrote all these letters and sent them off. Then ... nothing! Absolutely nothing!

Mom had got herself a new job, as a manageress of a little cake shop in Walsall, and we were now living in a flat above this cake shop, which was on the ring road. So there we were, the four of us – Mom, Joe and we two brothers. The others enjoyed living there and obviously it suited Mom to be on the spot, as it were. I was at home, fresh from drama school, with nothing to do, desperate to earn some money, so I was taking on any temporary work that came along. I did a couple of jobs at the bakery associated with the cake shop where Mom worked. I got in there for a few weeks putting pies together, making Eccles cakes and sometimes helping with deliveries as the van driver's assistant. I even worked on a building site for a while, but hated it.

So, this was me in 1968. Doing jobs I had no interest in whatsoever, desperate to hear from any rep company, and waiting to absolutely no avail. It was me and a few hundred others who had recently left drama school, so I was getting very despondent.

Then came a phone call.

Having done my shift at the bakery, I got an out-of-the-blue phone call from the college. My old drama school. This was from someone in the office, who told me they'd been contacted by Roger Redfarn, who was assistant director at The Belgrade Theatre, in Coventry. Roger had actually been a student at my college himself and, with proper loyalty in place, he'd contacted the college and asked them whether they had got anybody who had just left, because he needed three young men who were big and strong enough to do some push-and-pull and scenery shifting and to play some minor parts in a new production of, believe it or not, Leo Tolstoy's *War and Peace*. I was certainly interested and said, 'Yes!' It was work! 'Yes, please!'

Thinking about it now, a stage production of *War and Peace* was a little ambitious, to say the least. Frankly, it was a silly idea because it ran for three and a quarter hours. Two hundred minutes of quality historical drama and not a laugh in it! So, in retrospect, it was somewhat misguided, although having said that, it was a very good production. My involvement was to be minimal. They simply wanted a few bodies to shift furniture. You know, shove a desk off stage during this scene, push a cannon on stage in that scene. It was all very fluid, quite clever. So I was recruited, along with a couple of other chaps, and was going to Coventry for just this one production of *War and Peace* – or so I thought!

I got myself a digs list and chose, completely at random, to stay with a Mrs M. Murrin at No. 110 Maudslay Road in Chapelfields, Coventry, because it was only a short bus ride away from the theatre.

The day dawned and off I went by train.

When I got there I was given a very warm welcome by Madge, as she liked to be called, who was a larger-than-life character with a gravelly voice to match. It turned out that she had been on the

The First Rule of Comedy..!

stage herself back in the day, mainly as a concert singer with a strong soprano voice, and was known as Madge Collin. She was a widow by now, her husband having been an army officer and in charge of the defences of Coventry during the Blitz. Over the time I was there, she told me some hair-raising stories of the horrors he had experienced during that awful time. We would talk for hours and hours. I found her life and experiences fascinating. As regards the business that I love, I learned about the thrilling days when she had been a stand-in for that brilliant comedienne and singing star Gracie Fields, when she was making films at Ealing Studios. I was gob-smacked and endlessly interested, as I still am by showbusiness stories!

I was there on a bed-and-breakfast basis and I remember it cost me £5 per week. I started on 10 guineas per week (that's £10 and 10 shillings), so I was still well in pocket. The breakfast was huge and there were no exceptions. She got a great deal of pleasure out of feeding me up and I was often given an enormous piece of smoked haddock with an egg on top or maybe a full English – and I do mean full! I never left that house hungry, but as a 22-year-old I soaked it up.

Madge and I got very close and I think I must have become the son she never had. She was a delight, full of fascinating stories. Mind you, I was starting to gather some theatrical stories of my own because The Belgrade's production of *War and Peace* had offered me a couple of speaking parts as well. Oh yes, it wasn't always just shifting furniture around, you know. I think I must have impressed them because I got a few lines to say – one of which I will never forget until my dying day. I had to portray the entire Russian Army as one man! Me. On my lonesome! I had to rush onto the stage, in this huge greatcoat, which was almost down to the ground, and I had these huge Cossack boots on and a Cossack's fur hat, which must have been about 3 feet tall. It was huge! I ran onto the stage – in this ridiculous get-up – and I had to shout, 'Run brothers! All is lost! Lost!' And then I ran off the other side of the stage.

It was ludicrous and usually got a laugh! I should have said earlier that there wasn't an *intentional* laugh in it, but I got a laugh with that line – not least from the lads in the wings who couldn't believe what they were seeing. I wasn't even trying ... but there I was – an unwitting comedian! As with many other times throughout my career, I was helped out by the writer. Although dear old Tolstoy wasn't trying to be funny, the scene was so stupid, and my costume was so stupid, and the premise – that I, alone, was the entire Russian Army – was so ridiculous that it couldn't help but get a laugh! I thought, 'Here we go, maybe it's comedy for me?' I looked wonderfully comic, and I spent the best part of the next fifty or so years doing much the same thing. Looking stupid and getting a laugh – but on purpose!

And, with grateful thanks to the very stupid Russian Army, as a result of *War and Peace* The Belgrade Theatre people asked me to stay on for the next play. The play was *The Devils*, written by John Whiting, a piece that had been commissioned at the start of the 1960s by Peter Hall for the Royal Shakespeare Company. It had been based on the Aldous Huxley book *The Devils of Loudon*, so not a lot of intentional laughs in that one either. But I'm sure I found one or two in the couple of very, very tiny parts that I was given. I took them with grateful thanks, though. The best bit I had was as a jailer, and we beat the Ken Russell film, with Oliver Reed, by a year or so, so we were on the pulse of what the public wanted. It was groundbreaking in that the rules had changed and women were allowed to take their clothes off. And the men were allowed to take their clothes off too. No wonder it was so popular!

Anyway, after *The Devils* I was asked to stay on at The Belgrade and work on a season of plays, though not all *on* stage. I had been engaged technically as an 'acting ASM' – that's assistant stage manager to the uninitiated, which really means general gopher and dogsbody with the odd line thrown in if you're lucky. That's how my acting career got under way, quite by accident, at Coventry. I had just been recruited as what amounted to a scene-shifter on *War and Peace*, and it had ballooned from there. Wonderful! I've always said that life sometimes takes you around a corner where you didn't even know there *was* a corner!

Now, although I loved spending time with Madge, I did rather yearn for my own place, or at the very least my own space. A bit of privacy with girlfriends would be nice! As I soon discovered, there were several purpose-built flats at The Belgrade for the use of actors and staff, which was quite unusual for a theatre at the time, but I put my name on the list and waited. It took a good year before my turn came, but eventually it came to pass. Although I loved being at Madge's, I was a lusty young buck and those flats were a gift from the gods! There was a running joke at the theatre that every night at about 2 a.m., if you stuck your head out of the door, you would see several people sneaking back to their own bed from someone else's. It was called 'doing the Belgrade creep'. A great time was definitely had by all, including me!

I was very sad to leave Madge and shed a few tears on the day, but we kept in touch as she had become a very dear friend to me.

Roger Redfarn would loom large, later on, in the stage world of David Croft, but I must have impressed him in that early part of my career – in my early 20s – mainly, I believe, because he worked out that I could be very useful to him, as a rep company member. I could look different – and not just when I was dressed up as a Russian Cossack either! I could not only look different, but I could sound different as well. I was good at accents and impersonations, so they kept me on. They just kept on renewing my contract and I was delighted. After all, what better grounding could I get? I was learning my trade.

It wasn't all a bed of roses, though, by any means. I soon became of the opinion that all was not well with my status in the company. Now, while Roger was quite open about his sexuality and made no secret of it, I soon became aware that he had seemed to have taken a shine to me! Nothing was ever said but the feeling was there nevertheless.

The man who actually ran the theatre was a Welshman called Warren Jenkins. He had been an artistic director all his life and now he was in charge of The Belgrade. Roger was his assistant and then became 'associate' a little later, and Warren would certainly listen to what Roger advised in the best interests of the productions, the majority of which were of the highest standards. I was very happy with what I was being given to do, but I got the impression that things were a little blacker than they might have been. For some reason, I was being singled out in rehearsals as not doing things as expected and was getting publicly admonished – unfairly, in my opinion. On one occasion 'What does Jeffrey Holland think he's doing?' hit the airwaves. It got a few laughs from those assembled at the time, but I was very tempted to ask Roger what on earth he meant by that as I thought I was doing quite well! I let it go but it continued to niggle at me for some months. I began to think, 'Will it always be like this? Is this what the business is all about?' I was still very green and unsure of myself at the time, but I did my best to rise above it. You have to, don't you?

I had this issue with Roger for months and months and months, and it wasn't until a production of Richard B. Sheridan's *School for Scandal* that it was resolved. Roger had two renowned actors in that production. One was Garfield Morgan, who had many stage and screen roles to his credit and will probably be best remembered by comedy fans as the boss of Rodney Bewes in the ITV situation comedy *Dear Mother ... Love Albert*, in which he was appearing at the time. He was also Jack Regan's boss in *The Sweeney*. The other renowned actor was Brian Kent, who had been a star of *Crossroads*. He had played Dick Jarvis, the brother-in-law of the mighty Meg Mortimer, as played by the formidable Noele Gordon. Brian had been in 400 or so episodes of *Crossroads* and was just about to leave the soap opera, in 1971, at the time of our production of *School for Scandal*. So he was over in Birmingham, doing *Crossroads*, not a million miles away, and was brought over to Coventry for *School for Scandal*. Garfield played Sir Peter Teazle, Brian played Sir Oliver

The First Rule of Comedy..!

Surface – those were the two leading roles – and I played Rowley, the old family retainer. It's an old character part, played in the West End – rather brilliantly – by Bill Fraser, as my wife Judy was there to testify. I wasn't bad either, though!

Garfield's real-life wife, Dilys Laye, played his stage wife too, Lady Teazle. You may remember Dilys from *Carry on Cruising*, in which she was serenaded at her cabin porthole by a love-sick Kenneth Connor singing 'Bella Flo'! She had already been to The Belgrade before in 1969 to play Dandini in *Cinderella*.

I had quite a few scenes with Garfield and Brian in the play and Roger seemed to relish working with both of them; as a consequence, I got pulled into the happy little ensemble too. It seemed to me that I was now getting the same sort of respect that the other two men were getting, and it boosted my morale no end! The bonhomie flowed in both directions and, as a result, the scenes all went very well indeed. It seemed that all that nonsense was now over and I could relax more into my work. My relationship with Roger seemed to have changed and he was now treating me like an actor of some merit. Maybe he thought I was? He certainly figured many times later in my life long after I had left The Belgrade, as you have already read and will see in later pages. It was a valuable lesson in how the theatre sometimes works and, having ridden the punches, I bounced back. I stayed at The Belgrade for another three years or so after that and I can truthfully say that I learned my trade in Coventry. You name it, I did it! It's where I got my knees brown, as they say!

It gave me a lifelong love of theatre. The mechanics of theatre. The architecture of theatre. The fundamental energy of theatre. I fell in love with it. And talking of energy, the sheer dynamo of working in a theatre makes you totally match-fit to be an actor. You never stop ... and you really don't want to!

You would rehearse one play all day long and then in the evening you would perform a different play. Then go to bed. And start the process again. Rehearsing one play, performing another. It wasn't weekly rep, thank God! It was three-weekly rep. On very rare occasions we would have a two-week run of a certain play, but in the main, it was a three-week run. In that case, we had two and a half weeks to rehearse the next play. Luxury! Pity those poor devils in the old weekly rep, where you were juggling three different plays at once. Performing one, rehearsing one and looking at the next one with a view to learning all those lines.

That's one question every actor dreads hearing, and somebody always asks it: 'Just how do you learn all those lines?' The simple answer is, it's what we do! There is so little known about the brain that I have come to the conclusion that actors may use a part of the brain that many people don't use. Thankfully, though, I've always been a quick study. I've always been able to learn my lines with ease, touch wood, and that skill has certainly stood me in good stead. You know, often you get the call at the last minute to come in and replace an actor who is indisposed, and with my talent for being a swift learner, I can step in … and the show will go on. I'm touching wood and keeping my fingers crossed now, but at my age – fast approaching 80 years old – I'm still a quick study and I don't usually get nervous before a performance either. Now that *is* a blessing! Some actors even throw up in the wings before a first night. I've never understood that because, I suppose, I'm not made that way.

The old brain box is still working. I've always been the same, though. I simply cannot learn a line of dialogue before I start rehearsing. I've done a couple of plays with Judy just recently. Now, Judy Buxton is a classically trained actress and a brilliant one! Judy's credits with the Royal Shakespeare Company speak for themselves. Judy's technique is to start learning her lines as soon as she gets the play. She's off book – dead letter perfect – usually before we see the theatre! I'm the complete opposite. I need to get to know the director and the rest of the cast and have a proper feeling for the piece before my mind whirrs into action. But when it whirrs, it's very, very quick!

I think it's because the words and the moves both go in together. There's a muscle memory bond between where I am sitting or

The First Rule of Comedy..!

standing, where I'm walking to on stage and what I'm doing with my hands or what props I'm dealing with, and the words I am saying at the same time. Everything goes into my head then and sticks. Somehow. But beyond that, I don't analyse it. It just seems to work. It always did and it still does!

The other question actors who have made some impact in the business are always asked is: 'My little son Johnnie wants to become an actor. What advice can you give?' My answer is always the same, 'Don't!' I'm laughing as I write that, but it's true, because the question demands more questions to be asked, frankly. The established actor must ask, 'Does he really want to do it?' Yes! 'Right, is he prepared to work hard?' Yes! 'And be out of work a lot of the time?' Yes! Well, there you go. Little Johnnie might, just might, cut the mustard! The fact is that if he really wants to, he will. You have to be very determined in our business. I did it because I was determined to do it, but that cold hard truth is a great leveller. You have to really want it! So, if you tell a young person who wants to be an actor, 'Don't!' then, if they really want to be an actor, that will make them even more determined. If your 'Don't' puts them off, they didn't have what it takes to do it in the first place. I rest my case!

If, on that fateful day, when I went, with my heart in my mouth, and told Mom and her new husband Joe that I wanted to be an actor, and they had said 'No!' or, more to the point, if Mom had said, 'Don't!', then I firmly believe I would have got up and done it anyway. I would have fallen out with them over it, in actual fact, as I believe it was my destiny, a predetermined part of my life. I just wanted their permission. But I got it anyway and here I am!

This business will soon let you know if you are any good or not, because if you are no good, you won't get any work. Thankfully, I did get work. Coventry was the bedding ground for my entire career. I never ever wanted to be famous, though – I just wanted to be an actor.

A good friend I made in Coventry, a man called Pat Bradley, with whom I used to chat most nights in the pub after the show, once said to me, 'You're a team member, Jeff. You are a great company member. You like to work as part of a team.' And he was right. I really do. It's what I became known for. It's the quality that David Croft spotted in me. It's why I worked well in rep. I love mucking in with everybody, and getting my hands dirty, and helping out with advice or assistance with other members of the company.

I had a wonderful time in Coventry and met some amazing people. Not just within the rep company at The Belgrade, but at the other theatre too. From 1955 it was known simply as the Coventry Theatre, a lovely 2,000-seater. It had actually opened as the New Hippodrome, in 1937, but nearly twenty years later I suppose it wasn't new any more, so it was renamed. There I met and slightly befriended the ever-so-lovely David Nixon, the TV and stage magician and a very good actor too. He was brilliant in pantomime and, actually, he was starring in the Coventry Theatre pantomime down the road from The Belgrade while we were doing our three-week production. David was a lovely chap and so good in the leading comic roles, particularly Buttons in *Cinderella*, which he loved playing! For the 1971/72 season David was giving his Buttons in Coventry in a starry cast that also included Basil Brush, whom he often worked with on TV; impressionist Mike Yarwood, still a bright young thing but making a big name for himself; and a couple of young actors whom I would work with an awful lot, by the names of John Inman and Barry Howard, playing the Uglies (the Ugly Sisters). A wonderful production!

David Nixon and a few of the cast from that panto managed to come and see a matinee performance of ours, and after our run had come to an end, myself and a few members of our company managed to get down the road to see a matinee of *Cinderella*. David was very gracious and met us after the performance. He was so nice, and he was particularly lovely to me because he had seen me play the lead comic part in our pantomime. He was very complimentary about what I had done. I was bowled over! That a man of David

Nixon's stature would take the trouble to pay me a compliment ... little me! Honestly, David's lovely comments about my performance meant the world to me. I felt 10 feet tall! Those memories of his kind words and thoughts stuck with me for a long time. Actually, every time my wife saw David Nixon on TV from that point on, it was always, 'Oh, there's your friend David Nixon.' Not in a nasty, sarcastic way, you understand, but in a really warm, kind way, because David Nixon was just that: very warm and kind. A lovely, supportive man. I can bet you any money you like that you won't hear a bad word about David from anybody in our business. Genuinely loved, by everybody!

And the vital lesson I learned from that encounter was to try to be exactly the same. If I meet anybody after a show and I loved what they did, I tell them. It's just that responsibility of handing out a justified compliment to any new actor in the business. If he or she gets as big a kick out of it as I got from David Nixon, over fifty years ago now, then it's well worth doing!

Talking of pantomimes ...

Belgrade Panto – Enter Freckles!

My, what I can only describe as 'in-depth', repertory experience at The Belgrade Theatre in Coventry over several years, involved six separate pantomime seasons. I was young and energetic enough to be cast as the comic in most of them once I got established there, but my first panto was *Aladdin* in 1968 when I was cast as the Slave of the Ring, a character who is more often than not these days eliminated from the story, being deemed unnecessary. The Slave is a foil for Abanazar, the 'Demon King', in his machinations to acquire the magic lamp, but most productions now make do without the character – to save a salary, if we are honest! As far as a rep company is concerned, all those on the payroll are recruited into the panto to make it as spectacular as possible.

My second pantomime, in 1969, was in a supporting role in a production of *Pinocchio*, which starred the then unknown Sir Tony Robinson in the title role. He later went on to great renown as Baldrick in the *Blackadder* TV series and, of course, as a presenter of *Time Team*.

Over the next year or so I established myself as a fairly adept performer of comedy, and so I was cast in the next pantomime as Idle Jack in *Dick Whittington*. I had, during that year, appeared in a melodrama called *Dirty Work at the Crossroads* as the lovelorn local yokel Mookie McGuggins. After I had achieved some marked success in out-front audience contact, this gave Roger Redfarn the confidence to cast me as the panto comic, I'm happy to say, and that was the start of a pantomime career that stretched for forty-five seasons altogether! I had put some freckles on my face as Mookie, as it added a certain charm to the role, or so I thought, and it made sense to me to include them again when I played in panto.

The freckles idea continued as subsequent pantos came along for the next few years at The Belgrade, namely *Jack and the Beanstalk*, *Mother Goose* and *Babes in the Wood*. I had got into the routine of placing the freckles on my face in a fairly geometric pattern, which I thought was quite amusing. On each cheek there was a top row of three, a second row underneath of another three, offset between the ones above, and a third row below them of another three in line with the top three. It worked for me and always made the band laugh in the pit!

By the time *Babes in the Wood* had come along, in 1973, it had reached the point where some of the stage team and, of course, the band were trying to guess exactly how many freckles I would have on my face during each show! The idea of a sweepstake or company wager arose, I think mainly from the orchestra pit, although my friend Robin Carr who ran the show from the prompt corner may have had something to do with it. I left it until the final week of the run and then began to leave several random freckles off my face to see the reaction. Well, I have to assure you that it meant nothing to the audience, most of whom were completely unaware that I had any freckles on my face at all, but the response from the crew and band was hilarious! The band, which included bass player Ken Ingerfield and drummer Lionel Rubin, both of whom were regular members of the Jerry Allen Trio on TV's *Lunchbox* programme featuring Noele Gordon, became great pals and loved the competition. As I made my first entrance from the wings, I tried to keep my face obscured as best I could before stepping out onto the stage, when all hell would break loose in the pit as the spots were counted and the wager won. It gave me a problem, though, of how to end it in a way that was spectacular – and then I was inspired. On the last day of the run, at the matinee, I wore only one freckle. Then for the final performance in the evening I wore no freckles at all. Well, I thought the band would never stop laughing! I don't know what the audience made of it, but the band soon calmed down and the show went its usual way. That is a panto memory that really is unique in my experience!

I mentioned earlier the other pantos I did at Coventry during that time, but Robin Carr reminded me of an incident I had almost forgotten about in the 1971 production of *Jack and the Beanstalk*, in which I played Simple Simon and we had the wonderful George Moon as the Dame, the lovely Gemma Craven as principal girl and the amazing Joyce Blair, the sister of Lionel, as principal boy Jack. Joyce made her first entrance on horseback. It was a spectacular way to come on, most unexpected, and the audience loved it. What they didn't know, however, was that for some unknown reason, every time Joyce mounted the horse to make her entrance, it got a huge erection! Fortunately, this was spotted during the dress rehearsals – well, you couldn't miss it really. There didn't seem to be a logical explanation for this somewhat baffling occurrence, so to avoid public embarrassment, a member of the ensemble was dispatched to walk alongside with a lowered flag to camouflage the offending appendage!

A little way into the run, Robin, who was running the show, noticed that as Joyce came into the wings, the horse, which was standing by for the big moment, twitched his nostrils and his ears pricked up, if you'll pardon the pun. Robin suggested to Joyce that perhaps the scent of her perfume was the trigger for some reason. Well, the next performance came and Joyce didn't wear her usual perfume. Bingo! No erection! That was it and we continued without any erectile distractions for the rest of the run. The thought that it might just happen again wouldn't go away, however, and the flag bearer was left in place just in case!

A slight digression, or should that be diversion, to Wolverhampton ...

My connection with the Midlands has been a lifelong one. Not only was I born there, in Walsall, and then went on to train for the theatre in Birmingham and followed this with a long period of repertory in Coventry, but I also have strong connections with Wolverhampton.

I speak particularly of Wolverhampton's Grand Theatre, a beautiful building designed by Charles J. Phipps and opened in 1894. I have the honour to have been, for several years now, the President of the Friends of the Grand Theatre, or FoGs as they are known. However, my association with the Grand goes back over sixty years.

When I was a small boy growing up in Walsall, it was my custom, on a Saturday afternoon, to take myself off to the cinema for some Hollywood escapism. However, on one particular Saturday, as I was flicking through the pages of the *Walsall Observer* to see what was available, another ad happened to catch my eye. This was advertising a play that was showing at a theatre, not in Walsall but in Wolverhampton, just 6 miles or so down the road by bus. A play, I thought, is something this 11-year-old boy hadn't considered. I had only ever been taken to the theatre to see a pantomime previous to this and was quite curious! So I decided that I would give it a try, took myself down to the town centre and walked up Park Street to the bus stop behind the Savoy cinema. You see, I knew where the bus stop was but had never used it. Then I travelled the 6 miles across to Wolverhampton and made my way to the Grand Theatre.

I was quite in awe of this spectacular edifice, having never seen it before, and having spent my pocket money on a rear stalls ticket – I forget how much it was – I took my seat for the matinee performance. I remember being quite entranced by the whole feel of watching live actors on a stage right in front of me, acting out the silly tale of a most improbable love match. The play, I remember well, was called *Love on Ice* and was a modern take on a Romeo and Juliet-type relationship between two rival Italian ice-cream salesmen whose son and daughter were dating each other behind their rival parents' backs. It was really silly, I do remember that, and there was a very flamboyant man playing the Italian father, whose face was a strange, almost orange colour. I found it hard to believe, even at the age of 11, that he would ever have *had* a daughter! I have since, of course, realised what I was looking at – a very camp actor trying to be butch! I have never heard of that creaky old play since and think perhaps it might have been a Ben Travers farce. I do remember, though, that at the curtain call, the leading actor, having taken his bow, stepped forward to make a speech informing the audience about next week's play. It was still in the days of their weekly rep! Well, we are talking about 1957 here. That's my first ever memory of the Grand Theatre, Wolverhampton!

It would be many years before I returned, but it was the very first theatre in which I watched a play and something I have never forgotten. I have, of course, performed there myself on several occasions, a memorable one being the panto *Jack and the Beanstalk* with my wife Judy in 1999/2000. We have been back a few times, notably with a national tour of *'Allo 'Allo!* and have got to know

Adrian Jackson, who runs it, very well. I was delighted to play Danny for him in their first in-house production of *Brassed Off* in 2017. I also returned for what was to be my final pantomime performance there in 2019/20 with my dear friend Su Pollard in *Dick Whittington*. She gave us her wicked Queen Rat and I, ironically in my swansong after forty-five seasons over more than fifty years, played a man! I played Alderman Fitzwarren, having played Dame for the previous twenty-six years. I was delighted, though, to sit back and watch Ian Adams give us his wonderful Sarah the Cook. I followed this by playing the Headmaster in their last in-house production before lockdown, Alan Bennett's *The History Boys*. Fantastic!

I look forward to returning again in the not too distant future and, in the meantime, will continue to support this magnificent theatre as the President of FoGs.

My First Wife

It was sometime in mid-1970 when my attention was drawn to a rather attractive young lady who had suddenly appeared around the repertory company. 'Oh, she's a friend of Paul Beck's,' said one of my colleagues. 'She's just graduated at LAMDA.'

I remember seeing her from across the road as I was in the studio theatre rehearsing. I saw her from the dressing-room window, and I was smitten! She was wearing a full-length, bright-red maxi coat, and it caught my eye as I'd never seen one before. Well, as it turned out, she was a Coventry girl and had been accepted into the acting company after auditioning for the directors. I got to meet her later in the green room and she had the most beautiful, big brown eyes I'd ever seen! I tried not to stare but it was difficult not to. Her name was Eleanor. I must add here that I already had a girlfriend at the time, but that relationship was beginning to wind down.

The First Rule of Comedy..!

The play I was rehearsing at the time was *The Doctor and the Devils*, a powerful piece written by Donald Taylor and Dylan Thomas. Warren Jenkins was directing. I was playing three roles: Dr Barclay, the Lord Chief Justice, and a few lines as the Carpenter. Gareth Hunt, who went on to fame in *The New Avengers* and *Upstairs, Downstairs*, was a contemporary of mine, and he was cast as Dr John Knox, the Edinburgh physician who employed the body snatchers Burke and Hare – played by Richard Borthwick and Ray Callaghan. These chaps were to steal cadavers on which Knox would experiment to ascertain the workings of the human body. Not a lot of laughs in that one, either! We were very fortunate to have Carmen Silvera join the production. She was playing Nellie, a lady of the night, and would find national stardom as Edith Artois in *'Allo 'Allo!* for David Croft. There's that man again!

Anyway, back to meeting my first wife. We continued to work on various plays, and it soon became clear that we were attracted to each other. We did eventually become an 'item' after I ended my previous relationship, and then Eleanor and I were involved in a production that took us away from Coventry for a while. It was a new play by a rather brilliant young Dutch author named Hans Keuls. It was called *Confrontation*, and apparently the management had high hopes for it. The play examined the comparison between the assassination of an American president and the assassination of a Roman emperor. No prizes for guessing who! It had quite a complicated set combining ancient Rome and the modern USA, and we all had to flip between costumes for both eras. Confused? You soon will be! I was playing Paul in the contemporary scenes, and Paulus in antiquity. Genius!

Our leading man was Paul Massie, playing no fewer than three roles. In the early 1960s, Paul had been a film star of sorts. He had played the brilliant artist opposite the hopeless one of Tony Hancock in *The Rebel*. Paul was a very good actor, with an almost unfathomable other-worldly quality. My mate Gareth Hunt was back from *The Doctor and the Devils*. Gareth, a ridiculously good-looking cove, was on the verge of TV stardom then, as I have said. Also, Margaretta Scott was in the cast. She had been a very distinguished stage actress in the West End since the early 1930s. She had also made quite a few British films too. Peter Madden was in the cast as well, another very experienced actor. You may remember him as Bishop John Fisher in the film *Henry VIII and his Six Wives*, starring Keith Michell as the much-married monarch. Peter was playing Philocrates in Rome and the Cleaner in Washington. This business – you just have to love it! Peter had the most lived-in face I think I've ever seen. He pops up in TV screenings of old Hammer Horror films and I always smile when I see him. A proper old-school character actor!

Our director was Warren Jenkins. Now Warren, although an experienced director of, dare I say, the old school, had a very irritating habit of rattling the loose change in his pocket as he walked around the rehearsal room. It drove us all mad, but we dared not say anything! Another thing that he was notorious for was his fanatical devotion to Coventry City FC, or the 'Sky Blues' as they are known. He often spent a good part of our rehearsal time talking about their match the previous evening. I, of course, could not have been less interested! There was one occasion when a new production had an important opening night and this coincided with a cup-tie match for the 'Sky Blues'. Well, Warren came round and wished all the cast the very best of luck for this opening night and then promptly skedaddled off to watch the Coventry match! He thought we didn't know, but we had spies at the stage door. When the match was over – and thank goodness Coventry won – he got back in time to come round the dressing rooms and say, 'Well done, everybody! Well done! Good show!'

We took *Confrontation* to Norwich Theatre Royal and a few of us, Eleanor and I included, were put up in digs together. A wonderful old-fashioned landlady called Mrs Brown ran the house and gave us all a full cooked dinner around the table after the show. I'd never had

The First Rule of Comedy..!

that before and I've never had it since, but it was quite an experience. Needless to say, Elly, as I was now calling her, spent more nights in my room than in her own! I don't think Mrs Brown minded. It certainly wasn't a secret. For the Rome scenes in *Confrontation* we were all covered in brown body dye, and it came off on Mrs Brown's sheets. I don't think they ever quite recovered!

After Norwich we went to the Roundhouse in Chalk Farm in North London, where the set was condemned by the fire department as unsafe. It had to be torn down and completely rebuilt! Terry Parsons, our set designer, was beside himself, but we all rolled our sleeves up and got stuck in. We did eventually open on time but with no detailed technical rehearsal. Somehow we got through it on a wing and a prayer!

During this stay in London, Paul Massie had arranged with a friend of his, a lovely lady called Muriel, that Elly and I could have a room in her flat. It wasn't until almost the last day that we realised that Muriel only had one bedroom and we were in it while she slept on a sofa in her other room! We were devastated, but she assured us that she often did that for friends and regarded it as quite an adventure.

It was while we were in London that Elly and I decided to find a flat together, and did so in Earl's Court. We found a room at No. 41 Philbeach Gardens, just around the corner from the exhibition centre. This was in early 1971. It was an era when cohabiting while unmarried was still frowned upon. To avoid any unwanted wagging tongues, we were forced to tell a lie and pretend we were married. I remember the moment when we broke the news to my mother that we were moving in together. She burst into tears! The thought of her son 'living in sin' broke her deeply religious heart. She came to accept it eventually, though. I suppose she faced the fact that she had to move with the times – much as she didn't really want to.

During that early part of 1971, while we were in Earl's Court, I was still being called back to Coventry to do various plays at The

Belgrade. Naturally, all the time while I was away working in the theatre, I was missing Elly very much. By this time I had relinquished my theatre flat and, during show times, was lodging with mates. When Elly came up for a visit, my little cup of joy overflowed so much that I did the deal. I got down on one knee, well metaphorically, and I proposed to her. It took Elly completely by surprise! She still said 'yes', though, and we were engaged. During the next few weeks we applied for a permanent place to live back in Coventry. We were successful in getting a small studio flat, just across the road from the theatre, in a block called Mercia House. Slap bang in the middle of the city centre, it had a single room, kitchen and bathroom with a balcony overlooking the shopping precinct. We had to buy a sofa-bed to sleep on, but we were young and happy and loved it!

We arranged the wedding for a few months later, during the time that I was doing a show back at The Belgrade. The show was *The Pajama Game* (spelt the American way, just in case you're thinking of writing to the publishers!) and we got married at Coventry Register Office at 11 a.m. on Saturday, 2 October 1971. The entire cast was in the room with us! As the ceremony concluded and I kissed my bride, one of the more flamboyant boy dancers, a Canadian called Wally Michaels, shouted out from the back, 'Does this mean it's all over between us, Jeffrey?' Well, it brought the house down and was just what was needed. Thanks, Wally!

After the wedding I had a matinee to do. As the dress circle was closed for that afternoon's performance, Elly and all the family and friends from the wedding were guests of the theatre. In *The Pajama Game* I played a character called Prez who was a bit of a womaniser. Throughout the course of the show, he was reproached several times by various girls, saying, 'What about your wife, Prez?' Well, you can imagine the caterwauling that came from the circle when that happened! I tried very hard not to let it put me off. After the evening show, we had a party in the scene dock at the side of the stage, then Elly and I, having been given a hotel room by a local friend who ran the Leofric, retired to our marriage bed, only to find it 'apple-pied'. The sheets were so neat and tidy and tightly folded that we would have been in danger of getting stuck and trapped when we were only halfway in! It took a while to remake it, but all was well in the end.

After the run at The Belgrade, *The Pajama Game* was taken on a short tour around a few dates in the UK. The first stop was the Grand Theatre at Swansea and it was here that the unthinkable happened. After a couple of nights there, Elly had a miscarriage. We had no idea she was even pregnant at the time. She was whisked off to the hospital and taken care of while I had to get on a train and go to Hull the following day for our next date. I can't begin to tell you the anguish I was in, having to leave her behind in Swansea. Her dad drove down from Coventry and took her home to stay with them while I was away. Not a happy time.

The tour concluded. As night follows day, the tour was followed by pantomime, which took us into 1972. Having decided we did want to have a family, we had to think about trying to buy a house. We were still in our tiny flat and couldn't find room to swing the proverbial cat never mind raise a child.

I was still in regular contact with my lovely old Coventry landlady Madge. We chatted about my housing dilemma and it must have sparked a thought in her. A lovely thought. A little while later she suggested that we buy her house and that she could then move to our little flat. Madge reasoned that the flat would be much better for her. Her health had begun to decline and her big house was proving too much for her. We duly arranged all this and the move was made. I'll never forget going to the Bradford and Bingley building society to ask if I could have a mortgage. My opening line was, 'Before you say anything, I'm an actor.' I seriously thought I would be turned down, as a lot of worthy people in my profession had been, but the nice young man just looked at me and said, 'So?' Much to my surprise, I got the mortgage and we bought our first house!

Television Tales

That first house – Madge's home, one I was very familiar with – was bought in 1972, and we stayed there for four years. The deep sadness of Elly's miscarriage a little over a year earlier still hurt, but we had soldiered on, and she got pregnant again, soon after we had moved into our new home. Our doctor friend Louis Kelman kept a close watch on Elly and, despite a scare early on, she went full term and Lucy was born in April 1973. She brought with her much joy and was greatly loved!

I was in and out of work at the time. Mostly out, if I'm being honest – a feeling most actors can relate to. For the next couple of years, and for most of that first year of Lucy's life, I had no work at all! Being very conscious of my responsibility as hunter-gatherer, as it were, I got very frustrated and depressed about it. Frankly, I almost gave up altogether and thought about going off to get a 'proper job' somewhere, like maybe on the buses or something! For real. I couldn't even get a part in the TV series of *On the Buses* because that had come off air in the May of 1973. There's no comic justice!

Elly, I remember, was very supportive and berated me back to sensibility, saying words to the effect of 'Don't be stupid! You're a bloody good actor! What else would you do?' I needed that and came back down to earth with a thud!

I did, though, have a couple of very memorable moments. During a brief spell back at The Belgrade, I was asked to go up for an episode of *Dixon of Dock Green*. The role was that of a young husband. Whether I was a good actor or not, I *was* a young husband, so I thought I had a good chance of getting it. Well, I did get the part, which was very exciting really – my first TV speaking role! It turned out that there wasn't much speaking for me to do, though. I was a bit disappointed because it meant I had to turn down the part of Jonathan Harker in a production of *Dracula* that The Belgrade were doing and, having been a fan of the Count all my life, this was a wrench.

The First Rule of Comedy..!

However, doing *Dixon* was a great experience. It meant I got to work with the great Jack Warner. The character of Dixon, as played by Jack, had famously been killed – by a young Dirk Bogarde – in the Ealing film *The Blue Lamp*. This was back in the late 1940s, but the character had proved so popular that he was resurrected, still played by Jack, for BBC television in the 1950s. Twenty years on, Jack was still playing him, and now nearly 80! He was a gentleman of the old school with impeccable manners. I remember on the day we were recording in the studio at Television Centre, we were on a tea break, sitting in the little green room. Suddenly the door opened and the actress playing my wife walked in. Jack immediately stood up as a lady had entered the room! All of us chaps who were there also rose to follow Jack's example and the poor girl was so embarrassed she clutched her face saying, 'Oh, please, do sit down!' She simply wasn't expecting courtesy of this kind but she was working with a doyen of the 'old school'. The rest of us had lost the habit by 1974.

Jack was very arthritic by then and rising from his chair can't have been easy for him. They had put him behind the desk-sergeant's desk so as to give him respite from too much movement, but it wasn't long after that that he called it a day and retired. Well deserved. He was a great man, and that is a great memory!

The next adventure in Television Land happened that same year of 1974 when I was called into *Crossroads*. They wanted a young man to play a stall-holder in the Birmingham Bull Ring market and, being a local lad with a native accent, I fitted the bill perfectly. The character was called Mike Hawkins and was a friend of a regular couple in the show who also had a market stall.

There have been many stories told about *Crossroads* over the years, and most of them are true! The series, set in a motel, was the brainchild of two Australians called Reg Grundy and Reg Watson. In fact, years later, they both had a hand in creating *Neighbours*, so what they didn't know about long-running soap operas wasn't worth knowing. They also knew how to cut costs on the budget! I found that out for myself the day I arrived at the rehearsal rooms. Sonia Fox, who played my friend Sheila, had already been on the show for over five years. She clearly knew the ropes well. She took me under her wing and introduced me to various people. All these well-established *Crossroads* actors seemed to have their own designated chair in the rehearsal room, which was large and long with chairs against all four walls and a long table down the middle. This table had chairs all around it too and there was a throne-like chair at the far end of the room which was, of course, reserved for the use of Noele Gordon! Russell T Davies and his brilliant drama *Nolly*, with Helena Bonham Carter as the diva herself, was only half of the story. Noele was that – and then some! Unfortunately I had very little to do with her during my stay, so I didn't get to see the full range of her 'involvement'.

It turned out that a lot of the *Crossroads* actresses had picked up Noele's attitudes. Some of them behaved like Hollywood stars of the 1930s. Not Sonia, though, who very kindly pointed me towards a chair against the wall on my first day, saying that the actress who used it was on holiday for a week so I could use it for now. The following week, however, I had forgotten about the imminent return of the holidaying actress and, as I was sitting perusing my script, I was suddenly aware of a shadowy figure looming above me. I looked up and very politely said, 'Oh, I'm sorry. Is this your chair?' I sort of hoped she would say something like 'Oh don't worry, I'll sit over there', but no! She said, 'Yes, it is actually.' And I had to find somewhere else to sit! I ended up squeezing into the circle around the table. I wasn't there long anyway. I did about ten episodes spread over six weeks, and because they didn't know what to do with Mike Hawkins after that, I disappeared into the kitchen one day to make a cup of coffee and was never seen or spoken of again. That's showbiz, folks!

I was a little healthier at around that time too because, when Lucy was 2 years old, I gave up smoking – for the first time. What's that thing that Mark Twain said about giving up smoking being easy

– I've done it hundreds of times! Well, both myself and Elly gave up when Lucy was 2 because we had heard a story from a friend, who had been watching this programme on TV about a man who had smoked and now had terminal cancer. And he had a 2-year-old daughter too. This chap had one remaining lung, and he was 28 – the same age as me at the time. He said, 'My only regret is that I'll never see my daughter grow up', and I looked at my little girl in the cot and I picked this packet of cigarettes up and just threw it in the bin! And stopped at that moment. So did Elly. Done!

The time I wanted to go back to smoking – albeit briefly – was when I was just about to do the *Dad's Army* stage show. So a pivotal point in my life. I went away from home, to Chichester, to do a job. Being away from home actually helped me forget about my habit, so I didn't even think about the fact that I had given up smoking. I came back, after being away from home for six weeks, sat down in my armchair and the first thing I did was reach for an ashtray. How about that for muscle memory! I was hit then by the realisation 'You fool, you don't smoke any more'. I haven't smoked for years and years and years now, and neither should you. Here endeth the lesson!

It's probably safe to say that my life – or, at the very least, my career – started at this point. It certainly took a remarkable upward surge when I started working with Jimmy Perry and David Croft. And that, dear reader, all began with the stage show of *Dad's Army* ... but this is where you came in. However, let me go back and explain.

The *Dad's Army* assignment came off the back of my 1975 season at the Chichester Festival Theatre. It was a very enjoyable season, or half-season in my case, which was coming to an end for me now. Here's how it came about ...

I had been called to audition for the Chichester season early in the year for a production of *Cyrano de Bergerac*, which was to be directed by the great José Ferrer who had played the role himself in the 1951 Hollywood film. The theatre was being run at that time by Keith Michell and he was to play the title role himself. Why not? He also was to play Iago in a later production of *Othello* with Topol playing the Moor. It's quite handy being an artistic director because it means you can grab the best roles for yourself and nobody can say anything!

Anyway, I went along to audition for Mr Ferrer and we got on surprisingly well despite me being in total awe. I played guitar and sang something silly as there was a musical element to the production. They wanted people to play the Carbon de Castel-Jaloux Cadets, or 'Gascony' cadets as we were known in the play. He must have liked the look of me because I was then asked to read some pieces of dialogue. I got the job! I was only booked for the first two plays of the season, there being nothing for me in the final two productions. I was in *Cyrano* and also had a small supporting role in *An Enemy of the People* by Henrik Ibsen, which was to star Donald Sinden. His son Jeremy was also in the company, so it was lovely to have father and son working together. I became good friends with Jeremy and there was also a family connection there with Simon Cadell. Donald Sinden was Simon's godfather, the families having been very close.

As you know, Simon left us at far too early an age. The same thing, sadly, happened to Donald's son Jeremy, who contracted cancer and succumbed at roughly the same time as Simon. I will never forget Donald saying to me many years later that Jeremy and Simon were both born within six months of each other and they both died within six months of each other at the age of just 45.

Having said all that, I was having the time of my life! The theatre was surrounded by beautiful parkland then – not so much now as there has been a lot of building work – and it was a beautiful summer too. What could be nicer?

I went off to Chichester full of beans for very little money, but who cared? I was going to Chichester!

The First Rule of Comedy..!

Moving House

I found that living in Coventry was becoming a disadvantage when the theatrical world was centred in and around the capital. So, after much deliberation, Elly and I decided to move south. But where to go? Well, as life suddenly has a habit of doing, the answer wasn't far away!

One of our actor friends, Leo Dolan, and his wife Sheila MacIntosh, whom we knew as a casting director for London Weekend Television, came to dinner with us one evening and the subject of moving house came up. Sheila told us that her parents lived in Hemel Hempstead in Hertfordshire and it was really nice and a short train ride to London. Why didn't we look there? We thought it was a very good idea, so we arranged to meet her parents and get some advice. We duly did just that and they were so very helpful. Bearing in mind they had never met us before in their lives, they even invited us to come and stay with them for a day or two so we could have a proper look around Hemel Hempstead at our leisure. So we did just that!

We found a small three-bedroom, end-of-terrace modern house on a handy estate not far from the station at a price we managed to afford. The property was also near to a school for Lucy, so it suited us down to the ground ... and up to the roof! Sam was still only an unborn babe within the warmth of Elly at this stage. As it happened, we had managed to sell our Coventry house before Hemel Hempstead came up, so as I was embarking on the *Dad's Army* tour anyway, we put all our furniture and stuff in the garage of Elly's parents' house and went to stay with them for as long as it took. Well, it took just the right amount of time. It was also a great joy for them to have baby Lucy with them, whom they spoiled rotten, naturally, and to have Elly at home again without me being around that much! Because of my commitment to *Dad's Army*, I just came back after the show on Saturday evening, for a lovely Sunday with my family.

You Must Have Reality

This was the sweltering summer of 1976, during which poor Elly was carrying Sam. He was born in the July, during the *Dad's Army* tour when we were at Richmond.

Elly's dad and I hired a van when we were able to move to Hemel and drove down to the new house one Sunday later in the tour with all our stuff. We unloaded it, went back and promptly broke down on the M1! Harold, Elly's dad, was an experienced businessman and managed to talk the van hire people into wiping the slate clean when we eventually got the van back, so we got it free of charge. I should think so too! We moved down to stay a short while later and Lucy started at her new school.

We were there for roughly three years while I did my Croft guest appearances, and also, at around that time, I was doing a highly prestigious stint at the BBC, where I ended up appearing in three – not just one, but three! – productions of Shakespeare plays for the *BBC Television Shakespeare* series, which was broadcast on BBC2 and subsequently comprised the corporation's definitive interpretation of the bard's work for international sales and educational purposes. Gracious! The three I appeared in were *Richard II*, in which I was cast as the Duke of Surrey and the Earl Marshal; *Henry V*, as Corporal Nym; and *As You Like It*, as William.

The move south came at the right time and the work I got was much easier to reach than it would have been from Coventry!

Talking of those three Shakespeares, they were pretty memorable for me in lots of ways. The first two, *Richard II* and *Henry V*, were directed by David Giles, for whom I also later did a stint in *The Mayor of Casterbridge* with Alan Bates.

I remember a very funny moment that happened during rehearsals for *Richard II*, which starred Derek Jacobi in the title role.

We were about a week into rehearsal at the time, so had all got to know each other quite well. As a result, we were feeling a little more relaxed than we had been at the beginning. None more so than Jacobi himself! We had got to the scene where the King is being officially deposed by Bolingbroke and there was a lot of high anxiety and tension in this moment. Jacobi, who was being at his most emotional, turned to the people in the room, of whom I was one, and said, 'Give me the crown', at which point he was supposed to hand it to Bolingbroke. Nothing. No crown was forthcoming! I think it was still among the props across the room, so Derek repeated, 'Give me the crown.' Still nothing, and none of us knew quite what to do as we hadn't had a chance to rehearse that scene before. It was meant to be handed over by a page boy, and we hadn't rehearsed them in yet, so Derek, being the star he is, lightened the moment. He put his hand firmly on his hip, turned his left knee inward and hissed, 'Where's the fucking crown?' Hilarious!

Richard II was also the first time I actually got to work with Sir John Gielgud. Well, I say 'work with', but I only really got to share a scene with him once – but I did make sure that I made eye contact with him as I made my dramatic exit! That was a special moment I will never forget. He was playing John of Gaunt and made the classic 'sceptred isle' speech. I will never forget that either. I happened to be there on that day for something or other and was at a loose end, needing something to do. I found myself on the studio floor near Gielgud as he was making his way over to the set where he was to make that classic speech. He had to walk past the set for a bath-house scene in which the King's three minions, Bushey, Baggot and Green, were with the King in various stages of semi-nakedness as they shared a bathing moment. This scene is very often cut from stage productions, but here, at the BBC, it was included. Thank goodness it was, as it provided an opportunity for Gielgud to make one of his classic comments. He stopped as he passed, took a look at their lack of garb and, throwing his head back, emitted the unforgettable comment, 'Buttocks wouldn't melt in their mouths!' I was there for a classic Gielgudism!

He moved on to his own set where he was to make that famous speech and I, with nothing else to do, slipped into the gallery and sat at the back, out of the way, to watch him do it. He delivered it with typical Gielgud aplomb, at the end of which the man next to David Giles turned to him and said, 'Well, that's one for the archives.' It was indeed!

My next and, as it turned out, last encounter with the great man was in 1989 when I was asked by Roger Redfarn to appear in a one-off charity performance of *Mother Goose* at the Theatre Royal, Drury Lane. I was to be paired with Matthew Kelly as the Broker's Men for Donald Sinden's wicked squire. It was enormous fun, a high point of which was watching Sir John Gielgud wearing a costume that I myself had previously worn in another production of *Mother Goose* as the king of Gooseland, King Goosegog, doing a duet of the song 'Me and My Shadow' with none other than Elton John! Elton wore an enormous crinoline frock in silver fabric and looked amazing! He had worn it earlier in the show to sing 'There is Nothing Like a Dame' and kept it on throughout the show as he loved it. That's a special memory that I treasure!

My time in *Henry V* playing Corporal Nym was spent working closely with great actors like Bryan Pringle, Gordon Gostelow and the wonderful Brenda Bruce, who had played Nurse to Judy Buxton's Juliet at the RSC back in 1980. That in itself is worthy of great memories. Then, in *As You Like It*, I got to travel up to Glamis Castle in Scotland, birthplace of the late Queen Mother, where most of the play was filmed in that beautiful location. I played William, only in one scene as it happens, in which he attempts to pay court to Audrey and is forcibly seen off by Touchstone, played in this production by the incomparable James Bolam. We had such fun working on that scene together and laughed for hours afterwards. Great times for me!

During those three years, Elly's parents came down to see us as often as they could as they were potty about the kids. We were beginning to think about another move. The kids were growing, and the house wasn't really going to be big enough for much longer. I don't know who was first to mention it, but the idea came up of Elly's parents selling up and us doing the same and us all buying a bigger place that we could live in together. We all thought it was a brilliant wheeze, as I personally got on like a house on fire with my in-laws and had no reason to think anything other than that the scheme would work brilliantly. The plan was pursued, although Elly and her mother insisted from the start on having their own kitchens, otherwise it was not going to work – we all agreed to that! We also all thought it was important for everyone's independence to have separate living areas too, so we knew what we needed to look for. The search was on!

We didn't look too far afield as we wanted to stay around the same area. We viewed a few properties, but you never find what you want straight away. However, we eventually found something that appealed to all of us in another part of Hemel called Felden, just a mile or so away. It was an extended bungalow with three bedrooms and a bathroom upstairs in a lovely neighbourhood. The aspect was on either side of a central front door, which gave us two separate living areas and the prospect of a separate kitchen for Elly's mother. Perfect! There was also a massive ¾-acre garden at the back, which the kids took to immediately. Elly's father Harold, who was an avid gardener, couldn't wait to start work there!

There was a delay while Elly and I arranged another mortgage, which we got. Elly's parents were mortgage free on their own home and didn't want another, which we thought was fair as they were virtually at retirement age and we were young enough to carry that responsibility. Harold still worked independently, though, as a freelance machine tool consultant. After the usual 'will we, won't we?' doubts had come and gone, the move was made in the early part of 1979. I was called away to a job in Teesside, and as a result I got away with just sending a telegram to welcome us all to our new domicile. It was a bit of a lark as I went into the Billingham Post Office and filled in the telegram form. Then I was asked to 'Wait a moment, sir. I'll just go and consult my manager.' You see the telegram was to read, 'May the Bluebird of Happiness crap all over our new home!' I imagine there was some sort of protocol about sending mild profanities through the post. Ridiculous! Anyway, thankfully the chap came back out seconds later chuckling away, as the manager thought it was very appropriate and extremely funny. More to come!

A Sad One

As I have mentioned earlier, the time immediately after Lucy came into the world was not such a great one for me, professionally. I was unemployed for quite a while. Not fun. Well, it was during that time that Elly and I decided to go for another baby. We'd always wanted two children as, at that time with the population of the world on the increase, we thought it only moral and proper to have just two children to replace yourselves. That was our thinking at the time anyway! So we tried.

We were successful – or so we thought – as Elly became pregnant again. The time went by and we continued to have our fingers crossed for a successful outcome. She was about five or six months into the pregnancy when she started to get concerned as there was little or no movement going on inside. This coincided with a time when her parents had booked a trip to Sardinia for a holiday and wanted Elly and Lucy to go with them. I wasn't able to join them as something had come up – work, at last! So I couldn't say 'no'. It was agreed upon that I should stay behind and earn a bit of money, so off they all went without me.

When they came back, however, it had become very clear that something was seriously amiss. Elly wasn't experiencing any movement at all. She underwent various tests, but it was concluded that the baby was not alive. We had already decided that if the baby were a girl she would be called Susie, so she had already got a very clear identity in our hearts and minds.

The First Rule of Comedy..!

The next stage of the proceedings were very unpleasant, and almost unbearable for Elly, as she had to go into the maternity unit and be induced so she gave birth to our dead baby. It was apparently the only safe way to proceed at the time. I don't know if they do things differently now, but it seemed deeply unsympathetic and insensitive to me that she had to be on a maternity ward with other women who had their babies with them. Elly went through with the delivery and was, understandably, in serious distress. Worst of all was the fact that she never got to see Susie, who was whipped away as soon as she arrived. That I can understand, though.

It was a very traumatic experience for Elly, but the one thing we both wanted was a proper send-off for our stillborn daughter. We arranged a funeral and it took place at the Coventry Crematorium a short time later. I will never forget when the hearse arrived and the tiny little coffin was taken from it. The coffin was about twice the size of a shoebox with a beautiful cover of white quilting, and as the funeral director carried it into the chapel I had to fight off the urge to dash forward and take it from him. I would have loved to carry her in myself but knew it would not be seemly, so I gave her that final dignity of being in professional hands.

I often wondered what Susie would have looked like as she grew up, but Lucy, who is a very good artist, had a psychic experience and drew a wonderful sketch of this cheeky-faced little girl and told us that she came through to her and inspired that sketch! I also had an experience many years later when I went for a reading with a renowned psychic called Lee Van Zyl and she told me that there was a very small spiritual presence with me that had chosen to come back as a guardian angel. I often feel her presence and would love to think that she has always been there with me. I think she has and will always be with both her mother and me. It's a very comforting feeling to know that. Thank you, Susie!

THE FIRST RULE OF COMEDY...
DON'T ANTAGONISE YOUR AUDIENCE

Most Embarrassing Moment

It was in Plymouth in 2013 and we were doing a production of *Robin Hood* at the Theatre Royal. As was my custom, I was not wearing my glasses. I hardly ever did on stage. On the few rare occasions when I had to, I felt most peculiar being able to see people's faces clearly!

Well, Bobby Davro had given me a gag to do which involved talking to a man in the front row. You may already see where this is going ... I had to say to him, 'What's your name, sir?' To which he would tell me his first name. I would then say, 'Sorry?' And, of course, he would repeat it. I would then say, 'No, I heard you. I'm just sorry!' which usually got a big laugh from the audience.

On one particular day, I was scanning the front row with my limited vision prior to this gag for a likely male accomplice. It was a struggle on this occasion, but I eventually settled on an unwitting victim. The person I had selected was holding a toddler on their lap, which I thought might help. The moment came and I said, 'What's your name, sir?' Nothing. Total silence! I tried again but there was still no response. I got into the ad-libbing stage now and I don't remember what came out of my mouth, but as I was still getting no response, and the kids on stage behind me were beginning to find this all very amusing, at my expense, I started to get a bit cross. I leaned over and pointed, and almost shouted, 'You there, the man with the child on your lap! What's your name?' To which, after an embarrassing pause, a very faint and reluctant feminine voice uttered, 'Tracy' back to me. With my feeble vision I had selected a somewhat overweight lady and thought it was a man! I turned on my heels with 'Moving swiftly on …!' And continued with the rest of the scene feeling totally embarrassed and very sorry for Tracy!

Needless to say, I never did that gag again and in future pantos I wore my glasses! I was awarded the Golden Arrow Award for the most embarrassing moment at the wrap party at the end of the season. It was presented to me by a very amused Nigel Havers!

Going into *Run for Your Wife*

It was in the springtime of 1985 that theatrical impresario Paul Elliott first asked me to appear in *Run for Your Wife*, the brilliant stage farce by Ray Cooney. It had opened in 1982 at the Shaftesbury Theatre with Richard Briers and Bernard Cribbins in the main parts. I was very fortunate to perform *Run for Your Wife* with Bernard Cribbins later. What a wonderful actor, and what a lovely man! I'm not the first to say that and I know I won't be the last. He was something very special and, wonderfully, shared my attitude that comedy was a team sport. He once said, 'Look, Jeff. If I bend over and you kick me up the arse, we *both* share the laugh!' Bless him! Anyway, unsurprisingly with such a cast and such a great play, *Run for Your Wife* was going really well and had moved to The Criterion in Piccadilly Circus.

It was usual for the cast to be changed about every twelve weeks – nobody really wanted to do more than that as it was so physically demanding. As I had never seen it at this point, they asked me to go and see whether I wanted to do it. So off I went with Elly one evening to have a look-see!

Well, it turned out to be one of the cleverest pieces of theatre I had ever seen! It was about this London cabbie who lives a double life and has two wives in two different flats, one in Wimbledon and one in Streatham. The set was brilliantly designed by Douglas Heap and had one front door on one side of the stage and the other on the opposite side of the stage and a common central area which was used by both flats, very often at the same time. Brilliant! There was no doubt in my mind at all that I wanted to do it, particularly as the actor I was replacing as the taxi driver was so 'over the top' that I felt duty bound to go in and put it right. Rather arrogant of me, I know, but I remember turning to Elly at the end and saying, 'I've got to go and save this play!' My tongue is firmly in my cheek as I speak and the actor in question is still very much with us, and doing rather well too!

It was a very happy experience for me and I was playing opposite the wonderful Geoffrey Hughes, who had stayed on to do it with me. It turned out to be a great career move for me too, as I went back to do it at regular intervals for getting on for the next five years. This included a trip to Canada in 1988, when we went to the beautiful Vancouver Island for three weeks and played the McPherson Playhouse in the capital Victoria. We then took it on to Vancouver City on the mainland, where we played The Playhouse for the whole of the summer and had a glorious time! I even managed to get Elly to come over for a couple of weeks with Sam, who was 11 years old at the time. That was when I played opposite Brian Murphy as Stanley, and we have remained firm friends to this day. We were both asked to go straight back to The Criterion with it on our return to London.

The First Rule of Comedy..!

It turned out that I became what I then described as the 'itinerant' John Smith, which is the cabbie's name, as I usually took my costume home with me because it was basic and comfy and suited me fine. All the other actors playing the character were given their own anyway. There were several occasions when the phone rang and, having just finished a stint in London, I was asked to go and take over somewhere else, as whoever was playing John had become indisposed for one reason or another. On one of these occasions I was asked to replace Terry Scott for a couple of weeks in the summer production on Bournemouth Pier. Terry was off sick – again! – so I was off to Bournemouth like a shot. I loved that one as I was playing opposite the great Eric Sykes as Stanley. What a joy that was! You couldn't really mess with the play as Ray Cooney had honed and toned it so well that it was brilliant as written, so I found it no effort at all to step into another version of it.

That is, until the Les Dawson version came along. I had been home for only a few days after another Criterion visit when the phone rang and it was Paul Elliott's office to ask if I would go straight to the Orchard Theatre in Dartford that very night to play John in place of Peter Goodwright. It was a touring production, starring Les as Stanley. Peter Goodwright's father had died suddenly and Peter had been called away to Derbyshire to look after his mother – a quite acceptable reason for stepping down for a few days. This was on a Thursday and they wanted me to do the rest of the week. Off I went with my costume in its bag and I drove to Dartford in plenty of time for the evening show. I was there long before Les arrived with his wife Tracy and got settled in. I had met Les socially a couple of times but had never worked with him, and as he was one of my favourite funny men, I was very much looking forward to it!

Les was not only a brilliant comedian but a brilliant comedy writer. His erudition and intelligence in devising those wonderful, intricate, shaggy dog stories could have me rolling on the floor with laughter. It was that lugubrious face and the downtrodden Mancunian tones. Just brilliant. Les had first come to fame through

Opportunity Knocks, and then held court in the Yorkshire Television panel game *Jokers Wild* – an excuse to steal every episode with some brilliant gags! Les found his ideal domain as host on *Blankety Blank*. He once paid me a huge compliment on the show, on camera, when we did a *Hi-de-Hi!* special. As he approached me in the top-left seat, he said, quite unsolicited, 'Jeffrey Holland! A man who, by his very presence, gives this show some class!' I couldn't believe it! He hardly knew me, but that would soon change. His ability to ad-lib, and even make the scripted jokes sound like he made them up as he went along, was inspired!

However, you couldn't do that with *Run for Your Wife*. Like I said, you couldn't really mess with that wonderful Ray Cooney dialogue because it worked so well. I certainly had no qualms about that ... but I also had no experience of working with Les Dawson! What I didn't expect were the 'Dawsonisms' that accompanied some of the dialogue. There's a scene where John is trying to explain to Stanley why Barbara mustn't find out about Mary (the two wives) and he says, 'Who's Barbara?' To which I had to reply, 'She's a lady.' 'A lady?' says Stanley, to which John replies, 'Yes!' This time, instead of continuing with the conversation, Les just looked at me and pulled that funny little face he used for his character Cosmo Smallpiece, with the puckered-up lips, scrunched-up eyes and leery look.

Well, I'm proud of the fact that it is very difficult to make me 'corpse' on stage, but this was too much even for me! I had always loved the Cosmo character that Les had perfected over the years. Watching him on TV, he would make me howl with laughter! When I got that face, live, just inches away from me, I just dissolved into helpless giggles. The audience, knowing full well that I was a stand-in that night, fell in with the moment and started to roar with laughter. The more they laughed, and the more I laughed, the more Les laughed too. We were all standing there with our shoulders shaking for several minutes before I could pull myself together and continue! I have to tell you that there were four other separate occasions during that performance alone where Les had me in unlawful hysterics with his extra antics. It took me until the Saturday matinee before I was able to control myself sufficiently to ignore them!

Those performances of *Run for Your Wife* remain some of my happiest memories, and I followed the career of Les Dawson all the way. His books are both hilarious and poignant, and his TV appearances were always joyous. I remember seeing him on a chat show, grinning from ear to ear, when he was chatting about the birth of his daughter, Charlotte. He was so proud, so happy. Tragically, Les wouldn't live to see Charlotte grow up to be a fine, young woman. She was a babe-in-arms when Les died of a heart attack. He was just 62, and his death robbed his family of a loving husband and father, and all of us of a brilliantly funny man. Bless him, I loved Les Dawson and miss him very much!

Everyone who had been in a stage production of *Run for Your Wife* – and was still breathing! – was approached by Ray Cooney and darling Vicki Michelle, who were producers on the film version. Most were little fun cameos. Even Bernard Cribbins, as a hospital patient, and Richard Briers, as a man falling into a hedge, came back. All as a favour for Ray Cooney! The cast of comedy greats in that film is incredible, including a few notable performers like Frank Thornton and Bill Pertwee, for both of whom it was their final film appearance. Actually it was a slow fade out for Richard and Bernie too. I remember Ray saying to me after the film was completed that not one of 'the chums', as he called us all, had said 'no'. We all did it for him!

Frankie Howerd

Frankie Howerd was one of those conquering heroes from the Second World War, and when he returned to Civvy Street he became one of the greatest comedians of his day. To achieve this he had conquered a crippling nervous stutter. All those 'Ooh!' and 'Aah!' exclamations that he used to punctuate his funny stories with were there to give him time to pause and compose himself. His long and very amusing shaggy dog tales, mostly written for him by Eric Sykes, had made him a national sensation on the radio music-hall programme *Variety Band-Box*. This success notwithstanding, Frankie was always a frustrated actor. This, coupled with the roller-coaster course of his career, made him an extremely worried man. He was a bag of neuroses – a comedy hero who had no self-confidence whatsoever!

It was during one of his low ebbs, with the *Carry Ons* and *Up Pompeii!* many years behind him, that Frankie Howerd crossed my path.

For the 1979/80 pantomime season I was booked to do *Robinson Crusoe* at the Alexandra Theatre, Birmingham. It was starring Frankie Howerd, Anita Harris, Bernard Bresslaw and Tommy Trinder. Well, here's me with my mouth wide open! All of them were brilliant theatre people I wanted to meet and work with, and there was the added extra bonus of having the legendary Jack Tripp as Mrs Crusoe. His partner Allen Christie always worked with him in panto and was playing the ship's captain. In fact, most of that all-star cast had worked together in some capacity or other before, Frankie, Anita and Bernard in previous shows and in the film *Carry On Doctor*.

Tommy Trinder, of course, was a consummate old pro. A stand-up comedian you would discuss with bated breath! He was on a par with the Cheeky Chappie himself, Max Miller. Tommy was a wonder on stage – one of the greatest front-cloth comedians we have ever had. We were lucky people, for sure. I shared a dressing room with Trinder. I couldn't believe it! There were three of us in there: him, me and the boy playing Man Friday (Victor Osborne) – a very nice but rather posh lad whom Trinder couldn't resist taking the mickey out of.

The First Rule of Comedy..!

Tommy didn't have a spot as such. He did a balloon-modelling act as 'Uncle Tommy', making animals for the kids. Also there was a scene that included the good old 'busy bee' routine with me. Now, I have always been a stickler for the script with no deviations. It's how I work and I wasn't used to the ad-lib ability of someone like Trinder. But it was, after all, what made him the great comedian he was.

One night we were halfway through the 'busy bee' when someone near the front shouted something that Tommy picked up on. He started a bit of banter with this chap in the audience while I stood by and just watched. I was forgotten and Trinder was back where he loved being – chatting to his audience. This went on for a few minutes, much to my frustration, until, finding what I thought was a suitable moment, I volunteered, 'Now, where were we?' hoping to get him back into the routine with me. Big mistake! He turned on me with words to the effect of 'Don't interrupt me, son! I was doing this before you were a twinkle in your father's eye!' It didn't stop there and I was feeling really embarrassed, and smaller and smaller. I wanted the ground to swallow me! The great Trinder was in his element and my lack of experience was showing. I never did it again, though, and despite my faux pas, he continued to be really good company in that dressing room.

He told me so many stories of his early days, one of which I remembered and it is now part of my play, *...And This Is My Friend Mr Laurel*. At the 1947 *Royal Variety Performance*, Tommy was in the wings standing next to Laurel and Hardy, who were waiting to go on. The organiser, Val Parnell (he has become the Stage Manager in my play), was there too and Babe Hardy commented on the rather dead and unresponsive audience, who, in their finery, were really only there to be seen. Babe said, 'They're a bit quiet here tonight, aren't they?' to which Parnell replied, 'Oh yes. They're always quiet here on a Monday.' This was a reference to the fact that they always did the *Royal Variety* at the Palladium on a Monday night for technical reasons. Babe just looked at him, not really understanding, but I put that anecdote in the play and, if I play it right, it usually gets a laugh. Thanks, Tom!

Now, back to Frankie Howerd! He was playing Billy Crusoe and all the comedy burden of the show was on him. His insecurity soon became apparent as rehearsals got under way. Roger Redfarn was directing and, as was his wont, he surrounded himself with people he felt he could rely on to get the best results. I'm happy to say this included me, since my foray into *Dad's Army* and all things David Croft! Some of Frankie's scenes were with support from me, and as rehearsals progressed, I managed to gain his confidence and, eventually, Frankie started to look to me for help.

There was a scene after the shipwreck where he entered on to a beach to proclaim all was lost. Frankie being Frankie, he would really milk this scene for some hilarious mock dramatics. He thought he should come on singing the *Desert Island Discs* theme.

'Oh!' said I. 'You mean "A Sleepy Lagoon"?'

'If that's what it's called!' he said and promptly sang the title to the opening bars. 'We need a rhyme,' he said, and I quickly came up with 'A spotty baboon'. 'Brilliant!' he said. 'I'm going to have to watch you. You'll be after my job!' Little did he know then that I was also his understudy and that scenario was not far away!

On went the rehearsal period and I was going to and fro from home in Hemel Hempstead, where my daughter had returned from school one day with chickenpox. I thought no more about it until, a few days into the run, I started to feel decidedly unwell and noticed a couple of spots on my face that should not have been there. Apart from my understudy duties, I didn't have a huge amount to do. My duties didn't extend much beyond just a couple of pirate-type characters which they could cover quite easily. So I was packed off home for at least a week until my bout of chickenpox subsided. It was rather fortunate for me, as I was able to watch the pilot episode of *Hi-de-Hi!* when it was aired on 1 January 1980. I would have missed it otherwise!

The First Rule of Comedy..!

After about a week or so, I was clearly better from the chickenpox and so I returned to the show to pick up my 'pirate' duties, one of which was a comedy fight with Frankie. This stage battle royale ended with me putting a hat on his head. It was a jokey prop hat with a false axe in it, but to the audience it looked as if he'd copped it through his head. Very funny visually but, for some reason, every time I dragged him into the wings to stand him up, he found some reason to tell me that I had done it wrong! He did this every single time we did the scene and I managed to shrug it off and not let it bother me, as I knew how insecure he could be. It's sometimes best to keep shtum!

On we went into the New Year and it wasn't long before disaster struck – well, not for me as it happened. I was staying at my mother's flat in nearby Walsall where we grew up, and one day I set off to catch the train as usual to get to Birmingham, which was only half an hour away. It was late afternoon, as there was no matinee on that particular day, and I ensconced myself in the train. It was an old-fashioned model of train, with single straight-across compartments with no corridor. Off we went and before long we ground to a halt about three stops away from Birmingham New Street.

Thinking we would set off again soon, I tried not to get concerned. There was no way to communicate with anyone – of course we didn't have mobile phones then. But nothing happened and it soon became obvious that I was going to be late. I worked out that they would have decided to cover my first couple of entrances, but I was still hoping to be on the move soon.

To cut a long wait short, the train did trundle off again, albeit ever so slowly, and we arrived at New Street Station at 7.15 p.m. The curtain had gone up at 7 p.m. Well, I don't think I have ever run so fast in my life! I flew down the road and into Station Street where the stage door was, only to find Michael Bullock, the theatre manager, waiting white-faced by the door. I thought I was in deep doo-doo now and apologised profusely, explaining that the train had been stuck on frozen points.

'Never mind that!' he said. 'You're on for Frankie! Didn't you know?'

Well, of course I didn't know. I'd been stuck in an isolated train for the last hour and a half! Apparently Michael had phoned my mother, who told him I'd set off at the usual time but there was no way to get to me. It was the first icy snowfall of the winter and Frankie had set off that morning to his local shop for something and skidded and fallen on the ice. He'd fractured his hip and of course was out of the show altogether.

I went into the theatre in a complete mess, not even knowing which dressing room to go to, his or mine! With a lot of help from those around me, I got into his costume and made my way to the stage to make my entrance as Billy Crusoe. I remember saying to the audience, 'Ladies and gentlemen, this must be as big a shock to you as it is to me!' which got me a laugh and on we went into a somewhat potted version of our normal show. I remember at the interval being told that we would be cutting this and that and so forth, all of which I was delighted to hear as I was still in nightmare mode! We did, as I said, a rather much shorter version of the show, and when I went to the bar afterwards for a much-needed drink, who should be there but John Thaw and Sheila Hancock. Sadly, neither of them said a word to me. I can only imagine they were there to see Frankie and were bitterly disappointed!

I was brought in early the next day, and what I was and was not expected to do was all worked out. Everyone, it seems, was secretly pleased with what had happened as they all went up the bill a notch and Anita Harris got the song-sheet back. I was no threat to anyone and was now getting more money too. It was a very happy show after that!

I've often wondered how many people out front that evening had seen the first *Hi-de-Hi!* go out, and had made the connection that that silly Spike Dixon was also that silly Billy Crusoe. It was too early in the show's popularity for me to be shouting out 'Hi-de-Hi!' all the time and getting the expected response.

As a turning point in my career, that rather unhappy pantomime becoming a very happy job was a pivotal moment.

Bernard Bresslaw

One of the greatest elements of that pantomime with Frankie Howerd was that it was my first meeting with the gorgeously lovable Bernard Bresslaw – or Bernie, as we all called him. He was very philosophical about the fame that the *Carry Ons* had secured him – like I became with the fame that came with *Hi-de-Hi!* Bernie was a very accomplished stage actor, who could play Shakespeare with the same consummate ease as he could play a Ray Cooney farce. The *Carry Ons* had given him great marquee value for summer season and panto too, of course, and he relished it!

In this particular production of *Robinson Crusoe* in Birmingham, Bernie was playing Blackbeard the Pirate. His flamboyant and elaborate costume included very high-heeled boots and a very tall hat so that, on top of his own 6 feet 7 inches, he looked about 8 feet tall! As part of my process of taking over from Frankie's lead comic role, I had quite a lot of very funny scenes with Bernie. He was wonderful. So charming and calm and helpful. Discussing Frankie's bits and pieces in the panto with Bernie made the transition so much easier than it could have been with a less gentle man.

Frankie had a scene with Bernie where he, Frankie as Billy, came on stage dressed in a silly drag outfit, much to the audience's delight. As the scene progressed, Bernie, as the baddie, tried to hypnotise him as this 'fair maiden'. Of course, it all went wrong!

Jack Tripp, who was playing Mrs Crusoe as the dame, took exception to me taking over this scene as he claimed that, since I wasn't a professional drag artiste, I shouldn't be allowed to do it. Jack was doubly miffed because, as the show was overrunning, they had already cut some of his own drag routines, which he was very good at. To his great credit – and quite rightly being a little self-concerned too – Bernie came back and said he wanted that scene kept in, as he was getting some great laughs in it. I was in the middle of this debate, understanding both points of view but keeping quiet. In the end Bernie won and the drag scene stayed in, and we both thoroughly enjoyed it and got plenty of laughs between us! Jack relented eventually, seeing the sense of it, and was very helpful and supportive to me after that, for which I was very thankful.

I don't think I met Bernie Bresslaw again until I did my second term in *Run for Your Wife*, at The Criterion, during Christmas 1985. He was playing Detective Sergeant Porterhouse, one of the two policemen. He was perfect in the role as it was quite a sympathetic character compared to the other one, DS Troughton, played with a hard edge by Paul Darrow, still very well known at the time as the villainous Kerr Avon in the science-fiction TV series *Blake's 7*, which had been on until 1981 and had secured Paul long-lasting cult stardom.

During this particular production of *Run for Your Wife*, there was an unforgettable moment one night when Bernie missed an entrance. Geoff Hughes had a scene where, having had a row with me and one of the wives, he had to make his way towards the front door, only to be stopped in his tracks by Porterhouse, Bernie, who comes straight in. Well, Geoff took the first of the two steps he usually took before the door was opened by Bernie. In this move, Bernie is supposed to force Geoff back down behind the sofa, where he puts a wastepaper basket over his head so as not to be recognised. It sounds silly out of context, but in the action of the play it's hilarious.

But – no Bernie! Geoff had no choice but to continue walking towards the door – still no Bernie! Geoff reached the door, opened it – no Bernie! Geoff went off through the door, leaving me and Serretta Wilson, who was playing Barbara, glaring at each other.

The First Rule of Comedy..!

What to do? I had a flash of inspiration which involved me leaving the stage for a moment – something I have been known to do before when things have gone wrong! So I said to Serretta, 'You go and put the kettle on, darling. I'll see what's going on!'

Thinking she would go off stage left, into the kitchen, I left the stage through the door after Geoff, only to find him in a complete flap as Bernie still hadn't appeared. He started to tell me to go back on, but he never finished the sentence as I cut him off with, 'I'm not going back on there!'

Just at that moment a very sweaty Bernie arrived in the wings, still wearing his glasses, which he, like me, didn't wear on stage. Placing them hastily in his pocket, he apologised, saying, 'Sorry, I was chatting!' He had simply lost concentration momentarily. It's a 'first rule of comedy' that even Jimmy Perry and David Croft didn't give us: never lose your concentration!

Anyway we decided I would go back on, followed by Geoff and then Bernie, and we could then pick up where we'd left off. I went back on and, thinking Serretta would be off stage left in the kitchen, shouted, 'Darling, I'm back!'

She replied from the opposite side of the stage in the bedroom, 'I'm in here!' Serretta had very wisely anticipated her next exit, which was into the bedroom. All was resumed and we managed to rescue the scene and carry on – so to speak!

Bernie Bresslaw played Porterhouse a few more times with me after that, most notably in the Canada run in mid-1988, when his wife Liz and my wife Elly, both on a visit, struck up a very close friendship. Bernie was a delightful and loving man. Honestly, if you only know him from his brilliant, very versatile performances in the *Carry On* films or, for comedy fans with longer memories, his slow-witted Private 'Popeye' Popplewell from the Granada Television sitcom *The Army Game*, with his mournful cry of 'I only arsked!', believe me you have no idea just how good an actor he was. He has been greatly missed in the thirty or so years since he passed away suddenly, while he was playing Grumio in *Taming of the Shrew* at the Open Air Theatre in Regent's Park. Part of me knows that he would have wanted to go out, still working, and playing in one of the bard's most fun and funny plays ... just too soon, Bernie. Much too soon!

Panto with Ken Dodd

After the success of taking over from Frankie Howerd in the 1979/80 panto *Robinson Crusoe*, I was asked back the next year to appear in *Dick Whittington* as King Rat and to understudy Ken Dodd. How can you understudy Ken Dodd? By Jove, Missus! The fact is, I decided, you don't. You can't! What you do instead is understudy Ken's character, Idle Jack. It would have been virtually impossible to go on, really, as apart from a couple of front-cloth spots on his own, he only did a handful of scenes with other actors. These could be covered quite easily, but then he finished the show with a fifty-minute spot on his own!

The curtain was due to come down at 10 p.m., and knowing how long Doddy could go on and on and on, the management insisted that if he did overrun by even one minute he would be personally responsible for the band's overtime, the children's extra licence fees and the taxi fares for the usherettes' journeys home. All on him! Now, this was before Ken's much-publicised legal battle with the tax man – which he cannily incorporated into his act, which got even longer as a result! – but he certainly wasn't going to cut his routine. His integrity as a performer had always been that his public expected to get their money's worth and, by Jove, with Ken they really did!

During this run of *Dick Whittington*, Ken finished his final spot by one minute to ten every single night. Annie, his long-term partner, and now Lady Dodd, was in the wings every night to give him the 'thumbs up' when the time was up.

The First Rule of Comedy..!

One thing about Doddy was that he found it very difficult to part with money. There was an occasion early on in the run – it was dress rehearsal week actually, when we were all in the bar on a break. Something came over him and he asked the barman to get drinks all round for all the cast members who were there. Later on, we heard, he cornered the barman and accused him of ripping him off as the round he bought came to just over £10. That was quite a realistic price as it happened, but the very next day he had a barrel of lager, complete with air pump, installed in his dressing room and for the rest of the run he was never seen in the bar again!

I had introduced Doddy to Elly at some point during the run of *Dick Whittington*, and when he realised she was a costume maker, that clever brain of his knew he might be able to save a few quid. You see, it turned out that he wanted to replace most of the Diddy Men costumes. These little fellas from the Jam Buttie mines of Knotty Ash were a very popular part of Ken's comedy, particularly at panto time. Moreover, these merchandising man's dreams were Ken's own personal copyright property.

The little Diddy Men – a great hit with the little ones in the auditorium – wore colourful costumes for the various songs in the show. Well, Ken asked Elly to give him a quote to run off these costumes. She went away, did her sums, and came back with a rock-bottom price which barely covered her costs. The reason was she really wanted to make those costumes for Doddy! Quite understandably, she thought it would be a wonderful assignment to add to her curriculum vitae.

Doddy listened patiently to Elly's budget and then, very calmly, told her to go away and come back with what he called a sensible price for the job! She came to me and burst into tears as she was really shocked that Ken could be so mean. Needless to say, she didn't end up making the costumes.

I did reassure Elly that this was just Ken's way, though, and not to be too hurt about it. In the end, I think he stuck with those tatty old Diddy Men clothes for years afterwards. Nobody seemed to mind, and Ken saved a few bob – even the tiny charge that Elly had suggested.

This mild debacle certainly didn't affect my working relationship with Doddy, either on stage or off. In fact, during that lovely panto run in Birmingham, I had got quite pally with him. One day the subject of vocal wear and tear came up. Ken told me he was suffering from fatigue of the vocal cords. His voice was giving him cause for concern.

Well, as you know, I trained in Birmingham at the college we knew as Chappie's in Edgbaston, named thus after its principal, Pamela Chapman. I suggested that, if he was interested, I could take him there to seek advice from the great lady herself, who was adept at voice production – the correct way. Ken was happy to agree to this, so I got in touch and arranged an appointment for him. I met him one morning at the Holiday Inn where he and Annie were staying and we got a cab to Chappie's.

Sadly, Chappie herself had retired due to ill health but her daughter, Patsy Yardley, was then in charge, and she was just as adept as her mother had been. I made the introductions and then made myself scarce, catching up with my old college, which was very nice. The session went well and I brought Ken back for a second visit the following week ... at his request, I must say.

Patsy was a hit. The result was that Ken's talking technique was deemed faulty, in as much as he used his throat for effect and consequently put a strain on the vocal cords. However, when he sang, his technique was flawless, as he was producing the sounds from his diaphragm, which was the very method we had been taught. I was very pleased to have been able to provide support for the great man. It was something the college was able to be proud of too. What a legacy!

I mentioned that, as well as attempting to understudy the great Doddy, I was asked to play the part of King Rat, the baddie, in this show. I had jumped at the chance! You see, the first series of *Hi-de-Hi!* had been made that previous autumn but had not yet

The First Rule of Comedy..!

been screened. The pilot episode had gone out a year earlier, to huge success and interest, of course – it was a David Croft product! I was well aware that, as soon as the series was out in the wild, if you follow me, the panto producers would want me to capitalise on the fact that I would be recognised as Spike off the telly. The chance to play the baddie had never come my way before, so I jumped at it as I knew this would be my last chance. From now on, it would be the dame or the silly comic. Lovely!

I got the head of our make-up at the BBC, Jill Hagger, to help me devise make-up that would be suitable for the role of King Rat and we came up with a cracker! Dear reader, my archive of theatrical mementos includes a photograph of me in this costume, included in the photo section. We'll pause for a moment for you to find it and have a lingering look. There! Done? Great, wasn't it? Anyway, for those who are still reading, my King Rat involved a lot of silver paint and black eyeliner. It was really dramatic!

It was fortunate that we had a canteen backstage at the Alexandra Theatre, as I could not go out between shows with that face on – much the same as when I was playing the dame years later. I was trapped in the dressing room for the interval, and unfortunately for me, one of my dressing-room companions brought his cat in every day as he had nowhere else to put it, complete with litter tray! The cat was very well behaved but decided to use the litter tray just as we came up from the canteen with our food. The smell was really unbearable, to say the least, so I took to sitting on the landing outside the door to eat my dinner. Well, one day Annie, Doddy's partner, came across the landing and saw me sitting there, dressed as a rat, eating, and asked me what was going on.

'There's a cat in there!' I said, nodding at my dressing room door, and off she went with a giggle!

I found out later that she had told Doddy what had been said and he quoted this back to me years later, when we met again, as one of the funniest things he had ever heard. Maybe I should have put it in the show. Actually, I'm surprised Doddy didn't. He collected jokes like lads used to collect cigarette cards!

Despite the occasional ups and downs, needless to say, it was an experience of a lifetime working with that man – a comedy genius to put it mildly. Ken Dodd was probably the greatest 'clown' this country has ever produced. His work ethos and the palpable joy he got from making people laugh never, ever left him. He was working until the very end, at the age of 90, and I must say, those many, many times I watched him from the wings, which I did every night, are something I will never forget as long as I live!

Third Time Lucky

While we were doing the *Dad's Army* stage show at the Shaftesbury Theatre in 1975, I was thrilled, along with everyone else, to be told that we had been asked by the office of Lord Bernard Delfont to bring a short version of 'The Floral Dance' – with which we closed Act One of the show – to the *Royal Variety Performance* at the London Palladium. Needless to say, everyone was over the moon at the prospect, not least of all me. I remember Pamela Cundell, who played Mrs Fox, getting quite tearful about it!

The *Royal Variety Performance* that year was one of the busiest that there could have been and starred people like Charles Aznavour, Telly Savalas, Bruce Forsyth, Vera Lynn and Harry Secombe … not to mention the Count Basie Orchestra, the cast of *Billy*, starring Michael Crawford, and the KwaZulu company!

The veteran cast of *Dad's Army* – and me – may have been chuffed to bits to join such an impressive roll-call of talent, but, to a man, they were respected and loved as equally as the rest. The excitement really started to mount when we were told that the *Dad's Army* segment would come as part of the finale of the show. Crumbs!

The First Rule of Comedy..!

However, the debacle arose when the magnitude of this starry cast proved impossible to accommodate. There was simply not enough dressing-room space for all the shows! As a result, we of the *Dad's Army* company, along with the cast of *Billy*, were housed in the Marlborough pub opposite the stage door in Carnaby Street. We were all called to stand by in the wings for the big finish, which was quite unbelievably crowded! Arthur Lowe found himself with Bill Pertwee on his left and a lovely KwaZulu lady on his right. She was topless and was breast-feeding her baby. In typical Arthur Lowe style, he caught sight of this and, with a big double-take, looked down at her and said, 'He likes a drink, does he?' Well, Bill Pertwee dined out on that story for years, and I thought it was worth a mention here too. Arthur could be wonderfully witty and dry ... unlike the baby. Anyway, moving on!

Back to the actual performance. We were given our cue, and we were sent from the wings on stage right, across to stage left, to fill up from there. I was fairly ahead of the others and, because of all the pushing and shoving, ended up right in the wings on stage left and couldn't see the royal box at all. My national anthem was sung in the prompt corner! Because of the vast number of turns appearing that night, only the principals of the *Dad's Army* cast were lined up to meet the Queen. The rest of us were all dismissed to get changed. I was *so* disappointed, I can tell you, but what else could I do? I thought, 'There has to be another time.' Well, there was!

In 1983 the *Royal Variety Performance* was staged, not at the London Palladium, because they were experiencing technical difficulties there, but at the Theatre Royal, Drury Lane.

The *Hi-de-Hi!* company was invited to make a guest appearance in the show. Twiggy and Tommy Tune were appearing in the George Gershwin musical *My One and Only* in the West End at the time, and the number they did from it involved a lot of splashing of water on the stage. We were asked to come on after a front-cloth was dropped, all carrying mops, to clean up to the sound of our theme song. This we all did with great aplomb and to a rapturous reception from the audience! The Queen was in the royal box with Prince Philip on stage right and, knowing they never watched much TV, I thought she would probably be thinking, 'Who the dickens are these people?' Still, even if she thought we were real stagehands, it was a very funny moment. For everybody!

That fun notwithstanding, the great joy of the show for me was that it was compered by the great Gene Kelly. He was the perfect choice given the musical theme of the show. I'm hoping that the name Gene Kelly will be familiar to even the youngest of readers, but just in case you don't know, Gene Kelly was the master of the film musical and, quite arguably, the greatest dancer ever to work in Hollywood – apart from Fred Astaire, of course! For the uninitiated, do please search out such wonderful MGM musicals as *An American in Paris*, *On the Town* and *Singin' in the Rain*. Sheer celluloid heaven! Anyway, during a break in rehearsals I got to meet Mr Kelly in the middle of the stage and shook his hand. I'm delighted, and not a little relieved, to say he was charm itself to me. Everything I could have hoped he would be. What a coup!

Anyway, come the finale, we were all crowded together on the stage, much like before when I had been on parade with *Dad's Army*. But because this particular *Royal Variety Performance* had a strong musical theme, everyone apart from us had been told that they were to do a time-step when the curtain went up. Well, we were totally unaware of these instructions because we'd had to remain in our bus outside, as dressing room space was again at a premium. Imagine being in the middle of a crowded stage and suddenly everyone starts to dance! Well, we managed to bob up and down a bit as our feet couldn't be seen, so we got away with it. Then came the presentation to Her Majesty and this time I *was* one of the principals. During the time it took the royal party to get from their box to the stage, an almighty scrum began to grab the best places and Ruth Madoc, Paul Shane and I managed to get together. However, in the ensuing few moments, I found myself elbowed back into the second row, leaving Paul and Ruth in front

The First Rule of Comedy..!

of me in pole position. There was no way I could squeeze back in, so I had to watch as the Queen and Duke passed by without even a fleeting glance at me. It had happened again!

'I'm not giving up,' I thought, 'there *will* be another time' – and, amazingly, I was right!

So on to 1990. Back at the London Palladium, and because it was the Queen Mother's 90th birthday they decided that the show would be called 'The Queen Mother's 90th Birthday Gala'. The theme, this time, was musical shows again, but taking one from each of her ninety years of life. We started with 'Tell Me, Pretty Maiden' from *Florodora*, which was from 1900, the year of her birth. There was a small ensemble of names asked to do this one. Having recently appeared in a musical piece in a TV telethon, I was asked by Norman Maen, the choreographer, with whom I had worked on that telethon, to be part of that number for the Queen Mother. I was thrilled – a feeling that escalated when my dance partner turned out to be Anneka Rice! We did the song and it went down really well, which was a relief. It was *such* a strong line-up that year, concluding with a selection of music from Andrew Lloyd Webber's *Phantom of the Opera*, sung by Sarah Brightman.

Well, that year the presentation to the royal party was *so* well organised that I couldn't believe my luck when, because we were the first song in the show, we were the first to get to meet Her Majesty the Queen Mother! Anneka was on my left in first place with me next. When the theatrical impresario and head man at the Palladium at the time, Louis Benjamin, brought Her Majesty through the pass door to the stage, she was just a few feet from us. At that moment she stumbled and I thought she was going to fall. Thankfully, she didn't! She had seen a piece of white tape on the floor and thought it was a step, but it wasn't, so she recovered and came over towards us. Anneka was presented to her and then it was my turn. This was 19 July and her actual birthday wasn't until 4 August so, as she reached for my hand, I said to her, 'I hope you have a very happy birthday, Ma'am!' to which she instantly and

Don't Antagonise Your Audience

without hesitation replied, 'Thank you so much.' Then she moved on, but I was rapt with joy!

And it wasn't over yet. As if to make up for my previous bad luck, who should follow on but Her Majesty the Queen herself! You see, it had been a family affair and the royal box was full. As I was presented to Her Majesty, I couldn't help myself and, because it was a very warm evening, I said, 'It was very hot tonight, Ma'am. Was it hot where you were?' meaning, of course, the royal box. Well, unlike with her dear mother, there was an icy moment you could have cut with a knife. I had broken protocol! I thought, 'Oh no! That's me in the Tower!' I needn't have worried, though, because she recovered and replied, 'Yes, it was very warm.' As she moved on, I was then confronted by Prince Philip, and bringing up the rear was Princess Margaret, who said quite voluntarily, 'She's had a wonderful evening!', meaning, of course, her dear mother who loved musical theatre.

So there you have it. After two bitter disappointments, I was dealt a full house. I'd had to wait fifteen years but it was a day I will never forget – and it really was third time lucky!

Mom and Dad's wartime wedding day: 15 April 1944. The family line-up is (standing) Sam Parkes Snr, Joe Hope, Dad, Mom, Frank Harrison, (sitting) Emily Parkes, Clara Partridge, Betty Harrison and Rose Harrison.

The happy day when the gorgeous Judy Buxton became Mrs Parkes, 19 September 2004. Twenty years on … and we are still smiling.

The first taste of a holiday camp for 'Little Spike'! Little wonder my mom and dad are looking so happy. My brother was conceived during that holiday.

Playing Spike for the *Hi-de-Hi!* finale of *Dick Whittington* at the Grand Theatre, Wolverhampton, for the 2019/20 season. Little did we know that theatres would be dark soon after, and I've vowed this will be my last panto. Oh yes it is!

As King Rat in *Dick Whittington* at the Alexandra Theatre, Birmingham, in 1980/81. This was the last time I could do panto with full greasepaint disguise. After *Hi-de-Hi!* the audience wanted to see the face they recognised.

My Coventry pantomime performances all became known as 'Freckles', at least within the company, for obvious reasons. By the time of *Babes in the Wood*, in 1973, the number of freckles had inspired a sweepstake.

Alan Bates and myself in *The Mayor of Casterbridge*, in 1977. Or 'Two Elvis Presley Fans Do Thomas Hardy'!

My first involvement with the wonderful world of David Croft and Jimmy Perry: me with the hilarious Bill Pertwee, moonlighting as a couple of German soldiers in the *Dad's Army* stage show, in 1975.

James Bolam and myself in *As You Like It*, in 1978. Or 'A Couple of Likely Lads Do William Shakespeare'!

Quite simply, the happiest times of my professional life were with Paul Shane. Dear Shaney. We are here as Ted and Spike in *Hi-de-Hi!*, of course. The comedy gift that keeps on giving.

'Don't Tell Him Pikes!' Or 'Don't Tell Him Pike and Spike!' With Ian Lavender at the Grand Order of Water Rats Ball in 2015. It's no exaggeration to say we both owed David Croft and Jimmy Perry an awful lot.

As pompous footman James Twelvetrees in *You Rang, M'Lord?*: another smash-hit comedy from David Croft and Jimmy Perry, and one I'm extremely proud of.

As the officious railway station master Mr Parkin from *Oh, Doctor Beeching!* Oh, how I wish I could have played him for at least one more series ... or two ... or three!

The original line-up for David Croft and Jimmy Perry's *Hi-de-Hi!*, with Ruth Madoc, Simon Cadell and Paul Shane. All very much loved and very much missed by me ... and millions of fans.

With the brilliant cast of *You Rang, M'Lord?*: (standing) Donald Hewlett, Catherine Rabett, Susie Brann, Michael Knowles, Paul Shane, Su Pollard, Me, Bill Pertwee, Perry Benson, (sitting) Mavis Pugh, Brenda Cowling and Barbara New. What a company!

The amazing Russ Abbot surrounded by his Madhouse repertory company. *Clockwise from bottom left:* Sherrie Hewson, Bella Emberg, Les Dennis, Russ, Dustin Gee, yours truly and Susie Blake.

Recreating the wireless madhouse of *The Goon Show* in *Goon Again*, with Jon Glover, as Spike Milligan; Ray Ellington's son Lance Ellington; Sir Harry's son Andrew Secombe; our brilliant and esteemed producer Dirk Maggs; operatic singer and stooge Lizzie Glassborow; me, standing in for Peter Sellers; Christopher Timothy, handling the announcing duties of his late father Andrew Timothy; Harry Pitch, contributing harmonica in place of Max Geldray; and maestro John Wilson.

Probably my proudest achievement on the stage. Bringing my comedy hero, Stan Laurel, back to life for the solo show *...And This Is My Friend Mr Laurel*.

Talking to an imaginary Babe Hardy in his sick bed, in *...And This Is My Friend Mr Laurel*. So, a two-hander solo show, if you will. Why, certainly!

Aladdin, at the Birmingham Hippodrome for the 2010/11 season, was billed as 'The UK's Biggest Panto!' Oh yes it was! Jeremy Fontanet was the Sultan of Morocco; Lukus Alexander was the Cat; Julian Clary was the Spirit of the Bells; Joan Collins and Nigel Havers were Queen and King Rat. My dame Felicity Fitzwarren is next to Catherine Rooney as Alice, while special guest Keith Harris, aided by Orville the Duck, was the Rat Catcher.

With the incredible superstar and lovely person Joan Collins, out of our panto guises and in our civvies.

A happy way for Mr and Mrs Parkes to spend Christmas together. Do a pantomime! Judy is the elfin Fairy Organic – very green – and I was giving my Dame Trott, in *Jack and the Beanstalk*, at the Palace Theatre, Newark, for the 2008/09 season.

Carry On Cruising. Judy and I enjoying the 'Formal Night' on board. Don't we scrub up well?!

My dear friend Robert Ross and I, checking our diaries. We'll be coming to a venue near you … soon.

'Triple Velvet' in Victoria Wood's *Talent*, in 2009. Here I am flanked by Eugene O'Hare and Mark Curry.

Completing the sitcom connection as René, opposite Vicki Michelle reprising her role of Yvette, in the 2008 stage tour of David Croft and Jeremy Lloyd's *'Allo 'Allo*.

Family time: with son Sam, grandson Tom, and Judy.

With my grandchildren Harvey and Gracey.

A 2010 charity lunch in my honour: (standing) Yvonne Marsh, Nikki Kelly, Paul Shane, David Croft, Donald Hewlett, (sitting) Perry Benson, Susie Brann, that Jeffrey Holland, Su Pollard and Vicki Michelle. How thrilled was I!

THE FIRST RULE OF COMEDY...
NEVER TELEGRAPH A JOKE

Arthur Lowe and the Birth of My Son

You should never telegraph a joke, it's true ... but telegraph news of a birth? Maybe ... or phone? Let me explain. As we saw at my first and very near miss with royalty, at the 1975 *Royal Variety Performance*, Arthur Lowe — the mercurial Captain Mainwaring while I was touring in *Dad's Army* — could be a man of ready wit. But Arthur could also be pithy and petulant!

My son Sam was born on 15 July 1976 at 2.30 a.m., but the day before I was in Richmond doing a matinee of *Dad's Army* when I got the news that Elly had gone into labour, and I got it just as we were about to do the finale! I was called to the backstage phone and just had time to take the call from my mother-in-law. Elly had gone for a routine check-up and had been told that she was in labour. So they whipped her into the maternity unit straight away. As you will remember, Elly had a very delicate history of pregnancy, having miscarried just after we were married. Then she nearly lost Lucy in 1972. Thankfully, everything worked out with Lucy, but then she had the still birth in 1974, so it was always going to be a touch-and-go situation.

The First Rule of Comedy..!

My mind was in turmoil as I took the curtain call. What should I do? I knew the show was important, but in my heart I also knew where I needed to be. My two roles were covered: Private Walker was being understudied by Kevin Hubbard, while the German inventor would be played by John Conroy ... so I had a quick word with both lads on my way to the dressing room and said that I was legging it to Coventry because my wife had gone into labour. They were both very understanding, of course, and, in my haste, I asked whether they would kindly please tell the company manager, Tony Cundell.

After I had changed out of my Second World War garb, I raced through to Richmond Station and there was a Waterloo train waiting for me. 'This bodes well,' I thought, and we got to Waterloo in fifteen minutes, whereupon I dashed to the Tube to head to Euston. A train came straight in and again I was whisked up to Euston in no time at all. Running up to the main line, I found a Coventry train just about to leave and couldn't believe my luck. 'Someone is looking after me,' I thought!

I got to Coventry and ran to the taxi rank, where a couple of people were waiting, and I blurted something out about my wife being in labour and would they mind if I jumped the queue? They were very understanding and, within seconds, I was in the next taxi on my way to Walsgrave Hospital. I worked it out that my journey from the Richmond Theatre to the hospital had taken just over two hours. Incredible! I was there just after 7 p.m. I might not have bothered so much if I had known that the baby wouldn't actually arrive until half past two in the morning – but I was there.

In the end, there were problems and I was very glad that I was there, as Elly had quite a difficult birth and needed a blood transfusion afterwards. My friend, our local GP, Louis Kelman, had joined me at the bedside earlier in the evening and was a great comfort to both of us. He came home with me after we had said goodnight to

Never Telegraph a Joke

Elly and the new baby, and we promptly opened a bottle of scotch to wet the proverbial head! It wasn't long, though, before he left for home and I went to bed, exhausted but very happy.

The following day was a Friday. I paid a visit to the hospital before making my way back to Richmond for the evening show. When I got there, I went to get my key and found a note in my pigeon hole: 'Mr Lowe would like to see you in his dressing room.'

'Oh dear,' I thought. 'This does not bode well!' But I made my way to Arthur's room and knocked on the door.

'Come in,' came the gruff reply, so in I went.

Now you have to know that, by this time in his life, Arthur Lowe had become Captain Mainwaring and Captain Mainwaring had become Arthur Lowe. The two personae had amalgamated completely! He was sitting at the other end of the room, at a mirror at 90 degrees to me, and was brushing the colour into his hair and moustache, which he did every day for the show. He wouldn't look at me! He was staring at his own reflection as he said, 'What you did last night was very unprofessional!' He still wouldn't look at me!

I started to answer, but he cut me off with: 'You should have been here with the show!' And then he added, 'Babies are born all the time!'

Well, that was it for me. My hackles rose! But I answered with the due respect I held for him. I explained the delicate situation that Elly had been facing, and that my understudies had been primed. However, I also hoped to make him understand that my priorities obviously lay at my wife's bedside. That much must have been obvious to him as a father himself and I must have caught him off guard. He just 'harrumphed' and I was dismissed without further ado!

That all having been said, the first flowers to arrive at the hospital were from the Lowes. Although I think that might have been down to his wife Joan, who was also in the show with us. It's a nice ending to the tale of Sam's arrival.

Stage Door Moments

When I was involved in the *Dad's Army* show at the Shaftesbury Theatre in 1975, I was still living in Coventry. I was commuting by train daily, which was easy to and from Euston. At the end of the show, I would get changed and make my way out of the stage door to Euston, usually via the pub for a quick pint! One night, because I am a very quick changer and usually one of the first, if not *the* first, out of the stage door, there was a child waiting with their mother. The child had a small pad and pencil in their hand. As I emerged, I smiled at the child who stepped forward with pencil and paper raised, but before a word was spoken the mother stepped forward and pulled the child back, saying, 'No, darling, you don't want his autograph. He's nobody!' I let the moment pass and went on my way.

Bless me, only a few nights later there was a similar scenario with another child and parent. The child stepped forward and again the parent pulled them back, saying, 'No, no, darling, not yet. All the unimportant ones come out first.' You don't forget things like that!

Alan Bates

When I did 'The Superstar' episode of *It Ain't Half Hot Mum* for David Croft in late 1977, I was also in the middle of something else. Some people are quite surprised to find out that I had a rather impressive brush with the classics!

Because I had worked previously with director David Giles on *Richard II* and *Henry V*, he asked me to play a supporting role in a few episodes of *The Mayor of Casterbridge* by Thomas Hardy, which he was directing and which starred Alan Bates in the title role. Well, how exciting was that going to be? Something quite different for me, it has to be said! I played a character called the Carter, so

Never Telegraph a Joke

you can tell how important it was. I think I appeared in about four episodes altogether.

I remember my first scene was in the village of Corfe Castle in Dorset, which was playing the role of Casterbridge as it was so rural and quaint. The real Casterbridge was based on Dorchester, which by the late 1970s was far too modern to be used in a period piece. Corfe is at the top of a very steep hill and I was supposed to drive my horse and cart up this hill and round into the main square. Well, because I had no experience with that sort of thing, the man whose horse and cart we were using insisted on playing my double to drive the horse up the hill. But he would only do one take, as he said it was too much for the horse to do more and might give it a heart attack!

Thankfully, it went well the first time and the cart was parked outside the pub they were using. I was then switched with the driver and had to walk through the wagon to the back and jump down to help two ladies down from the cart to the road. One of these ladies was the esteemed actress Anna Massey. This is where it gets rather delicate because, you see, only two days before this filming session, I'd had a vasectomy. Part of my male anatomy was full of stitches, and rather sore! They had given me some very heavy studded boots to wear for the part and I had no idea, when I jumped down and hit the road, quite what the effect would be on my affected parts. Suffice it to say, a serious shudder went all the way through me and back again, but being the trouper I am, you would never have noticed – but I did! I never told anyone about that until now ... You'll keep the secret, though, won't you? Thank you.

All the location shooting for *The Mayor of Casterbridge* was done in and around Dorset, and it turned out to be a tricky schedule for the production team to work out. I had a gap of six weeks after that, until I was required again for a farmyard scene, and I was put on a modest retainer to secure my availability. I haven't yet mentioned that I had grown a full beard for the role, having had enough time beforehand – then the problem came! David Croft came through to ask if I would do an episode of *It Ain't Half Hot Mum* for just a week, during the six weeks I had off.

Well, what to do? I had a beard! RAF recruits did not have beards! I got in touch with the *Casterbridge* office and they were so helpful. Not wanting me to miss out on what I told them was a marvellous opportunity, they sent me to Wig Creations, one of the foremost wig-makers in the business, to have a copy made of my own real beard so that I could wear that for the rest of their shoot after shaving mine off for 'The Superstar'! I couldn't believe how co-operative they were. It worked an absolute treat. When I did go back to Dorset, there was an outside scene, which was already in the can, where I crossed the yard and entered a barn, then, when we cut to inside the barn, there I am wearing the false beard, and you can't tell the difference. Good old Wig Creations! Brilliant!

Another fond memory of my filming in Dorset was spending time with Alan Bates, and a few of the others, during the lunch breaks. Not only wonderful chats, but I also listened to the stereo in his brand-new Mini. He had acquired a copy of *Moody Blue*, the last album Elvis Presley had made before his death, and he was beset with admiration for him, saying his voice had become virtually operatic in quality by this time. He wasn't wrong and, as an avid Elvis fan myself, I shall always treasure those memories!

My absolute hero, though – throughout my life – has been Stan Laurel. Ever since I was a young actor – going all the way back to my early days at The Belgrade Theatre in Coventry – Stan has been my idol and my inspiration. Well, both Stan Laurel and Oliver Hardy really, but Stan in the main. Even in those earliest days I would always try to incorporate a gesture or a movement or a reading of a line – of either Babe Hardy or Stan Laurel. Every production, simply for my own amusement. Just so long as it was during a speech of mine. I wouldn't deliberately distract on a cue line or anything. But I would throw my arms up in the air in exasperation like Babe would do. Or I would just touch my tie – very subtly – in the manner that Stan might have done in a particularly bewildered moment. Little moments of that sort just made me smile. Made me happy! I used to do them all the time, just to keep myself amused really. Just to lighten a long run ... and to stop boredom, or a jaded attitude, encroaching on the performance. Perish the thought!

There was another actor, Terence Hillyer, who was a local actor, and went on to RADA. He's still working, bless him. He played a couple of long-running characters in *Coronation Street*, Sean Skinner and Terry Goodwin, and he was Lewis Walker in a few episodes of *EastEnders* ... a very good actor. He and I shared a love of Laurel and Hardy, and if I did a little Stan and Babe gesture, he would do one back to me!

Meeting Gail Lowe

Back in 2012, my wife Judy and I went to a charity event at Dorking Hall, which was being produced and directed by Judy's long-time friend Lindy Alexander. She was also taking part in it alongside Ron Moody and Virginia McKenna. It was a series of readings and stories, and the aim was to raise funds to prevent a plan for fracking in the area to go ahead.

During the interval, we bumped into another old friend, Elizabeth Counsell, Libby to her friends, and over a glass of wine we discussed our various projects. 'What are you up to?' I asked, as we always like to know that our friends are busy, and she replied that she was doing a one-woman play in the studio theatre at the Yvonne Arnaud in Guildford that week. It was a rather harrowing tale, based on a true story, about a blonde-haired, blue-eyed Jewish woman who had betrayed tens of thousands Jews to the Nazis during the Second World War in order to survive. The play was called *Blonde Poison* and she added that the writing was superb and that we should come and see it.

The First Rule of Comedy..!

I then mentioned that I was looking for a writer to help me put together a one-man show about Stan Laurel, which I had been planning for years. I had found someone earlier, but it hadn't worked out, so we had shaken hands and walked away. Libby said that her author, Gail Lowe, would be around at the theatre later that week, so Judy and I booked tickets to see the play on the Thursday.

Well, Libby was right – the writing was superb, as was Libby's performance in it, it has to be said! Quite brilliant! So after a question-and-answer session with the audience, we retired to the bar and, over the proverbial glass of wine, I was introduced to Gail.

She said to me, 'Oh, you're the one who wants to do a one-man show about Stan Laurel, are you?'

To which I replied, 'Ah, she told you, did she?'

Gail said, 'Yes. When do we start?'

Well, I was over the moon! We carried on chatting and it seemed that, although Gail wasn't too familiar with Laurel and Hardy, only having seen them a few times on the small screen, she was keen to get involved and collaborate with me on the piece. Having exchanged niceties and, most importantly, email addresses, we agreed a time for me to go to her house in Hove. My mission was to collect up great armfuls of books and DVDs – I've got hundreds! – for her to do her own research and develop the play from there. This we did on a few occasions over the next few weeks and, before I knew it, we had the framework of a play.

'I write quickly once I start,' she said, and she wasn't wrong! Gail wrote the bulk of the text and I added in one or two anecdotes that I wanted to include and all the comedy moments too. At various intervals throughout the play, the lights change and I, having donned the derby hat, give snippets of dialogue from some of their more famous films. You get Laurel *and* Hardy in this play!

As she is an accomplished playwright, for whom I have the utmost respect, I was happy for Gail to choose the best time and place historically to set the piece in order to tell their story. She chose to set it in Oliver Hardy's bedroom at home in September 1956, just after he'd had a massive stroke that had incapacitated him completely. He couldn't move or speak, which made it easier for me to talk to him throughout the play, as if he were lying on a bed in front of me. It was a great way to unfold the story that Stan was there for – to talk about their lives and reminisce about everything they did together. I chose to use a simple bed frame, which I had made out of plastic tubing and which comes apart to fold away and carry in a bag, with a simple wooden chair that I use to vary the movement on stage. It couldn't be simpler. It's so easy to travel anywhere with it!

For several years before this happened, though, Judy, knowing my desire to get this project up and running, had been nagging me to get on with it. I always told her that I believed it would all come together when the time was right. 'It will happen when it's meant to!' I always said, because I believed it. The fact is that in September 1956 Stan Laurel was 66 years old and when we had the play up and ready to go at the end of 2012 – guess what? Jeffrey Holland was 66 years old! I turned to Judy and said, 'See? I told you I was right!'

Now we needed a booking! Well, as it happened, Judy and I had booked to see Libby again in *Blonde Poison* at the St James Theatre in London at the beginning of 2013 and we found ourselves sitting with our friend John Plews, who ran The Gatehouse Theatre in Highgate. We knew John socially but had never worked with him. During our discourse I happened to mention the great writing we were watching and told him that Gail had written a play with me about Stan Laurel.

Out of the blue, John said, 'Would you like to come and do it at The Gatehouse as part of the Camden Festival in September?'

Well, I was stunned and all I could say was, 'Oh, fuck! I've got to learn it now!'

He said, 'There's nothing like getting a booking to get you started!'

Well, it did get me started and I got it together over the next few months. In fact, once I started to learn it, it took me around ten days to polish it off in my head. I did several performances for John at The Gatehouse, having done a showcase performance at the Tristan Bates

The First Rule of Comedy..!

Theatre which, being my very first outing with it, was terrifying! The audience for that was peppered with friends and colleagues, so that helped, apart from one fellow who suggested I start again and rewrite the whole thing. I don't see him now!

A solo show? Well, why not? It would be an interesting change! The amazing thing, I suppose, is that all through my acting life – from rep, and through all the other many productions I was involved in, and then the situation comedies for David Croft – I had always been a team player. That pal of mine, way back in the Coventry days, had made that very point to me that I was great in an ensemble ... and now here I was doing a solo show. Just me. Alone. The discipline of acting is very different.

The idea of doing Laurel and Hardy on stage, in some form or other, had been with me from my earliest days on stage. As I mentioned, I would sometimes add a Stan or Babe mannerism into my performances just for fun, and Paul Shane – a fellow Stan and Olly fan – and I had recreated the double act for the *Hi-de-Hi!* stage show, with great success. The audiences loved it! You see, Laurel and Hardy were back in favour by the 1970s. In fact, in 1975, their recording of 'The Trail of the Lonesome Pine', from their film *Way Out West*, went to number two in the charts, only to be kept from the number-one spot by Queen's 'Bohemian Rhapsody'! And, without spoilers, *Hi-de-Hi!* fans will remember a Laurel and Hardy reference in the episode 'It's a Blue World'.

But the idea of celebrating Stan Laurel was not a new one. From a very early age I had loved Laurel and Hardy. It started at the Saturday morning picture shows when I was about 7 or 8. I used to go every week and pay my sixpence or ninepence! There would be a Mickey Mouse cartoon, an episode of *Flash Gordon*, a Roy Rogers western and, hopefully, a Laurel and Hardy. If for any reason there wasn't, I was bereft! You see, they became my 'friends'. A small boy could identify with their antics, always getting into trouble with authority, which is what we used to do. But as you get older, as I did, your priorities change, and that's what happened to me.

Then, in the 1970s, when BBC2 started to show their films in the early evening as an alternative to the news, my love for them was rekindled and I started to think about what a good idea it might be to do a one-man show – the likes of which were becoming quite popular then – about Stan. Nobody had ever done a one-man show about half a double act before, and knowing all about him, I knew it was a great story to tell. The problem was, I was only in my 20s at the time. You can't tell a life story until you've had a life, so I had to wait. I actually waited over forty years to get that show up and running, but I did and it worked. It worked really well!

But, in actual fact, another thought about the Stan play came along in 1989. It was the first time I was playing the dame in pantomime at the Theatre Royal in Plymouth and I was working with comic actor and impressionist Peter Goodwright. Anyway, Goodwright was a good mate and he loved Laurel and Hardy almost as much as I did. One day, in the dressing room, Goodwright said, 'Let's write a play! Let's write ourselves a play about Stan and Olly!' But it never got off the ground. By the time we had page one started and almost written down, along came 3 February 1990 – the end of the pantomime run of *Sleeping Beauty* – and I never saw him again. Just as well really! Actually, I did see him again years and years and years later, not that long before he died, when he came to see my solo show of Stan, when I played it down in the West Country at Cheddar. He came round afterwards and said some lovely things about the play and my performance ... and it was so good to see him again!

I went on to take it to the Edinburgh Festival Fringe in 2014, and again in 2015, where we sold out both times, as we did again in 2018 and 2023! I tour it around the country as and when they ask me, and I will continue with it for as long as I can. It's a piece of work I am very proud of. Thanks, Gail!

I have to say those Edinburgh seasons were the making of the show ... and almost the breaking of me. In more ways than one. Let me explain.

The First Rule of Comedy..!

When I had ...*And This Is My Friend Mr Laurel* up and running by the end of 2013, the only way forward for it, so I thought, was to take it to Edinburgh. I knew of The Pleasance in London and that they also ran The Pleasance series of venues as part of the Fringe in Edinburgh, so I got in touch with Anthony Alderson, who runs The Pleasance, and met up with him and an assistant to discuss my idea.

Anthony seemed to think that a combination of my name and Stan Laurel's would be a guarantee of good attendance. I also asked about a producer who could handle the official side of everything, as I knew nothing about the procedures involved, and he gave me the name of Kat Portman Smith. Now, Kat had worked for some time for James Seabright, an established producer, but was now out on her own. Anthony seemed to think she would be ideal, so having acquired her details, I got in touch.

I was working at the Menier Chocolate Factory at the time in Ray Cooney's *Two Into One*. The cast included television's Robin Hood, Michael Praed, that superb farceur Nick Wilton, and Ray Cooney himself who, at the age of 81 then, was as funny and frantic as ever, as the waiter. The *Guardian* theatre reviewer Michael Billington gave us four stars and described the production as 'an orgy of door-slamming', which pretty much summed up my joy of Ray's brilliant plays! With this buoyancy under my wings, I arranged to meet Kat Portman Smith near the venue in South London.

Kat and I had a cup of tea together in Pret a Manger, opposite Borough Market, and she was very encouraging. We agreed to work together towards taking the Stan Laurel play to Edinburgh for the 2014 Fringe. I funded the whole project myself, which meant all the Fringe brochures, photos, copy, flyers, the lot. As well as my accommodation, which, if you have ever experienced the glorious highs and frustrating lows of putting on a show in Edinburgh in August, is outrageously expensive. You can't blame hotels and B&B owners for hiking up their prices. Rooms are at a premium that month, so it's a case of make hay while the sun shines for those with a bedroom or two to spare!

It wasn't a cheap enterprise and my investment came to approximately £8,000! August soon came around, though, and off I went to the beautiful city of Edinburgh. I had been allocated a 12.35 p.m. spot in a venue in The Pleasance Courtyard called The Attic. The Attic is so called because it is a very small space with just fifty-eight seats, high up atop two flights of stairs! Thankfully, it went extremely well. So much so that, having sold out pretty much the whole time, I was given a few extra performances, at a later time of day, in another venue across the courtyard called The Upstairs ... so called for very similar reasons! It was a larger room with around a hundred seats – if we squeezed them in – and that sold out too. We played for the whole month of August and I loved it! Judy came and joined me for the second half of the season and we managed to see lots of other shows while we were there. Some were good, some were not, but we were both amazed at the fact that so much talent abounded there ... all for that brief time of four weeks! An amazing experience. I urge anyone with even the slightest interest in live theatre to go and wallow in the delights of the Edinburgh Fringe at least once in your lives.

It is a fact, though, that by the time you finish your run at the Fringe, be it long or short, you almost certainly lose money. It was no exception for me and, although it had been great exposure for my play, I went home £3,500 out of pocket! That's showbiz, I suppose, but I was determined to give it another go, and so, the following year, in 2015, with Kat's invaluable help again, I booked it in once more. However, this time round, I placed it in the larger venue of The Upstairs, where I had done my extra shows the year before. You see, The Attic, being only fifty-eight seats, was unable to take enough money at the door to return one's investment. The Upstairs, however, was a different matter and I was fortunate to sell out most of the time. At the end of the season I actually went

The First Rule of Comedy..!

home with a profit – albeit a small one, but it was enough to put a smile on my face! I got my money back – and then some.

I gave it a miss for the next couple of years, but in 2018 I went back again to The Upstairs, where the show was just as successful as it had been three years previously! During my early mornings in The Courtyard, over several cups of coffee before my show, I made the acquaintance of a very personable young Irish actor called Edwin Mullane, who was doing his own one-man play in The Attic where I had been previously. We hit it off with him, both Judy and I, so much so that even though he wasn't able to see my show himself, as our times clashed, he got me acquainted with some people from Dublin who ran a theatre over a pub called The Viking. He thought my show would go well there and he arranged for them to see it. As it later turned out, Edwin himself took on the role of producer and took me and Judy, and *Mr Laurel*, of course, over to Ireland where, after two weeks at The Viking in Clontarf, Dublin, we spent the whole of April 2019 touring around the country. It was wonderful and the first time for both Judy and me to see such a great deal of beautiful rural Ireland. Thanks, Ed!

The COVID pandemic put a stop to most, if not all, theatrical activity for the next few years and everything ground to a halt. The whole world seemed to go dark, and it was a terrible time for many in the profession. The rallying round of actors, producers, directors, writers and crew formed an incredible support network. It was a tough time … but most of us got through it. However, those shockwaves are still rumbling through our business, and it took a long time for people to have the courage to go back into a theatre. There is still an anxiety about it with some older people, which I can fully understand, and the end result is that many people now only book tickets at the very last minute, wary of how they are going to feel, how the performers are going to fare and whether the show will go on. It invariably does, so please have faith in returning to live theatre. There's nothing like it!

Never Telegraph a Joke

COVID undoubtedly gave the business a massive whack, though, and it suffered huge losses. The Edinburgh Fringe was no exception and, although they ventured back to work in 2022, attendance was very poor and the box-office takings were down to around 50 per cent of their usual business. Things took a much healthier turn the following year, in 2023, and I decided to take *Mr Laurel* back for a fourth and, as I thought, final trip to Edinburgh. We booked it into The Upstairs again and had another morning slot at 11.20 a.m. I was doing the whole month again and, although time was marching on and the years were adding up, I thought, 'I can do this!'

As before, we borrowed a friend's flat in the New Town area of the city. As some of you will know, Edinburgh is all hills. We had a half-hour walk to the venue every morning and it was all uphill. Easy coming home, but tough in the mornings! I got to the venue in plenty of time for a fortifying cup of coffee, and then did the show. I honestly thought nothing of doing that complete run once more. We took the wearying slog to the venue in our stride until, in the last weekend of the run, my old frame could take no more. On the final Saturday morning, before we were due to finish on the Monday, I barely got through the show. In fact, I became very breathless and twice even thought about stopping the show completely. Still, good old 'Doctor Theatre' took over and I somehow managed to get through it. I took my bow and left the stage, but still had to climb up two steep flights of stairs to get to my dressing room! I ended up crawling on my hands and knees, and then barely had the strength to change my clothes. You see, apart from being on blood pressure tablets, I had been told I now had an atrial flutter in my heart and was also on beta blockers for that.

Judy arrived at the dressing room, wondering where the hell I was, as I always met her down in the bar area after the show. Seeing my state, she immediately sent for the first-aid medics, who were very kind but, much against my better judgement, persuaded me that it would be wise to get a cab to A&E and get myself checked out. Judy had a friend with her that day too, who very kindly accompanied us to the hospital and was able to sit with Judy while I got checked out. The hospital staff were wonderful and did a chest X-ray, blood test and electrocardiograph, and a very helpful doctor told me she was sending me home as I had simply become a victim of my atrial flutter. The month in Edinburgh had worn me out!

I couldn't bear the thought of trying to struggle through two more shows on Sunday and Monday, so I rang Kat and she cancelled them for me. Thank you, Kat! I picked up my stuff the following morning and said a very grateful farewell to dear Edinburgh's Pleasance. The irony of all that is that *Mr Laurel* made a bigger profit that season than I had ever done previously. I must remember, though, that I'm not 25 any more. There may come a time when even *Mr Laurel* has to take his final bow!

The Goon Show

The first Goon-connected thing I ever bought was Spike Milligan's 45rpm (that's revs per minute, if you don't know) single record of 'I'm Walking Backwards for Christmas'. It was originally released in 1956 but I must have found an old copy of *The Goons* EP from somewhere a few years later. I know that we didn't have a record player then, and we didn't get one until after my dad died in 1961. I knew Milligan's funny voice on that track, and I loved another track called 'Bloodnok's Rock 'n' Roll Call' because all three Goons sang on it. The record had 'The Ying Tong Song' and 'Bluebottle Blues' on it too.

Anyway, the Colonel Bloodnok song was the one that really was my introduction to *The Goon Show*. You see, I was never allowed to listen to it on the wireless in the 1950s when I was growing up. My parents said it was stupid, but basically they just didn't understand it. They simply weren't mentally equipped for that sort of quirky humour. I was tortured by the fact that my friend Colum Gallivan

Never Telegraph a Joke

at school always quoted chunks of *The Goon Show* to me the following morning, after he had heard it the night before, and it drove me nuts! I think it drove him nuts too as he was always very much 'off the wall'. I worked with him many years later in Chichester, as he also became an actor, and he was still as barmy as ever then! I don't know what has happened to him since.

The shocking truth of the matter is that I never heard a full episode of *The Goon Show* until 1980! When Peter Sellers died, they released a four-cassette package called *Sellers at the Beeb*, which included three or four half-hour *Goon Shows*, as well as various other things he had recorded. I had a couple of LPs of Sellers doing sketch comedies and I learned most of those monologues virtually off by heart and kept mates amused for hours. I knew what a talent he was but had never heard him in *The Goon Show*. Well, I was in heaven – I'd never heard anything so funny in my life! I completely understand why Milligan said that writing it robbed him of his sanity. It was the zaniest, funniest, cleverest stuff I'd ever heard and I was in mimicry paradise taking off all the voices!

After that set of recordings was released, I set about seeing if there were any other recordings out there. I found a few in LP form in certain record shops, so I started to buy every one I could get hold of. Then, to my great joy, the BBC decided to release a certain number of them on cassette, so I started collecting them and soon had all the ones that were available. Now, of course, they've released all of them, plus a few bonus ones, on CD, so I have the full collection. Bliss! When I was travelling many miles on my own to various jobs all over the country, I used to measure the journeys in how many *Goon Shows* it took to get there. Wolverhampton? Oh yes, that's five *Goon Shows* away!

Throughout my radio career, mainly in the 1980s and 1990s, I worked many times with the producer Dirk Maggs. Now Dirk was also a huge fan of The Goons and he had actually worked with Milligan! He produced a wonderful documentary about them and, to cut a long story short, was going to produce and direct a

The First Rule of Comedy..!

tribute *Goon Show* to celebrate the fiftieth anniversary of the original shows, which were then called *Crazy People*. The show was first aired in 1951, with Michael Bentine as the fourth member of the group, when The Goons were subtitled the Junior Crazy Gang. Bud Flanagan and the boys had been West End and British cinema sensations before and well after the war, and were still going strong in the 1950s.

It didn't take The Goons long to develop their own style. Bentine left them, though, because Spike Milligan apparently thought he was just too crazy. How about that! I think that they were on very different wavelengths, and that's why they couldn't agree on what was funny. In actual fact, Bentine became a brilliant visual clown, with his pioneering sketch show *It's a Square World*. The three Goons – Sellers, Secombe and Milligan – were perfect radio comedians. Those Milligan scripts – aided and abetted by Larry Stephens, Eric Sykes and others – could paint surreal pictures in your head!

It was a challenge for Dirk Maggs to recreate it, but the year he needed to deliver, to mark the anniversary, was 2001. He had to get it done quickly. A kind of Spike Odyssey, if you will. Dirk went to the then head of radio comedy, James Moir (no, not the brilliant Vic Reeves!), to clear it with him, and after much cajoling Dirk persuaded him to let it be made. The only thing Moir said as Dirk left his office was, 'Don't fuck it up!'

I couldn't believe it when Dirk rang to tell me about it – and then asked me to play all the Sellers characters! He had heard me do them for fun all the time when we'd done other stuff together and he said I was the first one he thought of. He had to get Spike's approval, though, and Norma Farnes' – she was Spike's manager and owned the rights to them – so I had to do a couple of test recordings to be sent to them. They liked them, thankfully!

I was a little worried because my one and only meeting with Spike Milligan had been more than a little awkward. I was well aware that he could be tetchy or off-hand. His history of mental health problems is well documented. As mentioned, anyone who had churned out those hundreds of *Goon Show* episodes would have had to be made of hard stuff to survive with their sanity intact! Not to mention his harrowing war years, also well documented in his memoirs *Adolf Hitler: My Part in His Downfall*, and its sequels, most of which I had read.

Anyway, when I met him, it was in the lobby of the Dorchester Hotel at a children's charity lunch, a decade or so after *Hi-de-Hi!*, and I saw him crossing the room and thought, 'I might not get another chance!', so I headed him off and stood in front of him so that he stopped dead. I suddenly realised he might take exception to his space being invaded, but it was too late. I put out my hand and said, 'Hello, Spike. I just wanted to say "hello"! I played a character called Spike in a sitcom on television!'

He looked at me, took my hand and simply said, in a monotonous mutter, 'How very interesting.'

Ouch! That didn't bode well, so I then said something about being a big admirer of his work, especially *The Goon Show*, and with half a smile, he said in that same monotone, 'You must be very old.'

I realised I had caught him on a bad day, or maybe I had made it a bad day for him, so I made my departure post haste. Not the best of encounters with the great man, but I blame myself!

Anyway, his appreciation of the voices of his late-lamented cohort more than made up for it. We were on! So we went ahead with it, and on Sunday, 25 March 2001 we recorded that wonderful show at the Playhouse Theatre in London! It was amazing as we had Andy Secombe, son of Sir Harry, to play 'Son of Ned'; Christopher Timothy, whose father Andrew Timothy was the original announcer for *Crazy People*; and Lance Ellington, son of band leader and singer Ray Ellington, to play the parts originated by their very talented fathers. These very talented sons sounded exactly like them! The Milligan characters were done by my old mate Jon Glover, who had worked with Dirk a lot. We also had a live seventeen-piece orchestra on stage with us, conducted by the great John Wilson, and I can honestly say that it was probably the happiest night I have ever spent in a theatre in my life! It is entitled *Goon Again* and is available on CD as we speak.

The only downside to it all was that the recording was done only a few days before Harry Secombe sadly passed away, and Andy was brave enough not to tell us how ill Harry was when we did it. Both Harry and Spike were invited to the recording, but had to decline for reasons of poor health. I hope Spike was able to hear the finished product, though. He died the following year, at the age of 82. He was the last Goon and, quite simply, a true comic genius. A pioneer, whose comic vision will make me laugh until I can laugh no more!

Kenny Everett

Kenny Everett was a true one-off. He had been pals with The Beatles in the late 1960s, and his natural Liverpudlian charm, wit and exuberance made him one of the most intuitive, talented and, yes, beloved broadcasters the nation had ever had. He wasn't called 'Cuddly Ken' for nothing. Ken had a passion for radio. He loved the microphone and, in turn, the microphone loved him. He had the great skill that every single listener felt Ken was talking directly to them, and only to them. He was also very, very funny.

It was no surprise when his wacky and wonderful radio characters were transferred to popular and influential TV shows. During the 1980s, while I was involved in *Hi-de-Hi!* and *Russ Abbot's Madhouse*, I also got asked to appear in three of Kenny Everett's sketch comedy shows, which was great fun. My favourite was a spoof of an *Ask the Family*-type quiz show, which pitched the Thatchers against the Royals. Sheila Steafel played Margaret Thatcher and Kenny played the late Queen, complete with beard and no concession to femininity whatsoever! I was asked to play

Prince Charles because I had been doing an impression of him on the *Madhouse* for a while, and had become known for it. I was there in the full polo outfit, helmet, riding boots and jodhpurs ... the lot. I remember I only had a three-legged stool to sit on as part of the comedy and kept falling off it. Needless to say, I was black and blue all over when we finished!

Another hilarious Kenny Everett sketch, later on in the series, was one in which I played a policeman in an adult-sized Punch and Judy show, with Kenny as Mr Punch and Vicki Michelle as Judy. I did another, but I had to appear as myself, telling Kenny off for not turning up on time. That was great fun too, and we got on like a house on fire! So much so that I was called in – at Kenny's request – to record some voiceovers for a set of comedy adverts that he was doing.

In those days, BBC TV always threw a black-tie Christmas party in the big executive suite on the sixth floor in early December. Although I couldn't always attend these, due to panto commitments, on very rare occasions I could manage to pop my head in. I remember, on this occasion, standing in the middle of the room chatting to someone, when in walked Kenny, a little the worse for wear, it has to be said. The moment he clocked me, Kenny made a beeline and cried out in a very loud voice, 'Jeffrey darling!' and planted a huge sloppy kiss right on my lips. I managed to remain cool, and tried to look as if we always did this sort of thing. I think I got away with it!

Two Kenneths: Connor and Williams

Now, a pair of comedy actors who are still beloved, and perhaps even better known now than they ever were, are Kenneth Connor and Kenneth Williams. Always considered two of the best in the business of comedy, they have both achieved something like

The First Rule of Comedy..!

comedy immortality, thanks to their brilliant leading roles in the *Carry On* films. It's wonderful to think that their antics in those very funny films, like *Carry On Sergeant* and *Carry On Regardless*, are still getting laughs, sixty-odd years after they were made. Proof that quality will always survive!

For me, though, for both Connor and Williams, it is radio comedy that holds and cherishes their finest work.

Like me, Kenny Connor was a long-time admirer of The Goons, but unlike me, he was a friend and contemporary of Milligan, Secombe and Sellers ... and many of the other great comedy talents of that bravest of generations! Kenny would, on occasion, substitute for an unwell Peter Sellers, or a poorly Harry Secombe, and was a seamless and intuitive team player in that craziest of shows. I have heard his efforts myself, and he was a noble match for those he replaced.

Kenny Connor's own brilliant character creation, Sidney Mincing, a wheezing, nasal jobsworth of a man, had first found a voice, and a following – me included – on *Ray's A Laugh*, starring Liverpudlian comedian Ted Ray, back in the late 1950s. I loved this show and tuned in every Sunday morning to listen to all the characters, Mincing being my all-time favourite. To my utter delight, when I was doing *Inman and Friends* with John Inman and Sherrie Hewson, nearly forty years later, Kenny had been booked to record an episode as a guest. And, yes, it was on the radio. BBC Radio 2, to be precise.

Now, I had this purely selfish thought that this was an ideal opportunity to get Kenny to revive – reanimate, if you like – Sidney Mincing. So I had a word, the week before, with the writers, who seemed only too grateful to have help with ideas. 'This bodes well!' I thought. I explained the character, voice timbre and catchphrases of the Mincing character and they wrote it into a Guy Fawkes sketch we were going to do the following week. The setting was the cellar of the Houses of Parliament in 1605, where John Inman and I are looking for intruders and explosives, and we see something suspicious.

Never Telegraph a Joke

'Look,' says John. 'What's that filthy pile of old rags there under that table?'

To which Kenny replies, 'Do you mind?' in the Sidney Mincing voice. That was always his opening catchphrase, and *I* got him to do it! I couldn't believe I was standing at the mic, next to Kenneth Connor, as he delivered that immortal voice forty years on from when I used to listen to him on 'the wireless'! It was a very special moment in my life, my career, that I will always remember – and treasure.

That wasn't the first time, though, that I had worked with Kenny Connor. That was after Leslie Dwyer had dropped out of *Hi-de-Hi!* because of ill-health and, sadly, during the life of the show, dear Leslie had died.

David Croft had been considering Kenny for *'Allo 'Allo!* for a while, and an opportunity for a guest character had arisen for a one-off appearance with us in *Hi-de-Hi!* There was to be a scruffy old kids' entertainer, found by Ted and Spike on their day off, on the beach, attempting to amuse some kids with a comedy puppet act. This, of course, was Kenny, playing Uncle Sammy, who turns out to be an old pal of our boss Joe Maplin. So Ted invites him up to the camp to get cleaned up, and to think about a job as the children's entertainer – 'to replace old Partridge', as Ted puts it.

Well, I couldn't believe it, as I was still in awe of the great man. Here I was, meeting Kenneth Connor, and the first thing I had to do was scrub his back in the bath! We had to 'force' Sammy into a bath as he was filthy. It was only meant to be a guest appearance, but I had a thought, and I drew Shaney into my confidence here, that it would be a brilliant coup to get Kenny Connor into the show permanently as the new, somewhat unsavoury, children's entertainer. Well, his contribution to the episode was such a success that Shaney and I approached David the following week with the idea, and he went for it. Kenny was in as Uncle Sammy!

Kenny was such a good actor, of course, but he was also a brilliant team player. No wonder he had shone so brightly in the *Carry*

The First Rule of Comedy..!

On films. Anyway, Kenny became part of David Croft's repertory company. He was cast as the delightful funeral parlour owner Monsieur Alphonse in *'Allo 'Allo!*, which David had already been considering. He of the 'dicky ticker'! And David brought him in for just a scene or two as Lady Lavender's psychiatrist in *You Rang, M'Lord?* sometime later, and it was wonderful to see him again. That was not long before his death, in November 1993. In fact, I worked with him on the last TV recording he ever did, which was a five-minute pilot, as part of a collection of five-minute pilots that Charles Garland had arranged for some new writers, on the premise that nobody ever watches more than five minutes of a pilot. Sadly, this seems to be the case!

This pilot was a potential sitcom based in a sex therapy clinic. The mind boggles ... I was playing one of the clinicians and Kenny was another. I will never forget his immortal gagline to me when he said, 'I'm free at the moment. I had a "premature ejaculation" at two o'clock but he came early!'

Kenny was in the final stages of cancer and was very thin, and rather grey, but as funny and sharp as he ever had been. It was only a short time later that I got a phone call from Charles to tell me that he had passed away. One of the true greats of comedy, and I am privileged to have called him my friend!

Kenneth Williams was another performer born for radio comedy. He first came to prominence on *Hancock's Half-Hour* with a gallery of grotesque characters, from pompous upper-crust gentlemen to that high-pitched, irritating figure that became known as Snide. You know, the one who would always say 'Good evening!' and 'Stop messin' about!' I remember hearing Kenny interviewed once, explaining that the character came from a friend of his who, with great detail, related horrid stories of being bullied at public school. All these horrendous humiliations were enacted while the chap telling them tried to put a brave face on it and smiled throughout. This made them very, very funny, and so Kenny adopted this strangled happiness for Snide. The character became a national obsession,

Never Telegraph a Joke

and Kenny became a star of radio with *Beyond Our Ken*, and then *Round the Horne*, in support of avuncular broadcaster Kenneth Horne. Kenny was hilariously funny as the folk singer Rambling Syd Rumpo – joyous!

Alas, I never got to work with Kenneth Williams, but I mention him because I really do wish I had. Indeed, my only encounter with him was when I was walking down Berwick Street in Soho on my way to do a voiceover. I was wearing a very unusual coat made of multicoloured tweed squares, and fleece lined, which Elly had made for me, and I loved it. Suddenly, I heard a very familiar voice behind me call out, 'Ooooh! That's a lovely coat!' I turned round and couldn't believe my eyes – it was Kenneth Williams! He was on his way to do a voiceover too, as it turned out, and we went our separate ways. Whether he recognised me or not, I don't know. He never said, and I didn't volunteer, but I do know he thought *Hi-de-Hi!* was a very funny show.

'How do you know that?' I hear you ask. Well, I'll tell you. Kenny was a panellist on *Did You See ...?*, the TV review show hosted by Ludovic Kennedy. Kenny was on a couple of times, but this edition, recorded in December 1987, was his very last TV job, although others he had filmed were screened later. One of the programmes under discussion was *Hi-de-Hi!* Our Boxing Day special, 'Tell it to the Marines', had kick-started our last series and Kenny Williams, very astutely, had made the comparison between our series and the *Carry On* films, saying, 'it's the sort of subject they could have handled easily. It's the same thing. You've got your heavy. We had Sid James; they've got Paul Shane. The comedian. You've got your funny girl. We had Joanie Sims and Barbara Windsor ... And Kenny Connor is indeed in this! Kenneth Connor was in all the *Carry Ons* ...'

Well, not quite, Kenny. Not as many, in fact, as Williams himself had done, but proof positive that Kenny Connor left an indelible mark on the *Carry On* films, and indeed on our series! Kenny Williams went on to say that Kenny Connor, as Uncle Sammy, has a lovely scene in the fish shop, the Happy Halibut, and then he lapsed into an impersonation of his old comedy comrade, about asking for extra gherkins to get the attention of the young girl serving. Kenny said, 'The pathos with which he invests that is truly delightful. It's remarkable. It's almost – like the whole thing – a touch of poetry. It's a very funny series.'

Thank you, Kenneth, and what a joy it would have been to have had Kenneth Williams as a guest star – although I know he didn't really enjoy doing TV acting roles. Still, I'm chuffed he liked *Hi-de-Hi!* so much, and, I suppose, to follow his analogy, my character of Spike was kind of the Jim Dale role: the gullible, likeable idiot. Young, fresh-faced and funny, but more than likely to have the pratfalls and the faux pas. That was Spike!

In fact, at one time, around 2003 and into 2004, there was some very serious talk that a series of new *Carry On* films was about to go into production, and would I be interested in joining the regular team as a leading man and character comedy actor? Yes, please! Alas, Kenny Connor and Kenny Williams were both long gone by that time. And, yes, you guessed it, I'm still waiting for the confirmation that we will start filming. Never believe it's happening until your teeth are sinking into that first tuck-wagon bacon sandwich! I may have aged into the old man roles of Kenny Connor and Kenny Williams by now, but I'm still available.

Ben Warriss

When we did the stage show of *Hi-de-Hi!* in the summer of 1983, I was delighted to find out that Ben Warriss had been booked to play Uncle Benjy, the children's entertainer. He was there to replace the Mr Partridge character, and to have a few banter scenes with Felix Bowness as Fred the jockey. Now, I had always been a fan of Ben Warriss, who, in comedy partnership with his very funny cousin

Never Telegraph a Joke

Jimmy Jewel, was in one of Britain's greatest and most popular double acts. Ben was the straight man, but a brilliant actor and an even better *re*actor! He was a powerhouse of fast-talking patter, and that style of aggressive comedy, in the late 1940s, was full of it – a cynical reaction to the war years. I still have an episode of their radio series *Up the Pole* in my archive. There is a typical wartime gag in it where Jimmy Jewel is kissing a girl and, after the prolonged sucking noise – for comedy reasons! – is done, she says to him, 'Ooooh, Jimmy! Where did you learn to kiss like that?', to which he replies, 'Siphoning petrol'!

Throughout the 1940s and 1950s, Jewel and Warriss were at their peak. They appeared on TV regularly and made several films for Mancunian Films in Manchester, most of which I had seen. These were my formative years – the years I was growing up and developing my own sense of humour – so they were very important to me. Hence, the very idea of sharing a stage with Ben Warriss was thrilling, to say the least.

Ben had decided to retire as the double act's popularity had started to dwindle slightly. The business was changing, so Ben, ever the astute businessman, went into the hotel trade. Jimmy Jewel, however, decided to continue working as an actor, and a very successful one, most notably in the TV series *Nearest and Dearest*, with Hylda Baker. When that partnership became untenable – there are enough stories about those two to fill another book! – the writers of *Nearest and Dearest*, Vince Powell and Harry Driver, created another sitcom for Jimmy. It was a much gentler one, called *Summer and Autumn*, in which Jimmy played a lonely old widower who befriended a cheeky little lad. It was lovely. So Jimmy was happy – and so was Ben, out of the business until David Croft and Jimmy Perry tempted him back ...

Ben had always kept his eye on what was going on – any proper vaudevillian couldn't help but have an undying passion for the variety scene. Thus, Ben was a prominent member of the Grand Order of Water Rats, along with Jimmy Perry, and it was Jimmy's idea to get him back on the stage. Obviously Jimmy was not only a lifetime admirer of the greats of music hall, but he was TV's noted expert on the subject, hosting the enchanting and educational BBC programme celebrating the greats of the past, *Turns*. So, Jimmy asked Ben and, to our utter delight, he said yes!

I didn't have a great deal of contact with Ben to start with, but I did have a soft-shoe-shuffle-type number with him and Paul Shane in the show. Jimmy had written this specially to showcase Ben and, fittingly, in light of Jim's TV odyssey of variety, the routine was called *Turns*! Boy, oh boy, Ben was one of the best turns it's ever been my privilege to be on stage with. I enjoyed that enormously, and I don't think I ever stopped thinking, each time I did it, 'Here I am and I'm dancing with Ben Warriss!'

He was very much of the old school, and knew the theatre game backwards, forwards and every which way. He also took his privileges of seniority seriously, and expected the respect he was due from fellow cast members and stage hands alike. I shall never forget one day, during rehearsals, he was standing centre stage, smoking a cigarette. He had always smoked them when I had seen him on TV and at the pictures; it wasn't a prop! Ben loved smoking. Now, of course, as I have mentioned, most of his scenes were with Felix, who was playing the jockey, which meant horse references ... which meant the stage was often covered with hay and straw and the like. You can see where I'm going with this, can't you? But no, the whole lot didn't go up in flames, although that was a distinct possibility.

One young lady, who was our dance captain, working with him on a number, thought she would put that particular fire out before it even got started, if you follow me! She rather nervously went up to Ben and said, 'Emm ... excuse me, Mr Warriss. Would you mind awfully not smoking on stage? It could ...'

But before this poor girl could explain the dangers and, single-handedly, start the very ethos of theatre health & safety, Ben whipped round and politely said: 'Darling [*deep drag*], I have never [*another deep drag*] smoked on stage [*one more drag*] in my life!' (*a flourish and another drag on the fag*). At which point *she* apologised to *him* for making a mistake and swiftly left stage right. Brilliant! No harsh words, no conflict, just a moral and physical victory for the old campaigner Ben Warriss. What a stubborn old pro!

We did the 1983 summer season at the Bournemouth Pavilion, after a week's run-in at The Alex in Birmingham, and it was the first time a lot of us had seen the 'House Full' sign up at the box office. *Hi-de-Hi!* was at its peak in 1983 and we were solid gold. Comedy gold! We went back and did another TV series in the autumn, and followed that with a Christmas stage season at the Victoria Palace in London. That, of course, was the old home of the Crazy Gang back in the day and my chin was once again on my chest every night. The *Carry On* gang had also held court there in the early 1970s, with their revue *Carry On London!*, so we were really standing on the shoulders of giants.

That season was so popular, and so successful, that it was extended to the middle of May. Simon Cadell was still playing Jeffrey Fairbrother with us, but had commitments elsewhere, so he had to leave the show before the extension. He was replaced, however, by Michael Knowles from *It Ain't Half Hot Mum* who did a wonderful, if not somewhat thankless, job of replacing Simon as Fairbrother. It wasn't an easy assignment, as David Griffin would soon find out on TV less than a year later. At least David had a very different character to play, fulfilling the same function, but in a very different way. Poor old Michael had to play it like Simon, with his own unique twinkle. Of course, Michael had been immersed in the DNA of Croft and Perry for a long time – not only had he played *It Ain't Half Hot Mum* brilliantly, but also, with the late Harold Snoad, he had been entrusted with those peerless *Dad's Army* scripts and adapted them for BBC radio. Superbly. He is a class act, Michael Knowles!

Anyway, back to Ben Warriss. It wasn't until we took the show to Blackpool's Opera House for the summer of 1984 that I got

The First Rule of Comedy..!

to know this comedy legend much better. I had rented a house in nearby St Annes for the season and, as it turned out, Ben had some digs that were on my way home. I was more than delighted when it was suggested that I give him a lift home each night after the show. He could get in on the bus, but it was so much easier for me to drop him home after the shows. He used to tell me some wonderful tales, in the car, about the old days with Jimmy Jewel.

The issue of stardom arose. It happens that a certain act, which had been on at another theatre while we were in Bournemouth the year before, took the name of the show as theirs but only appeared for the last forty minutes of the second half. Ben told me that, when he and Jimmy did their big shows, they came on during the opening number and did a bit of banter with the dancing girls, so that the first turn, after that, became the second turn – a status thing in variety at the time, Ben told me. It seems that nobody wanted to be 'first turn'! Then they did a five-minute spot halfway through the first act, and finished with a fifteen-minute spot to close the first half of the show. It was much the same in the second half, with a big finish at the end, so the audience really did see Jewel and Warriss throughout the entire show. That was how it used to be, and quite right too!

I've never forgotten that, and always try to give people full value for money. That includes throughout the performance, be it matinee or evening. The audience have given up their afternoon or evening to be there, and paid out a lot of hard-earned money – and after the show, if people have enjoyed it enough to want an autograph as a keepsake, then it's all part of the business. It's what we do it for!

These car journeys with Ben were simply glorious for me. One great story that Ben told me was about when they were asked to step in at the last minute to replace Laurel and Hardy at the Finsbury Park Empire in November 1953. Stan and Babe were on tour, and this particular week Stan Laurel came down with a nasty case of flu. It was so bad, he just couldn't work. Ben said that he and Jimmy managed to drop whatever it was that they were doing and go along to Finsbury Park to substitute for Laurel and Hardy. What a gig! What an honour, but what pressure! Oliver Hardy, though, made it a point to be there every night. He would go on stage to apologise to the audience that he and Stan were unable to perform for them, and to gratefully introduce 'your brilliant comedy team Jewel and Warriss who will perform in our stead'. Ever the Southern gentleman was Babe Hardy!

Ben said they were waiting in the wings, and without fail, every night, an enormous groan would go up in the audience at the disappointment they felt. Unfortunately, Jewel and Warriss, as popular as they were, died on their feet every night that week! They simply weren't Stan Laurel and Oliver Hardy. The one bonus for Ben was that Mr Hardy spent a lot of the evenings in their dressing room during the rest of the show, chatting about the old days in Hollywood, and Ben said, 'We had a million laughs.' What I wouldn't have given to be a fly on that particular wall!

It's a privilege to hear stories from the true greats of the business. And, it's funny, looking back on my long life as I write these memoirs, that the sheer thrill that Ben got from hearing Oliver Hardy's stories was duplicated for me, hearing Ben's amazing stories from Variety days long before I was born! I like to think that youngsters just starting out in the business are interested in my stories, these stories. I certainly answer any questions that the young performers may have for me, and there have been many over the years. It's the true meaning of comedy ... passing that funny baton on to the next generation, for them to do their bit, their slant on the old jokes and the old routines. We are all in it together, though, and moments like those with Ben Warriss make me rather emotional and very proud. I have been extremely lucky!

THE FIRST RULE OF COMEDY...
PRETTY GIRLS AREN'T FUNNY

Another House Move

Now, before I get complaints, this is one rule of comedy I strongly disagree with, but before I disprove it completely, there was upheaval at home. I have covered the rather eventful move to Felden, in Hemel, which was going on in the early months of 1979. It was a monumental time, for sure, as that phone call from Jimmy Perry came in the merry month of May that year, with the request to muster for the pilot script which was to become *Hi-de-Hi!* A life-changing phone call in every way. Elly and I and our family lived in that house in Felden from spring 1979 to 1985, through those wonderfully popular days of *Hi-de-Hi!* on screen and stage and into the squadron leader years of David Griffin coming in to take over the reins of romantic leading man from Simon Cadell.

Halfway through that most dazzling and exciting of decades, Elly and I made the decision to make another move. But before I tell you about that, I'll tell you about another exciting career move I had!

The First Rule of Comedy..!

In 1981, as well as being involved with Croft and Perry, I got a call to go to London Weekend Television to audition for a show that comedy performer Russ Abbot was going to do called *Russ Abbot's Saturday Madhouse*. The casting director was Nicki Finch, who had been growing up in Coventry while I was in rep at The Belgrade, and she had seen me there many times, in all kinds of guises and as many different characters. Although Russ was obviously doing a lot of the heavy comedy lifting in this show – his show – he always liked to have a reassuring gang around him. A good team of performers in support. Inmates in his Madhouse!

They wanted someone to play various characters in sketches with Russ, a sort of straight man for him really, so I knew I was more than capable. However, the director and producer John Kaye Cooper wasn't at all convinced that I would be right, having already established myself in *Hi-de-Hi!* at the BBC. A comedy conflict of interest was feared. In fact, it wasn't until I reached into my pocket and pulled out a pile of photos of me, in various different roles at The Belgrade, that his eyes lit up. 'Is that you?' he said a few times at some of the disguises I wore, and I knew it was beginning to go my way!

I had to wait a couple of long days for an answer, but I got the job, and I had the most wonderful few years doing the *Madhouse* with Russ and the gang. It was a starry line-up, with Dustin Gee, Bella Emberg, Susie Blake and also Michael Barrymore, who was in the first series but went on to do his own thing soon after ... and for many years after that. Les Dennis joined us then, and Sherrie Hewson brought an extra slice of glamour to the proceedings. We had such fun doing that show! And I hope it showed when huge audiences sat down to watch. We were so good, even Russ couldn't keep a straight face sometimes!

It was during the recording of an episode of *Russ Abbot's Madhouse*, in 1983, that we had a rare occurrence – a moment of helpless laughter – from none other than Russ himself. This was very rare indeed, as Russ was normally such a disciplined performer

– just as well, as he always had so much to do! It happened in a sketch involving his character Basildon Bond, a spoof on James Bond, and came as a complete surprise to all of us.

I was seated behind my desk playing Bond's boss 'P', Sherrie Hewson was Miss Funnyfanny and Les Dennis was a visiting Arab dignitary called Sheikh Ma-Handi ('Of coursey-worsy!' replies Bond, shaking hands!).

After a short piece of plot, it turns out that Les was none other than Bond's archvillain, The Gold Toenail, in disguise. Before a struggle ensues, the villain's identity is revealed by Les placing his sandalled foot on the desk to reveal a heavily beglittered gold toenail about 2 inches long, which was glued to Les's own toe! Combined with this apparition, and having to say an almost unsayable line, Russ dissolved into hysterics. The line was, 'Have you no soul, you heel, Gold Toenail?' Even he had trouble with that mouthful and it proved just too much to cope with!

He laughed and laughed – and, of course, we all joined him, and so did the audience! It went on and on for several takes until the floor manager had to relay a word of warning from the director, John Kaye Cooper, up in the gallery. We calmed down and tried again – and again Russ couldn't do it. More helpless laughter! The line tickled him so much that he just couldn't cope! We tried again – no luck again. More giggles! This went on for so long that John himself came down to the floor to have a quiet word in Russ's ear. This was a really embarrassing thing to do, in front of the audience, but they didn't mind – they probably didn't know Russ was getting a serious ticking off! Our audience was loving it, but it was getting very close to finishing time, and we had to get the sketch recorded before the deadline, or the plugs would have to be pulled. John went back to the control room and we were assured by Russ that, this time, all would be well. It wasn't! Off he and Les – well, all of us really – went again into fits!

It just so happened that the head of London Weekend Light Entertainment, David Bell, was up in the box too, unbeknownst to any of us, and he was having no more of this. He came down to the floor, walked over to the set and stood in front of us all with a thunderous expression on his face which didn't need an answer. As soon as he had disappeared back upstairs, we got the take. It concluded with Bella Emberg coming on as Bobbajob, an 'Odd Job' gag character in full Chinese make-up, throwing bowler hats at everyone, which was well worth the wait!

It was a moment none of us will ever forget, least of all Russ – but it never happened again. It's just a joyous memory of a very rare thing!

I was *so* lucky to be in that company. Russ used to take the mickey sometimes and ad-lib things like, 'This isn't your *Hi-de-Hi!*, you know', which always got a big laugh from the studio audience. I often got an Oliver Hardy-type 'camera look' in when that happened, just to acknowledge it, which was great fun! And talk about a brilliant two-way promotion for me – thank you, Russ!

Now back to Felden and our next imminent house move.

During those few years it became obvious that our daughter Lucy was developing a skill with horse riding. Elly and I had taken her to a school fête one summer and, as she was drawn to the horses, we let her have a go. Well, imagine our surprise when off she went on this pony with a perfect rising trot! It was meant to be – so we investigated locally, found a riding school nearby and got her started. It wasn't long after that that we decided to get her a pony of her own.

My agent, Jean Diamond, was an avid horsewoman herself, so I asked for her assistance in finding a suitable mount for Lucy, and she was delighted to help. Jean pointed us straight at David and Marion Mould, with whom she worked on a regular basis. David had been a jockey to the Queen Mother for many years and Marion, as Marion Coakes, had won many showjumping tournaments on her wonderful horse – well, pony really – called Stroller. They happened to have a pony available, which Marion was reluctant to part with as he reminded her so much of Stroller. She always said that if he had been an inch taller, he would not have been for sale! So there he was, Dudley, and we brought him home from their Lingfield estate to our riding school in Hemel.

We continued to spend time at the riding school with Lucy as she made great progress, but we collectively decided that it would be ideal to have our own place where we could stable and graze the horse ourselves. It wasn't long before we got another horse for Elly to ride as well. She had been a rider as a girl, so we went back to David and Marion and bought a wonderful sturdy mount for her called Coco. He was a chestnut cob and David had nicknamed him 'Cobby', but we preferred Coco!

So, with this escalating stable of noble beasts mounting, the search began for another house to accommodate not only our double family but also our two horses.

We found a perfect place, not far away, in a village called Chipperfield, where I had taken Leslie Dwyer for that pint at the local a few years before. It was another house which managed to suit our needs, with separate living quarters for both families, although we had to share a kitchen until one could be equipped for Elly's mother. The land at the back had a few outbuildings, a substantial stable block for the horses and a couple of acres of grazing land too. Lucy joined the local Pony Club once we were ensconced there, and she had some wonderful times, as did her proud parents. We moved there in 1985, but as it turned out, it wouldn't be very long before we were moving again!

The Move to Somerset

We had been in Chipperfield for nearly four years when we started to think about the future schooling for our children. Lucy had been at Berkhamsted School for Girls and was due to go into sixth form. Sam was at Beechwood Park, a prep school near St Albans, and was due for his secondary school years. We had friends who were already sending their child to Millfield in Somerset, and they were always talking about how wonderful they thought it was, so we decided to check it out for ourselves. The fact that I had been busy on TV for several years had given us the chance to use the independent school system for our kids. The children responded well to the idea, so we decided to carry on with it.

Having investigated Millfield, it turned out that the boarding fees were well beyond our reach. Was it out of the question? Well, not if they were day pupils – but we would need to move to Somerset! That was a big step and there was a lot to consider. I was just at the start of my time in *You Rang, M'Lord?* Having made the pilot, we were about to embark on the first series later in the year. The big issue was, would my parents-in-law want the upheaval of a move as far as Somerset? Well, as I have already said, they were potty about the kids and would do anything for them. They thought it was a wonderful idea and couldn't wait! Elly and I were astonished, as we thought that another move would be the last thing they would want. We arranged to take the kids for an interview with the headmaster and both Lucy and Sam passed with flying colours!

They were due to start in the September of that year, 1989, with Sam in the secondary class and Lucy in the sixth form. We needed to put the house in Chipperfield on the market and find somewhere to live in Somerset ... and that always takes longer than one thinks it will! What happened was that it swiftly became necessary for Elly to go and live with the kids in temporary accommodation, while Elly's parents and I resolved to stay in Chipperfield for as long as it would take. Elly found a flat conveniently near the school and the kids were able to start at Millfield without any problems.

In the meantime we started to look around the area for a property that would suit our growing family – growing, that is, in terms of cats, dogs and horses! Elly's dad, Harold, and I drove down on many fruitless journeys to the West Country, looking without any luck for a suitable property. We just couldn't find anything that would conveniently convert to accommodate our two families. Then one day Elly and I were sent details of a former farmhouse that seemed perfect. We decided to go and look at it and it *was* perfect! A little more expensive than we would have liked, but the pros very much outweighed the cons.

The house was situated at the top of a hill with a dairy farm next door, and was about a mile and a half from the school. It had a huge barn, a stable block and several acres of grazing land, which included a separate field at the end of the lane. We couldn't believe it! Elly's dad came with us to look at it and agreed with us that it was just the job. Her mum, however, now not being all that mobile, decided to leave the decision to him and took it in good faith.

We got a suitable mortgage deal and made an offer which was accepted. We were going to Somerset! It was a very exciting time in our lives, and a complete change of pace as far as lifestyle was concerned. Life was so much slower there, and almost stress-free. The best advice we had was from a lady that Elly and the kids had got to know while they were living in the temporary flat – if you are driving anywhere, always allow an extra fifteen minutes for the sheep! It was so true. Anywhere, at any time, you could guarantee a farmer would be moving his flock across or down a lane, and you just had to wait. That's country living!

By the summer holidays the moving date was fixed, and we moved down to our new home in the country – Hill Farm. Elly and I moved in first, with the kids, to get sorted before Elly's mum and dad joined us. I'll never forget, on our first morning there, having slept on the floor in sleeping bags before the vans arrived with our stuff, we had gone outside to smell the country air and Sam, being full of beans, ran down into the field screaming at the top of his voice with excitement.

'Be quiet, Sam!' I shouted, in a hoarse whisper. 'You'll wake the farmer!'

This was about 8.30 a.m., and when I told Graham, our neighbouring farmer, this story a little while later he was greatly amused, as by then he had done virtually a day's work. A different world, but I soon got used to it!

The big change for me came when I started work on *You Rang, M'Lord?* later in the year. I started by going up to London by train, to Paddington, but it wasn't easy. You see, although I could get a train from Castle Cary, about 6 miles away, coming back wasn't easy, as the only train back in the afternoon didn't leave Paddington until 4.30 p.m. As a result, I had to hang around the rehearsal room for hours because we didn't usually rehearse much beyond 2.30 p.m. I soon decided to drive, and although I enjoyed driving, I was doing about 1,200 miles a week!

The Somerset Years

The years we spent living at Hill Farm in Somerset were from the start, by and large, happy times. Harold loved it, and as a keen gardener, he kept control of the not insignificant space around the house. He dug out a huge vegetable garden along the side of the riding arena and planted everything from potatoes to runner beans, radishes to cabbages. We did not go hungry!

The girls continued to ride, and we even acquired some sheep to add to the menagerie. Our Cavalier King Charles spaniel had given birth to a litter, and we ended up keeping four of them. I was consulted, but it was only a symbolic gesture, as I just kept hearing myself say, 'All right then!' We also had about four cats by then too, and our border collie, Holly, who had made it her life's work to make sure the horses ran correctly around the arena! She had devoted herself to the horses so much that, when the sheep arrived, she didn't want to know them at all. A sheep dog who dislikes sheep. Typical!

Life went on, and *You Rang, M'Lord?* came up for a series every year for four years, with me driving up and down to London. I had also been seconded into the cast of Radio 4's *Weekending* by this time, which was recorded on a Friday morning and aired that same evening. It involved many different voice impressions, mainly of the politicians of the day, which was right up my street. I was working with Toby Longworth, who could do everyone, and Sally Grace, whose 'Margaret Thatcher' was second to none! Sally and her husband Richard have become firm friends over the years.

I had been a fill-in guest on the show many times before, but then I joined the cast permanently, taking over from the excellent Alistair McGowan, who had gone on to pursue his TV career. It was a wonderful opportunity to do some comedy voices, most of which were government ministers, one of my favourites being Kenneth Clarke. I remember once Alistair McGowan saying you could sometimes use one person's voice to create another, and he gave an example of how he used Dot Cotton from *EastEnders* to give him Albert Steptoe from *Steptoe and Son*. Using the same premise, I created an impression of Kenneth Clarke using the voice of Derek Nimmo. It must have worked because Sally Grace's husband Richard Edis, who was himself a retired radio producer, said it was the best 'Kenneth Clarke' he had ever heard!

I loved doing *Weekending* – proper funny satire for me to get my teeth into – and I'm glad to say I managed to stay around with the cast until early 1995, when the schedule just proved impossible. I had been unavailable to take part several times because of other work, touring the country with plays, location filming and the like, and I was beginning to feel very guilty about letting the producers and my fellow cast members down. Maybe I should have jumped ship earlier ... because I was eventually pushed! Yes, I was dropped from *Weekending*, much to my dismay – but you can't be everywhere can you?

As the 1990s went on, the rot began to set in, as it had become apparent to me that I was virtually married to three people. Elly's

The First Rule of Comedy..!

parents had strong opinions about most things, and when decisions had to be made, Elly always asked me to keep the peace and agree with them, as it usually meant that she would get a hard time from them if it went the other way. Well, this was all very well, but it soon turned out that I was unable to make a decision in my own house!

My marriage to Elly had started to take a downward turn and things were not really as they should have been. The fact that I spent a lot of time working away from home helped relieve the pressure to some extent, but things just weren't right. We continued to have visitors coming to stay, and in the summers we held barbecues and other gatherings, which were great fun. But – and it was a very big 'but' – in 1993 Harold was diagnosed with prostate cancer. He spent some time in and out of hospital in Bath, and one day, while he was in the hospital, he had a stroke. It was quite severe and he was robbed of his power of speech, and the use of his left side. I remember all the family from Coventry coming to see him. That consisted of Elly's two brothers and their families, and although Harold couldn't speak, I will never forget him grabbing hold of Elly's mum and giving her a squeeze with his good arm. It was such a hard squeeze that it made her cry out in pain, but it was clear to me that he was saying goodbye. His own father had died of a stroke just after Lucy was born and he obviously thought that this was his time.

Very soon after that, we were called into the hospital one evening as Harold had gone into a coma. Elly and I spent the night at his bedside, and early that morning he passed away in his sleep. I was very sad to see him go as, although our relationship was becoming strained, he was the man I had called 'Dad' from the day I married Elly, my own father having passed away when I was only 14.

Elly's mum continued to live in her half of the house for a while, until it became clear that she needed help with most things, as she was quite immobile due to a hip replacement that had gone wrong. The decision was eventually made that she would go into care and we found a lovely retirement home nearby, called The Cyder Barn. It was a lovely place, run by a lady who assured us that her residents did not come there to die. 'They come here to live!' she said. Elly's mum was very happy there and had a lovely room with a view of the garden at the back of the house.

At the end of that year, 1993, I was in a pantomime at the Birmingham Hippodrome in a production of *Dick Whittington*. There was an extraordinary array of stars in the cast! Lesley Joseph, very popular at the time as the man-hungry Dorien in *Birds of a Feather*, played Fairy Bow-Bells, and John Nettles, who was one of TV's favourite detectives, Bergerac, was a brilliant, almost Shakespearean, King Rat! That breathtaking dancer and actor Wayne Sleep played Tommy the Cat, and veteran entertainer Vince Hill, who had been a chart sensation since the 1960s, was Alderman Fitzwarren. Vince was having a really difficult time getting his head around playing an older man, Alice's father, about to turn 60; it was the first time that he was not playing the juvenile lead! We also had my old friends the Simmons brothers as Captain and Mate. The beautiful Rosemarie Ford, who was on TV as Bruce Forsyth's assistant on *The Generation Game*, was Dick, the principal boy, and because he was very popular at the time, Wolf, from the *Gladiators* TV show, was King Rat's assistant. What a line-up! Ross King, who now lives in Los Angeles, played Idle Jack, my son, as I was playing Sarah the Cook, the dame. It was such a brilliant show that it was video-recorded for the archives of the Theatre Museum in London!

The pantomime may have been as sweet as a nut, but my domestic bliss was anything but. When I was back for a weekend, things got very beady, and Elly and I had a major bust-up. It was so serious that it was decided that I would leave. Things had got very strained, and, to be frank, it seemed inevitable. I summoned Lucy and Sam and told them that I was going, and that their mum and I were splitting up. It was horrendous and I will never forget their faces as long as I live. I got in my car and headed back to Birmingham with tears rolling down my face. I found it really difficult to get through the next few performances, and I confided in a couple of close friends in the cast. They were very sympathetic, of course, but it was a strain on Christmas fun, I can tell you.

Not long after that, Elly came up to Birmingham to try to mend things, and we talked and talked and eventually decided to give it another go. For a time, things got back to a semblance of normality. After the panto season was done for another year, we carried on at Somerset. A little later in 1994, as summer drew near, the kids were finishing their education and Elly and I decided to throw a big party. Lucy had been at Christchurch College, in Canterbury, where she got a BA Hons degree in Radio, Film and Television Studies, and after his sixth form and A levels, Sam was due to go to St Andrews University, in Scotland, to study astrophysics. It seemed like a good idea at the time, but as it turned out, Sam became very disillusioned with the course he was on and asked his mother and me if he could leave. Not wanting him to be unhappy, we said 'yes', so he came home. That was all a couple of years later, though! In the meantime, my career on the stage was still wonderfully buoyant because of my ongoing situation-comedy fame – and I was about to meet someone who was later to become the new leading lady in my life.

Enter Judy Buxton

During 1994 I had been asked to do a play with the wonderful Marti Caine. It was *The Gingerbread Lady* by the absolutely brilliant Neil Simon. What a thrill! The play was to be directed, we were told, by Marti's husband, Kenneth Ives. We were to do a short run at the Theatre Royal, Windsor, followed by a week in Marti's home town of Sheffield. It was during this time that I met a lovely member of the cast called Judy Buxton. I had never met her before, but I remembered seeing her, many years earlier, in a daytime soap called *General Hospital*, in which she played student nurse Katy Shaw.

She and I were nothing more to each other than colleagues in the play. She was living with an actor called James Kerry, whom she had met during her time on *General Hospital*, and they had been together since then – over twenty years. I, of course, was still married to Elly.

We went on our trip to Sheffield, where it became embarrassingly obvious that Marti's husband, Kenneth Ives, had designs on Judy. So much so that he had threatened to come to her hotel room one afternoon! It's worth mentioning that the marriage of Marti and Kenneth had well and truly disintegrated by then, and although they were managing to work together, they drove separate cars. Judy came to me distraught, and we decided that it would be best to escape. The cinema seemed the safest option. The film we went to see was, of all things, Steven Spielberg's *Schindler's List*. A wonderful film, no doubt, but not a laugh in it!

In the event, however, I had to leave the cinema early to do a radio interview, so I left Judy safely ensconced in the dark and out of harm's way. I never did find out how that film ended! The week in Sheffield panned out, and at the end of it, I gave Judy a lift back to London. As I had another radio show to do, I dropped her off outside Broadcasting House and she made her way home from there. That was that – or so I thought!

1994 ran its course and I was due to do *Dick Whittington* again – talk about 'turn again, Whittington'! For this particular season, I was down in Southampton, at the lovely Mayflower Theatre. There were a few changes to the cast this time, and the always wonderful Windsor Davies came in to play Alderman Fitzwarren. Just terrific! The assistant to King Rat was another bit of gimmick casting, but great fun, as he was played by that fantastic Olympian with the most infectious laugh, Kriss Akabusi.

Ross King had dropped out of the company, while in place of Wayne Sleep, the Cat was played by one of the boy dancers. It was still a cracker of a show, though, and we went on to do it for a number of years after that. During the latter part of the year, while I was away, Judy had phoned my home to speak to me, but, as I wasn't there, Elly answered. Judy had phoned to tell us that James, her partner, had died of cancer. Elly very kindly offered her a break away at our Somerset house if she would like, and she thanked her, but nothing came of it.

1994 became 1995 – no surprise there! – and I was offered a tour of a new play called *Bare Necessities*. It was written and directed by Rob Bettinson, who was responsible for the great West End success *Jolson*, which was an enormous box-office hit for Brian Conley. In *Bare Necessities*, I co-starred alongside the lovely Geoffrey Hughes, with whom I had done *Run for Your Wife* in the West End ten years before. Marji Campi and Karen Archer were also in the cast, and it was a joy working with actors of their calibre! It was actually this tour which was the final straw for the producers of *Weekending*. Because I was committed to *Bare Necessities* for the three-month tour, they gave me the big heave-ho! It was such a shame, but you can't do everything, and to be totally honest here, the pay for touring theatre was far better than for radio. You know the old joke: I'm wearing my BBC suit – it's the one with the small checks – cheques! Get it?!

It may come as no surprise to you that these few years, in the early to mid-1990s, were quite eventful and, as a result, a bit of a blur in my memory. So much happened to change my way of life, and I am having great difficulty remembering things in the right order! One of the major events was the start of David Croft's series *Oh, Doctor Beeching!*, for which we made a pilot. The first and second series took us as far as 1997 and had its own drama to relate, so please see the separate section on that. It's well worth the read!

It was during this year, though, 1995, that I wrote to Derek Nimmo, who regularly sent tours of comedies out to the Middle and Far East. I thought that I was probably the only comedy actor who had never done one of these, so it seemed that it was worth a try. As it happened, Judy had already been cast in his next one, unbeknownst to me.

Anyway, Derek Nimmo seemed to be at a loss as to whom to cast for one particular role. As Judy was already on board, Derek phoned her to ask if she knew anyone who would be suitable to play George Pigden in this show, Ray Cooney's farce *Out of Order*, as he couldn't think of anyone himself. She said she would have a think and call him back. She thought no more about it for quite some time, and then suddenly, out of the blue, she thought, 'Jeff Holland would be good in that!' But she never got round to calling him back to tell him. Spookily enough, I got a message from my agent, Jean Diamond. Yes, you guessed it! I can only think that Derek had a brainwave and thought I would fit the company. Either that, or he realised he had used everybody in the vast company of British comedy thespians except me, and he wanted the complete set!

Whatever the reason, Jean told me that Derek Nimmo had asked if I was available for the part. I was, and clearly fate took a hand. Off I went in his production of *Out of Order*. We travelled to Hong Kong, Singapore, Kuala Lumpur and Bangkok. We then came back to the UK and did a spell at the Theatre Royal, Windsor, during which time it had become apparent that my marriage to Elly had crumbled away almost completely. The writing was on the wall, as they say; it was over. We went away again to the Middle East with the show and it was while we were there, and completely unexpectedly, that Cupid fired a little arrow at Judy and me, and we fell for each other like a ton of bricks! Neither of us was looking. I was smarting from my break-up with Elly, and Judy was still mourning the loss of James, but there it was.

When we came back, I returned to Somerset and started to put the wheels in motion to sell up the house. Elly moved out and went to share a flat in London with a friend. Lucy was still away at the time, in Bournemouth, where she had met her first husband Kevin. Sam was still up at St Andrews struggling with that course he didn't like, and it was still a year or so before he dropped out. I didn't know then, of course, that it was going to take the best part of two years to sell the house, but we pressed on.

Panto came round again and it was *Dick Whittington* again, at Woking this time. John Nettles wasn't available, so the lovely Robert Duncan played King Rat this time round. I stayed in Woking, at a friend's house, but was up and down to Judy in London as well as having to pop back occasionally to Somerset. It was a very gloomy time for me – well, all of us really. I went back to the house when it was necessary, but fortunately I was able to trust Libby – Graham and Paddy's daughter from the farm next door – to come and look after the horses for me on a regular basis, and to feed the dogs and cats! As time went on, we decided that the horses should go to a new home, as it was unlikely that Lucy would be back to do any riding.

We got in touch with David and Marian Mould again and they arranged for a horse box to come and collect the horses, grooming kits, the lot! They were taken back to a farm on the south coast and we did manage to arrange for Lucy to visit them once, although Marian thought it unwise as it would be too emotional. It was – but she coped, bless her! Lucy was very cross that her horses had been 'taken away from her', as she put it. She was right, but there was little else we could do.

The wait on the house sale continued. It was interminable. As a result, 1996 is a bit of a blur for me. I know we did the first full series of *Oh, Doctor Beeching!* at some point, and I remember spending a lot of time on my own at the house. I was running out of money and my debit card had been declined at Safeway! This may have been later in 1997, but as I said, everything is a bit of a blur. I did somehow keep going, though, and I remember putting on a video one night. It was the Kevin Costner film *Field of Dreams*. It's a wonderful story of hope, and I desperately clung onto the motto in it: 'If you build it, they will come.' I was keeping my fingers crossed that someone would come and buy the house!

But panto came round yet again, this time at the Theatre Royal, Plymouth. Nicholas Parsons played Fitzwarren this time and Maria Rice Mundy took over as Dick. And so we went, fingers crossed, into 1997.

Well, as it happens, someone did come. I wasn't there at the time, but the estate agent sent a lady to see the house and it was Libby from next door who showed her round. The potential buyer was recently divorced and, with a decent financial settlement from her ex-husband, she wanted our house. She too was a horsewoman with children, and to this day I only know her by her nickname, 'Bumble'! Her real name is on the paperwork, but she's Bumble to me! I happened to be in my agent Jean's office when I got a call that she had made an offer, albeit a low one, and I told the estate agent that if she could see her way to raising it to a figure that my head had settled on, she would have a deal. I left it at that, and I was still chatting to Jean minutes later when the offer came back. We did have a deal!

This was 1997 and the housing market was in a state of flux. Even though I was happy with Bumble's offer, it was still a few hundred less than I had originally paid for it. Still, I was thrilled to have it sold at any price. To be honest, I was completely exhausted by the whole process and so I was glad to be done with it. I managed, with Sam's help, to clear everything out. Elly, in the meantime, had moved into a house in Twickenham, so the dogs went there. They hated it, particularly Holly who missed her runarounds, and she would growl at me when I visited, as I was the one who had taken her away from all that she loved! It broke my heart and I feel dreadful about that even now, but what could I do?

Bumble moved in on 27 November 1997. I gave her the keys, wished her every happiness in the house, got in my car and drove to London. And I moved in with Judy on 27 November 1997 too!

The First Rule of Comedy..!

Barbara Windsor

Time for a small diversion! Another one? Yes, it's my book. So behave!

If one thinks of the *Carry On* girls, and I know my distinguished co-author has spent an awful lot of his time thinking about the *Carry On* girls – mainly in a professional capacity, it has to be said! – then most people would think instantly of Barbara Windsor. I first met her soon after she shot her last *Carry On* film in the summer of 1977, when she was playing the title role in *Aladdin* at the Alexandra Theatre, Birmingham, for the pantomime season of 1977 through to 1978. I remember the mighty David Davenport was cast as the Emperor of China. David had been a centurion to Kenneth Williams in *Carry On Cleo* and a torturer in the employ of Good King Sid James in *Carry On Henry*, so he fitted in very well!

Terry Scott, another *Carry On* luminary, was playing Widow Twankey, Alfred Marks was Abanazar, and yours truly was doubling as the Emperor's Vizier and the Genie of the Lamp. As the Genie, I remember having to make an explosive entrance through a stage trap which was operated by six burly stage hands. These chaps all had to heave together so that I could rise quickly through the hole and steady myself with a jump on to the stage. It was quite an exciting way to make an entrance, and, as it happens, I was the last actor ever to use that trap before the stage area was refurbished not long after.

Barbara Windsor was a great traditional principal boy, back in the days when the role was always played by a girl. She had such incredible energy and was a joy to behold! I encountered her a couple of years later, in 1979, when Roger Redfarn rang and asked if I could step into the breach at the Forum Theatre, Billingham, in *Calamity Jane*, replacing that lovely Welsh actor Dudley Owen, who had been taken ill. Jane was played by Barbara – brilliantly, of course! I took a train that very evening, and Roger met me at Darlington and drove me to Billingham, where I stayed in the hostel known as Billingham House. This was a notorious tower block directly opposite the theatre, where the narrow beds had those awful nylon sheets. Ghastly, but it was only for a week, as it turned out.

I rehearsed with most of the cast all that next day – not with Barbara, though, but with her understudy. Thankfully, this lovely lady knew it all, so it helped. I was replacing the character called Henry Miller, who owned and ran the saloon bar, and, luckily for me, was the only character in the show who didn't sing! I was able to carry the script around with me on a clipboard, being busy-busy as he was, and look at it if I needed to. As I say, I'm a very quick study of a script normally, and luckily I managed to absorb most of my dialogue during that day's rehearsal and found it necessary only to look at my clipboard once that night. Barbara was great in it, and very kindly presented me with a bottle of bubbly at the curtain call!

I did a panel game with Bar much later when she sang with the Ronnie Scott Quartet, and she later appeared in an episode of *You Rang, M'Lord?*, playing Paul Shane's music-hall partner Myrtle. I didn't have any scenes with her that time, though. I think the last time I met her was when she came to the panto that I was doing at the Theatre Royal, Plymouth, in 1996. That season it was *Dick Whittington* again, but a different production this time and with a different cast. As usual, I was giving my dame – this time playing Sarah the Cook – with Judy playing the Fairy on flying wires! We also had Gary Wilmot and John Challis as Dick and King Rat respectively. Bar was visiting Lesley Joseph and came and stuck her head round my dressing room door, hoping to catch sight of Judy Buxton, whom I had not long been with at that time – but she wasn't there.

Another memorable thing that happened during that panto season was that Judy, knowing that my heroes, Laurel and Hardy, had made their final ever appearance at the Palace Theatre in Plymouth in May 1954, secretly arranged with the company manager for us all to assemble one morning, not knowing where we were going. I kept quiet and went with the flow. It soon became obvious to me, however, as we walked down Union Street, that we were heading for The Palace! When we got there, I was very sad to see it in a terrible state of disrepair, having by then been neglected for many years. The company manager rang the bell and we were let in and told to have a wander round. Joy of joys, I soon found myself in the middle of that fateful stage, just thinking about what Laurel and Hardy must have felt like as Babe was keeling over and they were no longer able to work. We had a look in the dressing rooms too, which were now quite derelict. I swear I could hear him gasping for breath! It was very special, if not a trifle sad, to be there in that fateful place. A great memory, though, for any true fan!

Amanda Barrie

A friend, contemporary and fellow *Carry On* girl of Dame Barbara's was the truly extraordinary Amanda Barrie. It's not unkind to say that Amanda is as mad as a box of frogs, and ten times as beautiful. And talented. Her instinct to throw in disconnected ad-libs – particularly on cue lines – could confuse a less experienced actor but, happily, I had done my time in rep and could cope with it. The production was an outrageously farcical summer season play called *Kindly Keep It Covered*. If I tell you that Dave Freeman wrote it – he of *The Benny Hill Show* and the *Carry On* films writing fame – then you'll know the kind of play it was. One very kind BBC radio reviewer said, 'It's frothy, it's saucy – and it's very, very funny.' Well, quite.

I was actually a last-minute replacement for Terry Scott, so I was given top billing and a very good salary, thank you very much. I think they were desperate. 'They' being producer Bill Kenwright, who needed some sort of comedy name for the lead role. And I was available. I wasn't that keen, to be honest, but I can be bought, like anybody in this business. Producers, I hope you are taking note. Anyway, my co-star in this piece was the lovely and extremely good Robin Nedwell. Sadly, he came to a sticky end, at the far too young age of just 52, ironically – for an actor well known for playing sitcom medic Dr Duncan Waring – collapsing, after a fall, in his doctor's waiting room.

Amanda probably had the right idea to spice up the action and go off at comic tangents all the time. I say tangents, but her diversions had little or nothing to do with the plot – such as it was. It was all about an insurance company, hence the double-meaning title. Very Dave Freeman, that. Anyway, let's say Amanda would have a line like: 'I told you, I put the papers back on the table!' She would actually say, 'I told you, I put the papers back on the table. That brown one, over by the window ... nice, isn't it ...?' and just slowly drift off into nothingness. You had to be wary that these little curveballs could come your way. So I would pause after the cue and let Amanda do her disconnected mutterings, and *then* pick up with my line. It was bonkers, but fun. A bit like Amanda, really! Love her.

Judy Buxton and the 'Noughties' – Ooh!

Having moved in with Judy in November 1997, my life had changed yet again. I no longer lived in rural Somerset, but in a Victorian mansion block in Chiswick, West London. Not only that, but we were on the second floor and there was no lift. My thighs felt the benefit, but my lungs didn't! I was smoking again at this time, having started again when my marriage ended. Stupid, I know, but as Judy was a smoker as well at the time, it didn't seem to matter. But I decided I wanted to go on living for a while longer, so it had to stop. It did a short time later, when we both decided to go 'cold

The First Rule of Comedy..!

turkey' and stopped altogether, just like that! The diary says it was Friday, 27 March 1998, a memorable day for both of us. It wasn't easy, and don't let anyone tell you it is! We did have each other to answer to, though, and that really helped. Suffice it to say that we have never smoked since. We had to have the flat redecorated and new carpets fitted because the smell of stale tobacco smoke every time we came in through the front door was unbearable!

As we headed for the summer of 1998, I had been offered a season at one of our favourite places, Bournemouth Pier, in a production of *See How They Run*, which was to star Britt Ekland, Su Pollard, Victor Spinetti and Hilary Minster (from *'Allo 'Allo!*) as well as myself. After the season we were to do a tour of the UK, which was great fun! I remember, though, as part of the official launch for the summer season, we were all to be taken out on a luxury motor yacht from the side of the pier, and when Britt arrived, looking a million dollars it has to be said, Su, meaning well and in a very loud voice, shouted, 'Ooh duck, you look like a movie star!', to which Britt replied, in full Norma Desmond mode, 'I *am* a movie star!'

That was very much the state of play because Britt was very aware of her status in the business and behaved accordingly! She seemed to have a very American attitude towards waiters in restaurants, which I found a bit unnecessary and sometimes rather embarrassing. Never mind, I didn't mix with her that much. Su was much more my style!

During our tour, which took me right up to panto, Judy was back in the Far and Middle East for Derek Nimmo again. She was doing a production of *Move Over Mrs Markham* and it was during this time that I realised just how much I loved her, and how much she meant to me. We hadn't been apart really until now, and for me it was hell! She came back for a short while and then went off to Aberdeen for panto, playing Mrs Darling and the Magic Mermaid in *Peter Pan* starring Sonia! I was back in our *Dick Whittington* at Wimbledon, and this time, my old pal Bill Pertwee was playing Alderman Fitzwarren.

Pretty Girls Aren't Funny

I have already mentioned that *Run for Your Wife* had become a regular visitor to my life, and now it raised its head once more, in a most unusual way! Leslie Lawton, who had been assistant to Ray Cooney for a while, as erstwhile replacement director of said play, approached us to ask if we would like to take a production of it to Israel. He had been working over there for some time, directing shows in both English and Hebrew, at which he was becoming quite adept. He had a production of it up and running in Hebrew and wanted to bring an English version over to see what they would make of it.

Well, we rehearsed and flew to Tel Aviv in mid-February. We were only there for a couple of weeks and, having done several one-night shows in various venues across Israel, we were invited to watch a version of it in Hebrew. Well, it was fascinating, to say the least, as we didn't understand a word, apart from interjections of the words 'Wimbledon' and 'Streatham' every so often! The leading lady playing Mary, the part Judy always played, was Israel's equivalent of our Joan Collins, or so we were told, and dressed accordingly. She was determined to maintain her glamorous image, including her hair style. She was the most well-turned-out taxi driver's wife you would ever have seen!

It was while we were over there that we heard the sad news that Derek Nimmo had suffered a serious fall at his home, which had resulted in a stroke from which he never recovered, and he died only a few weeks later.

However, *Run for Your Wife* stayed around for a few visits in 1999. We did a cruise on the *Marco Polo* (more later) and then came a season for Judy on – yes, you've guessed it! – Bournemouth Pier again. It was for the summer season and starred Bobby Davro and Fraser Hines. It was another happy season for us but with a difference. Bobby Davro was playing Stanley and there was a tour of only a few weeks booked to follow it, but Bobby couldn't do it as he was booked elsewhere. So, as I was around there with Judy for most of the time, they asked me to take over as Stanley for the tour.

The First Rule of Comedy..!

I was thrilled! John Smith is a lovely part to play and I had always loved it, but Stanley was the fall guy and I relished the opportunity to have a crack at it! It soon came round and I loved it. It was only for a few weeks and was over far too soon, but it wasn't the last time I got to play Stanley.

Judy and I were asked by Qdos again to do a panto season at The Grand in Wolverhampton that same year, which I have already talked about in my Wolverhampton piece, but what I haven't said is that it was an extremely long season and ran for just over eleven weeks. It was *Jack and the Beanstalk* and starred John Nettles, Jesse Spencer from *Neighbours*, myself and Judy, and featured Tony Adams, late of *Crossroads* – oh, and Otis the Aardvark! We all had a wonderful time, although we were exhausted by the end of it. I didn't mind a bit, though, because as it turned out, I had dug a bit of a hole with the tax man at the time and that long run of panto earned me some good money, so I was able to square things in the end.

I told you Derek Nimmo had died, but the good news for us was that his son Piers decided to carry on his father's business and continue to produce these foreign shows. Piers managed four or so shows a year and said he didn't know how Derek had managed to do eight or nine!

He was doing *Harvey*, made famous by James Stewart in the old Hollywood movie, and when I heard that he was having difficulty casting the lead, I rang him and volunteered. His wife Marina answered the phone, and when I told her why I'd called, she shouted through to Piers who was in the bath at the time, and he was so excited he jumped right out of the bath and ran naked to the phone! It's a good job we didn't have FaceTime then! He asked me to do it and we had a lovely time going to all those exotic places that we loved to visit. Judy joined me in Abu Dhabi and we went on to Al Ain and Muscat, and then came home. It was marvellous and we were so lucky.

It just occurred to me that, while I am chronologically in 2000 at the moment, it would be appropriate to mention that my first grandson, Tom, was born on 17 August. Sam and Leigh, who weren't yet married – but, silly me, they do it the other way round these days, don't they? – gave me my first grandchild. I was now a 'grandad'! Wheeeee!

Our panto seasons were separate again in 2000, as I went to Newcastle with *Dick Whittington* once more, and Judy wasn't far away in Darlington doing *Cinderella*. She was playing Fairy Godmother with Stu Francis as Buttons and Ray Meagre (pronounced 'Mar'), Alf from *Home and Away*, playing Baron Hardup. I managed to get to see her show on a day off and it was superb! Stu Francis was inexhaustible as Buttons and wonderful with the children on stage for the song sheet. Judy wasn't bad either!

We both finished early January 2001 and came home to rehearse Ray's two plays and then off we went on the big cruise. Sorry if we are a bit out of sync. I've written some things by topic and not all by chronology. Still, it keeps you on your toes!

I think it might be safe to say that, between us, Judy and I kept the British theatre going during the next few years! We never stopped touring. Sometimes together and sometimes separately, but it was a busy time for both of us. Most of the plays we did were worthy of a good outing, but some, it has to be said, were just fillers which kept the money coming in. Well, a chap's got to eat!

One very worthy play that I will never forget was a production of *Travels with My Aunt* by Graham Greene. I had done a stint in a version of this play a few years before in 1993 with my friend William Gaunt at the Whitehall Theatre, but this one in 2002 was excellent! There were just four actors in it: Clive Francis playing the Aunt – wonderfully, it must be said – Gary Wilmot and myself playing the same man, Henry Pulling, and Andrew Greenhough who played everything else! He was brilliant and, with so much to do, he never let us down. It was a really classy show – if I can use that term – and was brilliantly directed by Richard Barron. We toured around the UK for several weeks and my agent Jean, who also represented Gary, worked tirelessly to try to get it into the

West End, but sadly to no avail. A shame as it would have worked there really well!

I went on to work with Gary again later that same year when we did panto together at Milton Keynes. It was my dear old friend *Dick Whittington* again with Gary in the title role this time.

A very sad memory for me, though, was having to break the news to Judy on the phone that her dear father had died. He was taken ill before Christmas and was in hospital, and Judy and I went to see him on Christmas Day on our day off. She was in panto at Wimbledon with Russ Abbot and so not far from home, and I was a short drive down the M1. Her father was very weak then and we were told to expect the worst. Judy's mother phoned me after the show on Boxing Day to say that 'darling Daddy' had passed away, and I had to break the news to Judy. He lived a very long life, though, finally giving way at the age of 94.

2003 was memorable for me, for a very special reason. After our pantos were finished, our various touring shows came back to the fore and we were both involved in a tour of Ray Cooney's hospital farce, *It Runs in the Family*, playing husband and wife Dr and Mrs Mortimore, which was to open, as well as rehearse, at our old favourite venue of Bournemouth Pier. We were there for three weeks all told, for rehearsals and a week's run. We arrived on Easter Sunday ready to start rehearsing on the Monday morning, so having settled our things in the digs, I suggested we go for a wander down to the beach. It wasn't the nicest of weather – in fact, it was blowing up a very strong wind – but we persevered and ended up on the pier.

Having got to the end of the pier, and looking out to sea, conditions were a bit nasty, so Judy said, 'Let's go back inside', but before we could go any further, I turned her to face me and, in the howling gale at the end of Bournemouth Pier, I asked her to marry me. Of all the reactions I could have got, I got one I wasn't expecting – she laughed in my face! I think I had taken her completely by surprise, though, because after the smallest of pauses, she said 'yes'.

I wanted that moment to be a memorable one for both of us, and it certainly was that! At the end of Bournemouth Pier in a howling gale? I think so!

We ended up in panto together again that year too, back at Plymouth Theatre Royal with Judy as Fairy again, up on the flying wire, and me giving my dame as usual. Something rather strange happened, though, which is worth a mention. We were approaching the end of the run when we had a visit from Jonathan Kiley, who was in charge of all panto allocation for Qdos at that time. He had invited all members of the company to the local pub, The Bank (on account of it once being a bank), for a 'thank you' drink after the show. The conversation, after being quite general, moved towards what pantos would be where the following year. I noticed that, having positioned himself some way from where Judy and I were sitting, Jonathan had become somewhat reluctant to give much away, and wouldn't look our way at all. I thought it rather strange, as I believed that she and I were thought of very favourably by the panto powers-that-be. We would, however, have to wait until much later in the year before the answer became clear. Watch this space!

In the meantime, 2004 became a very busy year for us in so many ways. Read on, dear reader, read on!

The first thing we did was fly to Cape Town in March to pick up the P&O ship *Arcadia*. We went on a two-week cruise and performed two Alan Ayckbourn plays: *Relatively Speaking* and *Confusions*. Judy and I had great pleasure performing the husband and wife roles, originally made famous by Michael Hordern and Celia Johnson, in *Relatively Speaking*. Both plays were directed by Michael Gyngell, and the second one, *Confusions*, was just that! A collection of short one-act plays which couldn't have been more different. It was a great experience nonetheless.

Next, having returned to Southampton via the west coast of Africa, we made ready for another trip abroad, this time to beautiful Vienna! We were booked to play the English Speaking Theatre in Vienna, where Judy had worked before, several years earlier, and we were to do another Cooney comedy, *There Goes the Bride* – well, it was written by both Ray Cooney and John Chapman. This was directed by Rex Garner and was an interesting prospect, because comedies need instant laughter to work properly, and in Vienna, unfortunately, we had to wait at least two beats after each gagline for the audience to translate it and then laugh – if at all! It was quite daunting at first, but we soon got used to it.

The lovely thing about being in Vienna was the opportunity to see so many beautiful sights and places of interest. We were there for seven weeks in all, and having done at least two, sometimes three, things in a day – as well as performing the play every night, of course – we still hadn't seen everything by the time we left!

Now, getting back to the mystery surrounding the panto situation: we were at a function one evening, in the company, as it happened, of Paul Elliott, who had employed us many times to do panto and, having sold his company to Qdos, still worked with them as consultant on the panto seasons. He took me aside to confide in me that, having asked out of curiosity one day where they were putting 'Holland and Buxton' this year, he was dismayed to find that we had been dropped and were no longer on their list! This explained Jonathan Kiley's shiftiness that night in Plymouth, I thought.

The long story cut short explained that it was a question of cost, and that together we were more expensive than two lesser mortals would have been! He told me that, if I took a cut in salary, he could arrange for us to be at the Opera House in Manchester that year with the Chuckle Brothers. Well, at first I was incensed but, when I realised it was probably too late by then to get a decent panto anywhere else, I began to think it made perfect sense. So I acquiesced, with Judy's consent of course, and we were booked to go to Manchester in another production of *Dick Whittington*. Same sets, different people! We had a lovely time, as it happened, but our days with Qdos had come to an end. Nothing stays the same!

Neither did we, because on Sunday, 19 September 2004 we got married! The civil ceremony took place at Pembroke Lodge in Richmond Park, with all of our closest friends and family there. It was a lovely day for all of us, and lots of friends made lots of speeches, some quite unheralded, like dear Su who stood on her table and thanked everyone for coming, only to be followed by the Master of Ceremonies banging his gavel and calling upon me, the bridegroom. Su sat down very sheepishly, saying, 'Oh dear, I think I've just done something terrible!' She hadn't, of course, having simply afforded me a huge laugh when I thanked her for saving me all that trouble! My best man was my old friend from way back in my Coventry days, Bill Johnston, who, along with his lovely wife Ann, was staying with Elly, who also drove them to the venue. Apparently she said, 'It's not every day you get to drive the best man to your ex-husband's wedding!'

Two days later we flew to beautiful Venice for our honeymoon. Such a wonderful place and we can't wait to go back! We were only there for four nights and have sworn to go there again.

On our return, we started rehearsals for a play at The Mill at Sonning, a favourite venue of ours, having visited and played there on many occasions. This was a play called *Murder by Misadventure*, a thriller. It's very strange that Sonning is the only place I seem to get booked for anything other than comedy! I'm allowed to stretch my 'serious acting muscles' there, I'm happy to say. We were both in it but never had any scenes together. I wonder why?

2005 was a busy year too, in its way. A tour of Ray Cooney's *Caught in the Net* took us around the country for most of the year, it seems, with our old friend Trevor Bannister.

The panto world changed hugely for us too, as we were offered a season with *Aladdin* at the Queen's Theatre, Barnstaple, by Ian Liston of Hiss and Boo Productions. I had known Ian from way back and bumped into him literally in the shops one day. When I told him roughly about our Qdos debacle, he virtually offered us Barnstaple on the spot. Oh, and I was to direct it too! It was quite an enjoyable experience on the whole, although I had some doubts, which isn't surprising really. We had our mates Rob Duncan to play Abanazar and Stan Pretty, whom we had known since Vienna, to play the Emperor of China. That made it great fun! It must have worked because Ian offered us a similar deal for 2006 doing *Dick* at The Hall for Cornwall in Truro. Not quite such a happy experience but, again, something different!

It was in the spring of that year that we went on another cruise – this time doing two of Ray Cooney's plays, *Run for Your Wife* and its sequel *Caught in the Net*, and with Trevor Bannister again too. I played John Smith, of course, and because my hair was quite grey at the time – it's greyer still now! – Ray, who was directing, wanted me to darken it for *Wife* and leave it grey for *Caught*. It made sense really, as there is a fifteen- or sixteen-year gap between them. As John wears a bandage around his head in *Wife*, it was easy just to mascara the bits that showed!

We flew to Cape Town and this time, when we got there, we had some time off, so we decided we would take a trip to the top of Table Mountain. We wanted to do that on our previous visit in 2004 but we couldn't, as the cable car had been closed due to high winds. We were so disappointed but so glad this time, so off we went, with Trevor Bannister leading the way like he knew it. He didn't – but we followed him just the same! When we got to the top, it was spectacular. What a view!

But who should we bump into on the top of Table Mountain but Bobby Crush! Bobby is an old friend, and I first worked with him in Plymouth when I played my first ever dame with Hinge and Bracket in 1989. He played Sleeping Beauty's handsome Prince. Well, he had just finished a stint on the same ship that we were joining, and was due to fly home, but he had wanted to do the same as us before he went, so there he was. It was lovely to see him, as always!

The two plays were a great success, and when we came home, we repacked almost immediately as we had a short trip booked to Carcassonne in the south of France. It's a wonderful old walled medieval city, and has been used in so many films that it seemed quite familiar when we got there! We only had four nights there, which we find is usually enough, before coming home.

I had a very happy time doing *By Jeeves* for Chris Jordan at the Devonshire Park Theatre in Eastbourne in August 2007. I played Jeeves, and I always felt it was a part I was born to play, particularly having played James Twelvetrees in *You Rang, M'Lord?* It was lovely to put on the black jacket and slick my hair back again! We did three weeks there and then took it on tour for four weeks after that, finishing in late October in Plymouth, from where Judy and I went for a two-night break to the wonderful Burgh Island. It's such a special place to go, even if you do need an extra arm and a leg. It's well worth it!

Two weeks later we were off again for a four-night stay in Barcelona. Wonderful!

We do get about, don't we?

Another very special thing we did in 2007 was a *Hi-de-Hi!* special on *The Paul O'Grady Show*. I first met Paul on the first night of Jean Fergusson's Hylda Baker play *She Knows, You Know!* and we had a drink together afterwards at the Greenroom Club, and Paul told me what a huge fan of our show he was! He said he and his mates all used to watch it on a Saturday or Sunday night and then meet down the pub to discuss it. They used to analyse it in detail, they loved it so much!

It was such a lovely surprise, then, to be asked to go on his show as special guests. What I didn't expect was to see him dressed in a full Yellowcoat jacket and whites! He looked wonderful and would have fitted into the show very well. There were the main four of us: Shaney, Ruth, Su and me. The show got under way with Paul on the ding-dong and the mic doing an 'announcement', while Ruth came on at the back in her Gladys outfit and a black wig – her own hair was different then, but the outfit, the original, still fitted perfectly! She did a wonderful exchange with Paul about not having his hands in his pockets and showed him how the job was done properly. It was lovely to see her back in full 'Gladys' mode again, with the broad accent, which was so funny! She went off to change to enormous applause, and he took it into a break while we all got ready to come on together.

When we did, I was seated at the extreme left end of the banquette on Paul's right, screen left, and as the chat intensified, it became clear to me that I wasn't going to get a word in. I think Paul realised this too, and threw some direct questions straight at me to get me involved, but no sooner had I started to answer than one of the others would leap in and take over. I've never seen three people so competitive to hog the limelight! I don't know why, as we were all in it together, but it turned into a competition – a Maplin's type of 'Who can talk the loudest and drown the others out?' competition!

There was a funny moment, though, when Shaney, in the middle of another free-for-all, turned to me and said something like, 'Shut up, Jeffrey!' which got a nice laugh from the audience and a reaction from me! The chat went on and some nice stories were told, and after another break, and to finish the show, we did a version of the 'Who can stuff the most spaghetti down their trousers?' competition, where Shaney went back into 'Ted' mode and got the audience at it again. The competition, with the floor crew as punters, raised £1,200 for Children in Need. It was wonderful to see the effect that *Hi-de-Hi!* was still able to have on the people who were watching us talk about it! It's on YouTube if you want to look it up.

Which brings me on to the pantomime season of 2007/08, when Judy and I were in *Jack and the Beanstalk*, at The Assembly Rooms in Derby, for producer Paul Holman. Paul had made us an offer, as Ian Liston had nothing else for us.

I was playing Dame Trott, of course, and Judy was the Fairy. Lisa Scott-Lee, from the pop group Steps, was playing Princess Amelia, and that very talented American actor Antonio Fargas was giving his Fleshcreep. Antonio was still basking in TV fame from having played Huggy Bear in *Starsky and Hutch* in the 1970s. It was a lovely production and it was towards the end of this run, in early January 2008, that I got a phone call from my agent, Jean Diamond, saying that Ed O'Driscoll from Calibre Productions was putting out a 25th Anniversary Tour of David Croft and Jeremy Lloyd's *'Allo 'Allo!* later that year. The amazing news was that Ed wanted me to play the role of René Artois! In tandem with this, Judy got a call from her agent asking if she could play Michelle of the Resistance too.

This came right out of the blue for me. I had previously been asked to go up for an audition for Ed and his director, James Robert Carson, who were going to do a tour of *Dad's Army*, with Leslie Grantham taking top billing in the role of Private Walker. I was asked to give them my Corporal Jones impression, which I had been known for giving, having worked with the original, the great Clive Dunn, in the first stage show. I did it for them and it made them laugh heartily, but I think we all knew that I was totally wrong for it. Physically, I was far too tall and, despite the heaviest rep theatre make-up available to mankind, I was the wrong age. Clive Dunn got away with it, but I couldn't! So, Ed and I said our goodbyes and off I went home, and thought no more about it. We did go and see the show when it was touring and it was a great success with a perfect actor, Richard Tate, playing the role of Corporal Jones brilliantly. Judy and I socialised with Ed and the cast afterwards, and they really got to know Judy then too. It's all about networking in this business!

So, when the opportunity of *'Allo 'Allo!* came along, we both jumped at the chance. To be part of such an iconic show was too good an opportunity to miss. Besides, our dear friend Vicki Michelle was to reprise her own TV role as Yvette. It was wonderful and enormous fun! I was somewhat worried, though, that I would not be accepted completely in the role, made famous on TV by Gorden Kaye. He was a very hard act to follow – not only brilliant in the role, but so beloved by millions of ardent admirers of the show. I needn't have worried at all, as I was told by several people who saw it that, when I came on to start the show with one of René's chats to the audience, it only took about a minute and a half before they had forgotten it wasn't Gorden at all. For this relief, much thanks!

Apart from Vicki, Judy and myself, we had a wonderfully talented cast of look-alikes and sound-alikes in the main roles from the hilarious TV series. These included the wonderful Richard Tate, who had played Corporal Jones in *Dad's Army* and remained in Ed's comedy company, now playing the fiendish Monsieur Le Clerc – lifts glasses and mutters, 'It is I, Le Clerc.' Glorious – a laugh every single time! That's great writing for you. It soon became clear that it didn't really matter who was in the show because the show itself, *'Allo 'Allo!*, was the star!

As a fringe benefit of doing the *'Allo 'Allo!* stage tour, I got to know Jeremy Lloyd for the first time too. It might seem funny that I'm saying that, because I had actually been in two episodes of *Are You Being Served?* that Jeremy and David Croft had written in the 1970s. It was that year 1977 again, the same year in which I was on television with the *Dad's Army* team, and did every showbusiness trick in the book for 'The Superstar' episode of *It Ain't Half Hot Mum*. As if to display my versatility beyond doubt, I was cast as what my script called the 'Afro Pants Man' in an episode called 'The Old Order Changes'.

Now, no names, no pack drill, but when my literary agent was offering this memoir to various publishing houses, one, a quite senior one, which was very interested, dropped out at the last minute because I was accused of doing 'black face' comedy in *Are You Being Served?*! Now, apart from the fact that the 1970s is a different country, and they did things differently there, the joke in this little scene is that I'm very much a white man trying to be cool and hip, and donning an Afro wig for that purpose. The plot – what there was of it – was that I wanted a new pair of trousers. My exclamation, with some glee, was 'Pant me, man!' Well, quite! The 'man' I was addressing this request to was none other than the wonderful Frank Thornton, as that pompous shopfloor walker Captain Peacock. The hilarity of the moment lies in the fact that Frank is dressed just like me, with the hippie gladrags and drop-out beads around his neck and, yes, an Afro wig. It's wonderful!

My second trip to Grace Brothers, the following year, was a bit more sedate, in an episode called 'The Apartment', in which I was an aloof and supercilious kind of cove, being pounced upon by three of the store's most dogged salesmen, Mr Lucas, played by Trevor Bannister; Mr Goldberg, played by Alfie Bass; and Mr Humphries, played by the most popular member of the cast, John Inman. Now, despite the fact that Alfie Bass seemed to behave more like Mr Humphries off camera, if you follow me, it was a fun experience, and John Inman, in particular, was a joy. He was one of our greatest comedy actors, and a brilliant pantomime dame. It's in the genes rather than the jeans! The item of clothing they managed to fob me off with was a rather natty sports jacket and a walking cane. My character was called 'The Blazer' because of how I was dressed.

Anyway, that is by the by. While I was making these – admittedly tiny – forays into *Are You Being Served?*, Jeremy Lloyd was very much around the place. Like David Croft, he was keen to keep a close eye on his creations. That notwithstanding, he didn't attempt to welcome me or have a chat with me. Nothing. This situation didn't alter at all throughout the rest of the 1970s or through the 1980s, when I was working on *Hi-de-Hi!* and Jeremy, with David, was working on *'Allo 'Allo!* Throughout all those years he had been around a lot at the BBC rehearsal rooms and in the canteen, while we were doing all the other Croft shows as well, but he had never managed to talk to me at any time. Not once!

Understandably, I think, I was soon under the impression, mistakenly as it turned out, that he didn't really like me. All the way up to the first day of rehearsal for *'Allo 'Allo!* when we were sitting having a coffee before we started, I felt the same. It seemed strange to me at the time that he ended up at the same table as me, but then, as I was sitting chatting to my fellow cast members, Jeremy suddenly got up out of his seat and came round the table towards me. He leaned down to confide in my ear and said, 'I am so glad you're doing this show!'

I was gobsmacked and delighted at the same time. I thanked him very much, and from that moment on we got on like a house on fire! He was so helpful to me during rehearsals, and he suggested all kinds of business, which was so useful and so good of him – and great for my interpretation of the role. Thirty years of mild worry ... for nothing! We do get rather paranoid sometimes. Bless you, Jeremy Lloyd, for your kind words to me, and for the hilarious words you entrusted me to deliver to a packed audience!

We opened *'Allo 'Allo!* on Friday, 29 August 2008 at the Gordon Craig Theatre in Stevenage. Although I knew Jeremy Lloyd was there in the audience that night, what I didn't know was that both Jimmy Perry and David Croft were also there, along with David's daughter Penny. I literally walked into David in the foyer afterwards, on my way to the bar, and I just automatically came out with 'Hello Guv'nor!', which is what I always called him.

His reply was simply, 'Bloody marvellous!' That meant so much to me!

The only drawback for me was that we had to miss my daughter Lucy's wedding to Darren on the following day, due to a matinee which I couldn't get out of. But having sent a letter from 'The father of the bride', I was told later that it wasn't needed, as it 'wasn't that kind of wedding'. I'm so sorry I couldn't have been there, though!

I'd managed to appear in almost all David Croft's TV sitcoms over the years, but never *'Allo 'Allo!* By the time it first aired in 1983, I was already involved in *Hi-de-Hi!*, so it was just impossible. Doing this tour of *'Allo 'Allo!*, though, was my way of 'completing the set'. And it was, as the Guv'nor would have said, 'Bloody marvellous!'

Going back to early 2008, our dear friend Barry Howard, who had been so brilliant in his ballroom dancing role in *Hi-de-Hi!*, passed away. He had been rather poorly for a few years with a form of blood cancer and had finally given way. Barry's funeral was one I will never forget. It took place at Bournemouth Crematorium, as Barry had lived at nearby Branksome, and when we were all assembled outside the building, the funeral director, who happened to be a friend of Barry's, came out and asked us all to follow him into this anteroom. When we got inside he apologised for the secrecy and explained that we should know about Barry's last wishes concerning his funeral. There was to be no music, no hymns, no prayers, no readings and no tributes of any kind – in fact, basically nothing at all! No reception afterwards either! He asked us to respect all that and to go into the chapel, sit with the coffin for as long as we were happy to do so, and then just leave. Well, I think we were all stunned but, knowing Barry's quirky nature, not entirely surprised!

Judy and I took a seat together on the front row and everyone else just sat in odd little groups, not knowing quite what to do next. After a couple of minutes, I got a bit naughty, and knowing Barry as I did, I turned to the room and said, 'If Barry was here he would say, "Look at them all, sitting there ... pretending they liked me!"' Well, it broke the ice to a certain extent, and people did feel able to leave after a while.

Barry and I had a rather camp greeting we had always used when we saw each other. Barry started it many years before and it had stuck. He or I, whoever said it first, would approach the other and say, 'Oh, morning Mrs ... er ...!' Just a bit of nonsense that made us both laugh, so, as I took my leave from this most singular of funerals, I went up to his casket and, putting both my hands near where his head would be, I just whispered, 'Goodbye, Mrs ... er ...!'

In July, we went to Canada. Not working, this was a holiday! I wanted Judy to see that wonderful country as I had seen it when I played there in the summer of 1988. We went to Trailfinders, and they put together a package for us so that we would fly to Calgary, stay overnight, pick up the Rocky Mountaineer train and, with an overnight stay in Kamloops, arrive in Vancouver three days later. It was amazing! The train was wonderful, and we had a lovely hostess who looked after all the passengers in our coach for the duration of the trip. She loved us Brits, but kept telling us that we 'talked funny'. We were sitting next to some old Australians who talked 'even funnier'!

The journey through the Rockies was breathtaking and I took a lot of photos. One that I was particularly proud of was my screen saver for several years! It's like being on another planet when you see something as alien as those mountains, but *so* beautiful. We stopped in Kamloops for an overnight in a lovely little hotel, and saw a show in the local hall full of dancing Indigenous people! Very 'show-ish', but the majority of the tourists loved it. Don't get me wrong, we did too, but being in the business, we could see all the flaws!

We continued on to Vancouver the following day, where we left the train and went to our hotel. From the twenty-second floor, we could see the whole of Vancouver spread before us. It was amazing, especially at night with all the city's lights on!

I took Judy to the Capilano Bridge, which is a suspension bridge across a canyon, made of cable and steel. As she had a rather delicate foot at the time, due to a sprain from slipping on a stairway, she found it rather alarming, to say the least, getting across it while all these kids were trying to make it rock from side to side! She did it for me, though, as she knew how much it meant to me. We collected a pine cone from the far side of the bridge and it now sits on our mantelpiece, along with our tourist badges from the train and a Canadian quarter coin, as part of a 'shrine', if you like, to our visit to Canada in 2008. Call me sentimental – I suppose I am!

I mention later in my cruise section that I took Judy to the Elbow Room café on Davie Street. Well, of course we went again to see our friends, Patrick and Bryan, who ran it. It was so good for me to order my favourite breakfast, the 'Eggs Brett Cullen', named after the actor of the same name, which I used to have every day in 1988. It's a version of Eggs Benedict with sides of streaky bacon and avocado. Yummy!

We visited my cousin Lorna and her husband Len too, who have been over there since the 1960s, and we had dinner with them before we came back. Lorna is the daughter of my father's sister Emily, and I used to see her as a teenager when I was a little boy visiting them on a Sunday morning in Walsall with my dad. She still had the dimples that I remembered from then!

We came home very reluctantly, but we had only a few days before we started rehearsals for *'Allo 'Allo!* We opened at Stevenage, as I've said, and ran until mid-November.

We took a break out to do panto again, this time for Paul Holman in Newark. The theatre was a bit pokey, but the town itself was gorgeous with the most wonderful market square. We had a happy season, albeit quite short, ending on 4 January 2009. Coming home, I had a good few weeks to grow my 'René' moustache again for more *'Allo 'Allo!* in early March. We did another big tour up until 20 June and had a ball. A great memory of a great show!

Victoria Wood

I have long been an admirer of Victoria Wood. What an extremely talented young lady she was! Those Acorn Antiques sketches she wrote and performed on television – with brilliant chums like Julie Walters and Celia Imrie – made us howl with laughter ... not least for me because I had experienced the shaky delights of *Crossroads* for real! Victoria Wood had also proved herself as a brilliant serious actress. Who can forget her superb performance as Sadie Bartholomew, relentless mother of young Eric Bartholomew, who would become Eric Morecambe, of course, in the BBC2 play *Eric and Ernie*? Or the drama *Housewife, 49*, in which she played Nella Last? Victoria had adapted Nella's wartime diaries for this TV film. Quite wonderful.

The First Rule of Comedy..!

I was very fortunate to appear in a production of Victoria's fantastic play *Talent*, at the Menier Chocolate Factory in London, in 2009. Amazingly, Victoria had written the play thirty years earlier, when she was only 25! It had been commissioned by the director David Leland, for performance at the Crucible Theatre, Sheffield. The play is all about the world of the talent contest – a world Victoria knew a lot about, having appeared on ITV's *New Faces*, when host Derek Hobson was in charge. Victoria starred in the original production of *Talent* and then, thirty years later, she directed us in it at the Menier Chocolate Factory!

I remember going there for an audition with Vic, and how shy she was! I was called into the room where she was sitting behind a table, alone, and I shook hands with her, and then she told me all about the play, or musical, as it now was. She got me to read a very convoluted piece about this ageing magician character, explaining how he wanted his music to be interpreted as he did his act. It was very funny, but because I was nervous – I get nervous at things like that, but never on first nights! – I gabbled it a bit, so she stopped me and asked me to do it again. Well, I knew what I'd done, so I slowed it down, and then she seemed happy enough. We chatted for a bit and I asked her if she had been busy with these auditions, which she said she had. I asked about the people she had seen, by way of conversation really, and she was rather non-committal, understandably enough, and then she finished with, 'We know who you are, though!' I was quite chuffed when she said that and left the room thinking that it hadn't gone too badly. Later that afternoon my agent Jean rang to say that they wanted me for the show. I was thrilled: I was going to work with the one and only Victoria Wood!

I was asked to play the old magician, who was a pensioner – I was only 63 at the time! There was a new extension to the piece, which she had written to make it more into a full-length play. It involved a tired 1970s rock band which she had called Triple Velvet. I thought the name sounded familiar, and then I discovered it was the name of a popular loo roll in the shops! Not in the 1970s, though, she explained, and I, along with two of my fellow actors, Mark Curry and Eugene O'Hare, were dressed in bright-blue velvet suits with wide flared trousers, long 1970s wigs and 3-inch-high platform shoes in which we were expected to dance and sing! Well we did. It was wonderful! We had such fun doing it, and there were no casualties – although we did get close in rehearsal, as we also had to cope with hand-held mics with long cables attached, which did get tangled up from time to time.

The one thing I do remember quite clearly was what a stickler Vic was about the dialogue. She wouldn't tolerate paraphrasing of any kind! Now, I am notorious at it and was admonished for my sins a few times, which I found a great leveller. I have written a few things myself, most notably speeches for villains in pantomimes, and have had to tear my hair out a few times when they were badly performed and my careful composition was ignored, especially if it was in iambic pentameter! So I knuckled down and made sure it wouldn't happen again. It was a very happy show to be involved in!

One day I was sitting in our dressing room with the three other male actors in the cast: Eugene O'Hare, Mark Curry and Mark Hadfield. We were chatting away, as we did most days, while getting ready for the performance that night, and the conversation had run its usual route of plays, TV shows, etc., past and present, that we had been involved in, and the many actors – good and bad, in our opinion! – that we had worked with in our respective careers. One theme led to another as we wound down the years and many names were mentioned, well known and not so well known, but we tended mainly to adhere to the 'well known' whom we could show off about!

As the time went on, I kept hearing myself – quite automatically, I might add, and with no ego attached – saying more and more frequently, 'Oh, I worked with him!' or 'I worked with her!' It later occurred to me that if a book was ever to be written about my life and career in showbusiness, a suitable title, summing up my time working as an actor, might well have been just that. I've been very lucky in my life to have worked with some remarkable people and I'd like to think that the same title might work in reverse too, and that they would be pleased to say, when my name was mentioned to them, 'Oh, I worked with him!'

It could almost have been the title of this very book you are reading now … if David Croft and Jimmy Perry hadn't given me a much better one!

We finished *Talent* on 15 November and we had all hoped it would be taken into the West End, as so many productions from the Chocolate Factory regularly are, but it was not to be. Sadly, the reviews were not quite up to the required standard, so the chance slipped by. Never mind! Then Judy and I went on to do our third panto for Paul Holman, another *Jack and the Beanstalk*, at Redditch in Worcestershire, from 7 December until 3 January 2010.

Before I go on, I think it's time to mention that my second grandchild was born this year. On 4 June 2010, Lucy gave me my second grandson, Harvey. As I write, he is turning 14 and is a dedicated Spurs fan. I won't make ribald comments of any kind here, as I know some might, because, as you know, I have no feelings for football at all, except that I would rather avoid it at any cost. As Queen Victoria once said, 'As long as they don't do it in the street and frighten the horses!' She may have meant something else, though!

In the early part of the year we did another tour together, which kept us busy, and then, later on, around Tom's tenth birthday, we were in rehearsals at The Mill at Sonning again for a wonderful play, *Spring and Port Wine*. I mentioned that Sonning is the only place I seem to get asked to do drama, and here we are again! I played the father, a very strict and money-careful northern man, and Judy played my wife. No surprise there, and it was easy to remember too because, throughout the play, I always referred to her as 'Mother'! It's a time-honoured piece and is now regarded, I suppose, as a modern-day classic. We were very lucky with the young people who played our children. They were very talented and we all gelled together perfectly! It was a very satisfying experience.

The week after we finished at Sonning, we went to the south of France for a holiday. Heaven knows, we were both ready for one, and this would be very special. Judy had always wanted to visit the Colombe d'Or in Saint-Paul de Vence and also, as it had been mentioned in a play she had recently done, Èze! We booked two nights at the cheaper Mercure in Nice first and had a lovely time, dining and drinking in the old town area, then we took a bus to Saint-Paul de Vence, which was so easy to do from Nice's bus station, and spent just one night there, having dinner in their sumptuous restaurant. I think I had another arm-and-leg transplant for that one too, but it was *so* worth it!

Next day we went to Èze and stayed for just one night again at the Château Eza. It wasn't terribly busy as this was mid-October, so they upgraded us to a very swish room with a bed that looked like a giant birdcage! It was wonderful and we had a balcony that looked out over a long and lush valley where we sat and enjoyed our evening tipple. What a life we lead! After a delicious dinner there too, we went back to the Mercure in Nice for two more nights before returning home. It was a dream holiday that neither of us will ever forget.

Joan Collins

The 2010 pantomime season came out of the blue for me and was something I certainly wasn't expecting. Having thought that my days with Qdos were over, they came through to Jean, yet again, to offer me the dame in a new production of *Dick Whittington* at the Birmingham Hippodrome, starring none other than Joan Collins! Because she was a bit of an unknown quantity as far as panto was concerned, they wanted people they knew they could rely on as the supporting cast. She was to play Queen Rat, a part especially created for her, supported by a King Rat played by Nigel Havers. The Fairy, or 'Spirit of the Bells' as the character was renamed for him, was to be played by Julian Clary. Judy was *so* out of the picture for this one. She has never forgiven Julian (not really)! They also booked the wonderful Keith Harris and Orville, a tried-and-tested old pro, if ever there was one. I got on so well with Keith that we stayed in touch well after the show had finished, right up until his passing.

When rehearsal started, Joan wasn't there, and we were told that she would be with us in a couple of days. 'This bodes well!' I thought, and when she did arrive, I was introduced to her along with the others, but she refused to shake hands, saying something about spreading germs, so I thought again, 'This does bode well! Not!'

Joan was Hollywood royalty and *not* an experienced panto performer, and although she gave it her best shot, I think she simply didn't have what it takes. Not her fault! Things could have been better, we others thought, if they had spent a couple of weeks with her beforehand on panto techniques and style, but this hadn't been possible. She opened to great applause, but after only a few days, she was taken ill with a chest infection. She was confined to her bed for about eight days altogether, and, as there was no suitable understudy available, they put the head boy dancer on – in drag! Well, being rather camp and *loving* it, he played it like an angry 'Ugly Sister' and, in my opinion, was much better than Joan ever managed to be. As I said, it was not her fault. She just didn't have the necessary wherewithal to carry it off. Having said all that, though, it was a very successful panto season, both for the Birmingham Hippo and for Qdos!

Terry Scott

Now, having revealed that I took over from an indisposed Terry Scott, when he proved unavailable or unwilling to take the lead in Dave Freeman's *Kindly Keep It Covered*, let's go back to Terry the comedy actor. A brilliant comedy actor but a rather tricky customer! I'm not the first to say it and I'm sure I won't be the last. His career was incredible, though, first working in partnership with Bill Maynard, and then with Hugh Lloyd in the wonderful *Hugh and I*, produced for television by none other than David Croft. There's that fantastic name again! Terry was given his own sketch show on BBC television, called *Scott On* ... various topics, from marriage to Christmas. He also became a frequent member of the *Carry On* team.

Before I report on the times I worked with him, let me tell you about the time he indirectly did me a nice favour. I never thought I would ever say that! But in 1988 I got a call from Jean to say that a tour of a play called *Kindly Keep It Covered* by Dave Freeman was in trouble, as its star, Terry Scott, had gone sick and they needed a replacement for the rest of the tour. It was produced by the late Bill Kenwright, and they wanted me to come and rehearse for just five days in Richmond while they had the understudy on, and then open in Bath the following week.

They sent me a script to my home by courier, and when I saw it, I nearly fainted. The part was huge! He was never off. No wonder Terry Scott had gone sick! Just a minute, I thought, do I need this? Even my quick-study brain would be hard pressed to learn all this in five days. Then, when I heard what pay they were offering, I definitely said 'no' to myself. I went back to Jean and said that I would do it, but only for a certain sum that would make all the stress worth it. Otherwise, no deal! We went to and fro a couple of times, but in the end I got what I wanted. So I did it! I had Bill cornered really, but I wasn't going to do it for any less. Although he appreciated me stepping into the breach and came to see me when I opened in Bath, he never used me again!

The First Rule of Comedy..!

I first worked *with* Terry Scott in 1974, at the time he had just started filming *Happy Ever After*, his domestic situation comedy with June Whitfield, which would morph into *Terry and June*. Our first production together was the pantomime *Mother Goose*, at Richmond, followed by *Aladdin*, at the Alexandra in Birmingham in 1977, and lastly *Dick Whittington*, at the Bristol Hippodrome in 1982. He played the dame in all three productions and I have to say that I probably learned more from him about panto daming than from anybody else. He was, though, not a very easy person to work with, in as much as he was very selfish and a bully to boot!

In the first show at Richmond, he did a scene with a jalopy car, which he drove on to the stage with lots of noise and explosions. Very funny for the audience, but not from where I was standing! I was given the role of a policeman in this scene, who came on and had an argument with the dame about the car generally and why 'she' shouldn't be driving it. The usual banter business! Having got the bonnet open, I had to lean in and examine the engine, and for some reason, he thought it would be very funny to fire a pistol near my head! Terry had it hanging on the upstage side of the car, out of sight of the audience. It was for giving the effect of the car backfiring and was quite a good gag – but not for me. The first time he did it, I thought perhaps it was a mistake, so I let it go, but when it happened again, I knew it was deliberate. I thought it was extremely dangerous, not only to my hearing, but also because the flame that came out from the blank could have been seriously damaging! I was quite incensed and picked a moment when we both happened to be in the wings to confront him about it. I can't remember my exact words, but I know it took him by surprise and he seemed amazed that I had stood up to him. I'm glad I did, though, because it never happened again!

The next time, in 1977 in Birmingham, I didn't have any scenes with Terry directly. As I mentioned earlier, Alfred Marks was Abanazar and Barbara Windsor was Aladdin, and most of Terry's scenes were with those two seasoned professionals. Thankfully!

Again, in Terry's favour, I do remember watching his striptease routine with awe. It was as his dame got ready for bed, and Terry was absolutely brilliant at it. The audience was transfixed, as was I! Every performance! It was a regular piece he did in every production he could. He knew it always went well and, my oh my, he was good. I never attempted anything like that myself, as it was far too much like hard work. I tried to keep things simple!

But Terry's bullying ego did resurface in 1982 when several of us from *Hi-de-Hi!* were billed with him at the Bristol Hippodrome. Because of his well-established career, he was given top billing, and Paul Shane, Ruth Madoc, myself and Barry Howard were billed below him on the poster. We were quite new to TV at the time and accepted this situation. The show was directed by a well-known and established director in the theatre business called Richard Hurran.

Richard and Terry had obviously been in cahoots before we started, because as Paul and I read our first scene on day one as Captain and Mate, we came on to our entrance with a shout of 'Hi-de-Hi!' to the audience, who then shouted 'Ho-de-Ho!' back. Richard turned to Terry and quite openly said to him, 'And that's the last time we want to hear that, isn't it Terry?', to which he replied, 'Yes!'

Well, this was too much for Shaney, who looked at me and then said, 'Just a minute. That's why we're here!' which just about summed it up!

Richard mumbled something like, 'Well, we'll see', and left it at that, but we could see what we were up against. It was clearly going to be a struggle but we soldiered on!

The ultimate insult came at the finale when we took our curtain calls. It has always been a tradition in pantomime that, whatever the billing is, the principal boy and girl are last to walk down together and take their bow, as it is symbolically their wedding. Not in this production! Terry Scott had insisted, and was supported by Richard, that he would walk down last as he was topping the bill. He, more than anyone, should have known better, but there it was. It made no difference to the audience, but it was a deliberate slight to us!

First Time as a Dame

In 1989 I played pantomime dame for the first time. It happened quite by chance really, as there was no definite plan afoot!

I was appearing in *Run for Your Wife* at the Criterion Theatre, again for Paul Elliott, and we came to the end of that particular leg, as we only did about twelve weeks at any one time. The human body can only just about stand that length of time, running around the stage in a Ray Cooney farce for two hours a night at 90 miles an hour! Paul was giving his customary end-of-term party at his house, which he always very kindly did at the end of each company's run. This was in the spring, sometime in April, and he had already booked me for panto later that year to play Muddles, the lead silly comic role in a production of *The Sleeping Beauty* at the Theatre Royal in Plymouth. The show was to star those two inimitable characters Doctor Evadne Hinge (George Logan) and Dame Hilda Bracket (Patrick Fyffe), and I was very much looking forward to working with them as I was a huge fan. Honestly, those two could have me in fits! If you don't know them, please search out their TV and radio programmes. 'Hinge and Bracket' – hilarious!

As Paul Elliott was seeing me off the premises at the end of the soirée, I just happened to ask him, 'By the way, Paul, who is playing dame with us at Plymouth this year?'

I could see I had touched a nerve because he winced and said rather reluctantly, 'Well, nobody at the moment, that's the trouble!'

I said, 'Oh, why's that?'

To which he replied, 'Well, everyone I've asked has said "no". They all say it would be like having three "dames" on the stage with Hinge and Bracket on the bill.'

Well, I was amazed and said, 'That's ridiculous because those characters are totally, one hundred per cent female! A dame is very much a bloke in a frock!'

He mumbled a sort of grudging agreement, and then I heard myself say those three fateful words: 'I'll do it!'

I had taken him – and myself, I think! – completely by surprise. He looked at me with a half-smile on his face and, after a considerable pause, he said, 'All right!' The deed was done!

This was Saturday night and on the Monday following I got a phone call from Roger Redfarn, who was not only directing the production but also running the Theatre Royal at that time. He said what a good idea it would be if I were to play the dame instead of the comic, as we needed a new generation to succeed the old school, and I would be ideal. My decision had suddenly become his idea. He was good at that!

Strangely, I had always maintained that no man should ever attempt to play dame until he is at least 40 years old, as he doesn't have the right 'weight' to carry it, and it looks like he's doing it for the wrong reasons. Here was I at 43 ... long overdue! Everything fell into place and, come December, I was donning frocks for the first time and loving it. I took to it like a duck to water and went on to play the dame in every panto I did for the next twenty-five years! The only two things I couldn't tolerate were lipstick and a padded bra. I felt choked and restricted in a padded bra, so I had pads sewn into the frocks, and I used a red carmine greasepaint stick on my lips, which was odourless and tasteless. I've never looked back!

Su Pollard

I really have to finish this section of the book with another couple of memories of the funniest pretty girl I've ever been on television

The First Rule of Comedy..!

with: Su Pollard. It was early days on *Hi-de-Hi!*, but Su had already become one of the nation's favourite characters.

Su and I were in this pantomime horse for a hilarious sequence and, luckily for me, it was Su who got the thankless task of being in the back end! It's a very funny scene. One of the funniest! The episode was 'Empty Saddles'. You remember the one, with the pantomime horse riding the real horse and old Mr Partridge looking at his booze and his banana and quickly deciding that the fruit was at fault and chucking that away before having a big swig of the scotch. Wonderful comedy reactions from Leslie Dwyer and one of the funniest visual gags ever dreamed up for television! However, the whole set-up for that joke proved a little too close for comfort for Su, for, you see, we naturally had that real horse in the scene too. Well, when this real horse clocked the pantomime horse, it took rather a fancy to it. The real horse was getting more and more interested in the pantomime horse, and more and more aroused! The real horse then started sniffing round the back end of the pantomime horse. 'Oh, 'eck!' said Su – at least that was the gist of what she said! Then she gave a brilliant Olly Hardy 'Why don't you do something to help me!', but I was helpless. If this real horse was going to mount the pantomime horse, there was nothing I could do! I was up the front end and all I could think to say was: 'Su, you'd better brace yourself! I'm going to eat grass!' Anyway, Su lived to tell the tale because David Croft, an experienced horseman himself, leapt forward and saved the day by grabbing the horse by the reins before any damage was done. Great story, though, and we will never forget it!

Talking about dumb animals that aren't so dumb, I'm very pleased to reveal a comedy secret within these pages. 'What another one?' I hear you cry. Yes, another one. It concerns Lady Lavender's parrot in *You Rang, M'Lord?* Being rather canny back then, I offered my vocal talents to play the voice of the parrot. Yes, folks, it's me! Every squawk and scream of that parrot is me! Percy Edwards was probably too expensive. At any rate, I picked up an additional £80 fee for the parrot. Su was tickled pink by this as she'd had a history with parrots. I'll never forget a real-life parrot that lived in a cage in the hotel at Dovercourt when we were filming *Hi-de-Hi!* Well, dear Su became rather fascinated with the bird and spent quite a bit of time with it and taught it to speak. It was only one word, but it was a beauty! I think that was the only parrot in hospitality that, when a guest walked by, said: 'Fuck off!' Thanks for all the laughs, Su!

THE FIRST RULE OF COMEDY...
ALWAYS HAVE A GREAT FINISH FOR YOUR ACT

It'll Be Alright on the Night

There wasn't much that ever went wrong on a David Croft set. His was a tightly run ship and everyone knew their place. We actors were no exception and, practised as we were in Croft discipline, we all went about our craft as efficiently as we could.

There was, however, one occasion when, during the studio session on the pilot episode of *Oh, Doctor Beeching!*, we had a 'comedy calamity'. It was unfortunately down to me! I have always been in the habit of removing my glasses whenever I am working, and although it might benefit me in an obvious way, I've never been a friend of contact lenses. I did wear them for a while back in the 1980s, when we were doing *Hi-de-Hi!* but, as they were hard lenses then, I didn't get on with them very well. I have an astigmatism in one eye – I'd always managed on stage, though, and indeed in the TV studios without 20/20 vision ... until this occasion!

It was the arrival of Mr Parkin, the new Station Master, played by yours truly, and we were on the main set, where the Station Master's office was all locked up, having been used as a store cupboard for the last several months. I asked for the key to unlock the door and, after much comedy searching and lots of 'I haven't got it!', the key was located eventually and handed to me. With a curt 'Thank you', I stepped up to the door to insert the key and let myself in.

Could I find the keyhole? I could not! The whole door was an unfocused blur to me, and there was no way I could get that key where it needed to go! I fumbled for a few seconds, but by then I realised that the moment had passed, and Mr Parkin's authority had disappeared completely. The only way out was to admit defeat, so I looked sheepishly up to the gallery and, with an embarrassed grin, said words to the effect of, 'I'm sorry, David. I can't see the keyhole!'

Well, I thought the rest of the cast would die laughing! It was the last thing they expected from me, and the audience thought the same. It got a wonderful laugh for all the wrong reasons, and after much fiddling about, I made myself very familiar with the keyhole's location and did it next time in one take. It really was a genuinely funny thing to happen, and it was the only time I have ever been a guest on TV's *It'll Be Alright on the Night*!

Oh, Doctor Beeching!

For those not reading these memoirs in order, I shall emphasise, once more, that due to my domestic upheaval at the time, the years 1995 to 1997 are a bit of a blur for me. One lovely part of the year 1995, however, was a third starring role for David Croft – my happy place of TV comedy employment! The series was *Oh, Doctor Beeching!* We had made the pilot in 1995, after David Croft had phoned to say he wanted to get the 'A-team' back together again for a new sitcom. The A-team being myself, Shaney and Su. How lovely! How flattering!

Always Have a Great Finish for Your Act

There was one big difference for this series: David was not collaborating with Jimmy Perry. Instead, the co-writer was Richard Spendlove, who was a broadcaster for BBC Radio Cambridgeshire and who had also, in his younger days, been the youngest station master on the railways when he was just 23 years old! Richard had been a very vocal admirer of Jimmy and David for many years, and had gone to them with this idea for a situation comedy. Following that old writers' rule of always writing about what you know, Richard's idea was centred around a railway station in 1963. This was a traumatic time for the railways, for it was during the days of the Beeching cuts, named after Dr Richard Beeching, whose report for the government, *The Reshaping of British Railways*, saw the enforced closure of many small community railway stations around the country. To Richard and to me, even now, this seemed like a brilliant basis for a situation comedy. And, yes, it was very Croft and Perry!

Not surprisingly, David was very keen on the idea, but Jimmy, who only liked to write about subjects he was experienced with, backed away. Moreover, he professed that he didn't particularly like railways! Jimmy couldn't invest time and effort in an idea that held no interest for him, so David decided that he would team up with Richard Spendlove himself, albeit in name only. Richard would be the first to admit that he wasn't really a writer, so David recruited various other writers to join the team, including my dear old friends Paul Minett and Brian Leveson. I had first met Min and Lev, as they are known, in the early 1980s, when they joined the sketch writing team on the Russ Abbot shows. They were also known by Roy Gould and Charles Garland, who were on David's production team, and had worked with us all for many years. It was all coming together for a reunion of a familiar and jolly comedy family!

So, we made that pilot episode in 1995 in an ideal location. They found us the most wonderful and perfect venue for our needs at Arley: a station on the Severn Valley Railway line, which was actually closed during the Beeching cuts of 1963. Thanks to the

The First Rule of Comedy..!

machinations of the Severn Valley Railway preservationists, it had been reopened in 1974, and it has been used in many films and TV programmes since. Visitors to the station are often baffled by the fact that the row of cottages where the 'staff' lived don't seem to be there. Well, the truth is that those 'cottages' were a brilliant piece of scenery and nothing more! A piece of genius created by our design team. They looked perfect, though, which is why they featured so much!

Being back with Shaney and Su was just delightful, as we all enjoyed each other's company and loved working together. It's always good to work with someone you know, as it saves a lot of time getting to know one another. Someone else whom I knew very well, and who was, for me, another connection with the old Russ Abbot days, was Sherrie Hewson, who was cast as Paul Shane's wife, May. Sherrie, as May, was also my love interest – with a secret past!

The pilot was a great success and a series was commissioned for production the following year. However, when it came to organising that first series, there was a bit of a blow, to say the least, as Sherrie had got herself a great part in *Coronation Street*, so she wasn't available to join us! David was very quick to cast around for a replacement, and the wonderful Julia Deakin was found. When we recorded the first episode in the studio – including the location footage – we had to re-record all the scenes with May in them, now being played by Julia. It went very well, though, and Julia made May her own right from the start!

The series went out later that year, although not in a very good time slot. As a result, it didn't get the viewing figures they had hoped for. A second series was commissioned, though, and that went into production in 1997. Unfortunately, they decided to schedule transmissions at 6.45 p.m. on Sunday evenings ... in July! Not only was nobody at home in the summer, as they were all out picnicking, but they took the programme off halfway through the series to accommodate an athletics tournament! By the time they put it back on, two weeks later, everyone had forgotten about it.

The viewing figures were disastrous! Shockingly, it seemed to turn out to be deliberate sabotage, as the then controller of BBC One had gone on record to say he didn't want any more 'net curtain' comedy. What I think he meant was no 'good clean family fun'!

You see, the BBC was changing in the mid-1990s, as was the world in general, and families were no longer sitting down with granny and the kids to watch the telly! Comedy was going the way of *Men Behaving Badly*, and that sort of genre was dominating the comedy scene. I have no axe to grind with that, as it was a wonderful series, well written and very well acted by the superb cast, but that was how it was going. The sort of stuff that we had been involved with was no longer wanted and, sadly, *Oh, Doctor Beeching!* was axed from the BBC's schedule. They used the excuse that the viewing figures were so bad that they couldn't justify recommissioning. It was the end of an era!

Goodbye to the Guv'nor

We had another little three-night break in mid-February and went to beautiful Prague. What we didn't realise was how cold it could get there, and we weren't really equipped with suitable attire! The temperature was around -7°C for the whole of our stay. We managed as best we could, and saw all the things we wanted to see, but it was rather a strain on our energy! The bonus was our hotel. We did an off-season deal with the Hotel Paris, a very nice old member of the Hilton group, and, just as we like it, it was possessed of 'faded grandeur'. Gorgeous! A very nice restaurant too. But if we go again, we will go in spring next time!

Judy was on tour again for a lot of the early part of the year, and then I was offered another 'drama' job at Sonning. It was a new play called *Guilty Secret* and was directed by Anthony Valentine. Tony was a lovely director and great fun, as well as knowing just

The First Rule of Comedy..!

what was what. It was a lovely thrilling crime drama and I got shot at the end. That was a first!

Another 'first' was the first week of August, which saw me filming my contribution to the film of *Run for Your Wife*. I got the part of the journalist, which actually doesn't exist in the play! I turn up with my assistant, played by Vicki Michelle's daughter Louise, to interview John Smith about his heroic deed rescuing a bag-lady – again not seen in the play but played in the film by Judi Dench. And I end up meeting his friend, played by Neil Morrissey, thinking it to be him! As I was on set for three days, I got a proper fee – fee? Well, we did it for Ray, didn't we? All the 'chums' in the background got a bottle of Pimms!

That same weekend, we were at Honington Hall, the home of the Croft family, for a wonderful black-tie 'ball', if you like, in a marquee at the back of the house. The occasion was to celebrate Ann's eightieth birthday, as well as David and Ann's fifty-ninth wedding anniversary. The next one, of course, would be their diamond, their sixtieth, but according to Penny, their daughter, earlier that year David had secretly bought Ann a diamond bracelet for that one already, and had given it to Penny to hide until the big day. Anyway, David must have had a feeling that he might not make it to that one, so he decided to give it to Ann on this occasion instead. Penny said, 'That was very "Dad"!'

Given that little tinge of sadness that none of us knew about, it was a grand evening nevertheless. We stayed in a guesthouse in the village along with a few other guests whom we didn't know. There were so many of us at the party – lots of their friends whom we didn't know and lots of our friends whom we did! Su arrived, escorted by Philip Lowrie, who had just gone back into *Corrie* as Dennis Tanner, a part he had created when the show started in 1960. When I did my day on it later that year, Philip looked after me royally, for which I was very grateful!

Even with so many people coming and going, David seemed very pleased to see me. But sadly, because of the deterioration of his condition, I found it impossible to hear what he was saying to me in the melee. He didn't say much, though, as it was mostly in passing. I just muttered something in reply and hoped I got away with it! Everyone was having a wonderful time with lots of food, wine, music and dancing. I found myself surrounded by lots of beautiful young ladies dancing round me at one point, only to find out that most of them were Croft granddaughters. Lucky old David and Ann!

I remember thinking, as the end of the evening drew near, that I would probably never see David again – a feeling I somehow shared with the Guv'nor. That's why, when I left, I snuck up behind his seated form and planted a kiss on the top of his head as I turned to go. Be it ever so humble, it was my 'thank you' to him for all he had done for me, in case I never got another chance to say it. As it happened, I was right. He died peacefully at their house in the Algarve just over a month later, aged 89.

It was a joyous occasion to remember, though, for all the right reasons. Penny told me that when Ann died, according to David's wishes, she inherited the bracelet. Wear it with pride, my darling. You had two amazing parents!

A Soap and Lots of Stage

As I mentioned above, I did a day on *Coronation Street* in December that year. I played a HMRC tax inspector called Clive Drinkwater, who turned up at the taxi office to examine Lloyd Mullaney's books. I only had two small scenes with Craig Charles, but I did most of the talking, while he just grunted 'yes' and 'no' to me. I think all I talked about was my mother's collection of Daniel O'Donnell CDs! I thought there was potential for more of the same, but it was not to be. But at least I did *Corrie* like Shaney!

Panto this year was *Aladdin* at the Derngate Theatre in Northampton. I had only been to town once before – for a week at the old Theatre Royal with *The Ghost Train* (written by my old friend Arnold Ridley) a few years earlier. That's a lovely little Georgian theatre, which is part of the same building now, the modern Royal & Derngate being somebody's idea of what a good thing it would be to incorporate the two. I think it's terrible! Never mind, they do a lot of big shows there, so you can't argue with that.

The panto starred Bobby Davro and, in second place, Brian Fortuna who was, at the time, very big on *Strictly Come Dancing* and had a lot of fans, who flocked in! We had a good supporting cast too and the show was a success.

I'll outline next a play that Judy did without me, which was quite significant for her at the time and, in the long term, led to us both doing another new play by the same author.

The play was called *The Art of Concealment*, a reference to the way that homosexuality was hidden away before it was legalised. It was about the young Terence Rattigan, one of our most celebrated playwrights of the twentieth century, as he was growing up and beginning his illustrious career. It was written by Giles Cole, who is a member of the Rattigan Society, an organisation that celebrates the life and work of Rattigan in this country.

Judy was cast in two roles, the first being Rattigan's mother Vera, who was constantly trying to get him married off! And she also played another role called Aunt Edna, who was a fictitious character that Rattigan had invented for himself to act as a critic and judge in his mind when he was writing his many works. Judy had to 'age up' throughout the play. She was beautifully 'grande' as Vera Rattigan and quite dowdy as Aunt Edna, for whom she wore a tweed Norfolk jacket with skirt to match and a suede trilby of mine over little round specs, which was perfect! The play was booked into the Jermyn Street Theatre for a couple of weeks in January and transferred to the Riverside Studios in early May for a three-week run. Nothing more came of this very clever play, which is a great shame for Giles, as he is a brilliant writer. More of him later!

Around this time I was a Vice President of the Heritage Foundation, a fundraising organisation which had lunches and evening events to raise money for good causes. One of the events I was involved in was a lunch in honour of Richard Wilson, best known as Victor Meldrew in *One Foot in the Grave*. Vicki Michelle and I were charged with having to interview him on stage about his life and career. This we did with great trepidation, but we need not have worried as he turned out to be a pussy-cat. I don't believe it!

Another of these events was held at the old Teddington Studios, which are no longer there now, to unveil a blue plaque celebrating the life of the brilliant writer John Sullivan, who was perhaps most famous for *Only Fools and Horses*. The top guests for that event were none other than Sir David Jason and Nicholas Lyndhurst, who both made very funny speeches in Sullivan's honour. I knew Nick and it was good to see him again, especially as I got to introduce him to my son Sam, who was there as my guest.

Panto 2012 took me back to The Mayflower in Southampton for *Jack and the Beanstalk* – again! This time Jack was played by Lee Mead, who a few years earlier had won the talent show *Any Dream Will Do* and had gone on to play Joseph in *Joseph and His Amazing Technicolour Dreamcoat*. Lee was making his panto debut as Jack and, of course, was honour bound to sing the aforementioned song! We were ably supported by Julian Clary as the Spirit of the Beans this time, Nigel Havers as the villain Fleshcreep, and the remarkable Paul Zerdin, a ventriloquist of extraordinary talent, as Simple Simon.

In the remarkable year that followed, nothing remarkable happened – unless you count the launching of ...*And This Is My Friend Mr Laurel*! I wrote copiously about it earlier, but it all started in 2013 with a rehearsed reading at The Tabard on 26 April, a showcase performance at the Tristan Bates Theatre on 24 July and an opening on 21 August at The Gatehouse in Highgate. All present and accounted for elsewhere! But I did go back to The Tabard for one performance only on 5 October – oh, and I did it at the

Laurel and Hardy Museum in Ulverston, Stan Laurel's birthplace, on Saturday the 19th too!

I say nothing else remarkable happened this year, but that is not entirely true! On Tuesday, 19 November my granddaughter, Gracey Eleanor Elder, was born to Lucy. I have a granddaughter – and she's beautiful!

The panto in 2013 was one of two consecutive ones with my old mate Bobby Davro topping the bill. This one was back at Plymouth in *Robin Hood*, starring Bobby as Will Scarlet, Lee Mead as Robin and Nigel Havers as the Sheriff of Nottingham. I think it's such a shame that they renamed this panto, which used to be called *Babes in the Wood*. As it involved kidnapping young children and taking them into the forest with the prospect of murder, political correctness had its way and they changed it. It always worked for me, though, and the kids who watched it. They loved the thrill of the chase, especially in the hands of two silly incompetents like Shaney and myself. But, as I've said before, nothing stays the same!

As I've already mentioned, around the time of doing *Mr Laurel*, I also did Ray Cooney's *Two into One* at the Menier Chocolate Factory. I love that name! It did, apparently, use to be a chocolate factory in years gone by, and it is certainly a unique name for a theatre venue. Nobody forgets it! But I was working there when I first approached Kat about producing *Mr Laurel* for the Edinburgh Fringe that year. *Two into One* is a sequel to *Out of Order*, which is what Judy and I were doing when we got together while working abroad for Derek Nimmo in 1995. I say sequel, but it just has some of the same characters in it, up to their usual shenanigans!

I was very happy, at that time in my life, to play the part of the manager of the hotel where it is set, as I was far too old then to want to play one of the agile leading characters! I remember one day saying to Ray, who was appearing in it himself as the old waiter at the age of 81, that I was very grateful to be playing the part I was, to which he replied, after giving me a good long look, 'You will always be John Smith to me, Jeff.' That really touched me and made me realise that I had contributed something permanent to the Ray Cooney world of comedy! But it wasn't over by any means. Read on!

As I mentioned above, panto came round again before I knew it and, as I said, I was back at Plymouth with Bobby Davro again in *Jack and the Beanstalk*. Bobby played Simple Simon, and I always remember him saying once, 'I love working with Jeffrey! He reins me in!' He was right, as I always tried to keep him on track as best I could, and stop him wandering off the story, which he would with great relish! Fleshcreep was played by John Challis, while I gave my Dame Trot, and Jack was played by the unique Chico. What a lovely man he was to work with – very spiritual and very generous on stage! It was a lovely season. I remember a gag that really tickled me. It was when John, as Fleshcreep, was pretending to 'buy' the cow, and, as he handed over a bag of beans, he sang a little ditty, 'We-buy-any-cow-dot-com!' after the car ad, and it was so funny I used to laugh in the wings with the audience every night. One of those silly things one remembers that makes panto so unique!

As 2015 began, Judy and I found ourselves working for a chap we knew very well and who we had worked with when he was an actor, but who had moved into producing. He had set up a tour of Arnold Ridley's *The Ghost Train*, which we had both done before – me about ten years before, playing the silly ass character Teddy, and Judy with a long history going back to 1976 at The Old Vic, when she played the honeymooner. This time, however, I was playing the old station master and she was playing the ageing spinster. You see, our friend Patric Kearns, for whom we were working, saw beyond the obvious, being an actor himself.

It was a really good production with a great cast, most of whom we knew anyway, and a good set. We did a few weeks first, some being split weeks, as certain theatres didn't want a whole week, and then a little break. I slotted a couple of *Mr Laurels* in between – we were keeping busy. The tour went on, and when we played The Grand at Wolverhampton, I had also been booked to fit in a

The First Rule of Comedy..!

matinee of *Mr Laurel* on the Thursday afternoon, so I had all the cast of *The Ghost Train* in to see me do that, as well as a good crowd of 'Friends of the Grand'. A triumph!

That tour took us right through to the middle of July, so we were really busy – and I had a few more *Mr Laurels* slotted in too. It wasn't long before I was due in Edinburgh again for what turned out to be a very profitable season with *Mr Laurel* this time. I was home soon after, but had quite a few *Mr Laurels* to do in September and October, including a lifelong ambition fulfilled to play at the Georgian Theatre in Richmond, Yorkshire. That was another busy time, and then, for a break, or so it seemed, a cruise with Chris Gidney, which was always fun!

Then we were lucky enough to be invited by King Rat, Rick Wakeman, to be his guests at the top table, for the second year running, at the Grand Order of Water Rats' Annual Ball in the Great Room at the Grosvenor House Hotel in Park Lane. That's always a great evening, and we were sitting next to Danny La Rue, who, it must be said, was not looking his best at that time, which was not long before he passed away. His great friend Annie, who made most of his frocks, was sitting next to me and it was lovely to chat to her as the evening went on about Danny. I remember him, in healthier days, saying to me at a pantomime launch for the company Qdos, 'How dare they put straight men in frocks!' It made me laugh because, as you know, I have always maintained that the best dames in frocks *are* straight men. Speak as you find!

I am devastated to report here that this year, 2015, was the first time in years that I did not have a panto in the book! It was the first time for thirty-seven years that I had been unemployed at Christmas. The last had been in 1978 when I took time out deliberately. But, you know, I didn't mind a bit! I felt I was getting too long in the tooth to carry on much longer, as playing the dame was such a drain on my energy and getting older slowed me down considerably. Would I ever do another? Wait and see!

We continued to work for Patric and did another play on tour in 2016: a new comedy murder mystery called *Secondary Cause of Death*, written by Peter Gordon. I played a retired colonel and Judy played Miss Maple, a 'Miss Marple' spoof! Again, it was great to be given the chance to play parts that we wouldn't normally be expected to play. We toured for nearly three months all over the country. Then I had a few *Mr Laurels* to do, including a tour of one-nighters around Cornwall, which was quite new to both of us. Oh, and a quick visit for him to Guernsey too! My next one was a week later at Thetford as part of the *Dad's Army* weekend. Then Judy had a wonderful time playing Madame Arcati in *Blithe Spirit* for Patric, while I did a few more *Mr Laurels*. I never did get to see her in that, which is a shame!

Farewell to Jimmy

After my 70th birthday in July, there were a few more *Mr Laurels* in August. Nothing really then until a fifteen-night cruise with Chris Gidney around the Canary Isles! That was nice, but while we were away, we heard the very sad news that my other great mentor, Jimmy Perry, had died on 23 October. Apparently he was brought home from a visit to hospital by ambulance staff and, as they got him up the stairs and into the flat, one of the medics turned to Mary Husband, with whom he shared the flat, and said, 'I'm sorry, my dear, he's gone!'

When I got home, I rang Mary to say how sorry I was, and she replied, 'Oh well, darling, he was 93!'

A few days later there was a chat show at The Gatehouse in Highgate where John Plews interviewed Su and me. That was great fun, and we were able to talk about Jimmy and what he had meant, not only to us, but to a lot of other people besides. His funeral was at Mortlake Crematorium on 7 November and he was lauded to the high heavens by the great and the good! It was a great send-off with a reception afterwards at Pembroke Lodge in Richmond Park, where Judy and I had got married twelve years earlier.

More Stage Fun

Despite my earlier doubts, panto did rear its head once again for me. After weighing up a choice of two, I chose *Robin Hood* at The Mayflower in Southampton, starring Shane Ritchie and Jessie Wallace from *EastEnders* as Robin Hood and Maid Marion, respectively.

I was hoping for a fun show, but as things turned out, although I was cast as the dame and called 'Nurse Nancy' (I never did find out why!), I was really nothing more than a 'Merrie Man' in a frock! I just milled around in the crowd scenes with only a few unmemorable lines to say, and found it all rather sad, really, that this might well be it for my panto career.

However, having finished the interminable, or so it seemed to me, panto in Southampton, after a few days I started rehearsals again for Patric, without Judy this time, in another new Peter Gordon play, *Dong Ding, Murder Me On High*. It was another improbable comedy murder plot with our old friend David Callister, or 'Cally' as we know him, playing the ever-bungling DS Pratt. I was playing a cuckolded gin-soaked aristocrat, and it was great fun! We even had Mark Little in the cast, best known as Joe Mangle from *Neighbours*.

This went on tour and ran until mid-March when I, having had time off to rehearse, went straight on to do a brand-new Richard Harris play, *Dog Ends*, at The Tabard. Richard took the trouble of asking me personally if I would do this play for him, and that meant a lot to me! It was quite a sinister plot about getting rid of unwanted old folk, as well as ageing canines, to put it in a nutshell, and it went very well indeed. It ran for nearly four weeks.

Always Have a Great Finish for Your Act

During the penultimate week, I got a call from Jean to say that someone needed help. Not *Run for Your Wife* this time, God forbid! But there was a tour in rehearsal, which I had read about, of *Waiting for God*, an old TV sitcom by Michael Aitkens starring Graham Crowden and Stephanie Cole, which had been adapted for the stage and starred Roy Hudd and Nichola McAuliffe. Well, Roy had to pull out at the eleventh hour. Nichola had apparently mentioned my name, and they phoned for me to come and open the following week.

Well, you know me. Ever one for a challenge, I put my 'quick-study' brain into gear, said 'yes' and went for it! So, after only a few days of rehearsal, we opened in Letchworth, Hertfordshire, at the cinema. Yes, a cinema, where a very enterprising lady was trying to introduce theatre to Letchworth as well. It was quite disconcerting when I arrived and asked where I should go, only to be told 'Screen One'! And we opened with only half a set as the rest wasn't ready, but it all worked nicely and everyone was pleased. It ran for eleven weeks altogether, but during the second week, Judy started rehearsals for a play called *Trespass* by Emlyn Williams for Patric again. That was another one I never saw – but you can't be everywhere, as I've said before!

Two weeks later I was in Wolverhampton, at my very own Grand Theatre, starting rehearsals for *Brassed Off*. I played Danny, the leader of the colliery brass band, and apart from a few miming actors, the band was played by the local community brass band. They were wonderful! I had to conduct everything live on stage and I loved it. I have been a 'front room' conductor all my life, and not bad if I do say so myself, but I got plenty of help from Adrian Jackson, the theatre's CEO, who actually *is* a musical director. Lucky me! We opened on 23 August and were a triumph!

After two weeks we went to Eastbourne, to the Devonshire Park Theatre, for another two weeks. We were meant to tour after that, but it was just not logistically possible, so that was that. Just as well, really, because on the opening night at Eastbourne there was an accident. In a scene where I, as Danny, had to collapse with a bad chest, one of the lads ran on to tend to me as I lay on the ground, but on this occasion, he mistimed it, and as he squatted down over me, his kneecap hit my shinbone like a hammer. Well, I thought I was going to die of pain! It was excruciating, but on those sorts of occasions, 'Dr Theatre' takes over and you get on with it – which I did. I carried on and got through the rest of the play only to find that, not only did I have an 'egg' growing on my shin, but my calf was swelling up too!

I was finding it difficult to walk, and after talking to the director, Gareth Tudor Barnes, the next day, I was able to make some adjustments to make it easier to get through the show. I even put a line in about having 'done me leg in!' One of the Eastbourne band was a GP and he arranged for an x-ray the next day, but nothing was broken, so I soldiered on as best I could as my leg got worse and worse. How I drove home the next Sunday I don't know, but I did, and Judy and I hobbled to my GP the next day as I had a blood pressure check booked in anyway.

As I limped into his consulting room, the doctor looked at me and then looked at my leg, my calf, which had swelled to twice its size, and said, 'Hospital now!'

I didn't argue, so we got a taxi to Charing Cross A&E where, after a short examination, I was told I had cellulitis! It was incredibly painful and I was put on intravenous antibiotics, which continued daily for about ten days, and I had to rest with my leg in the air for all that time too! It was just as well I had no work on at that time. I had trouble with my blood levels too, they told me, and after several tests, including a bone marrow test – ow! – I was diagnosed with a blood condition called Polycythemia Vera – although how our Vera got in there I don't know! Seriously, it's caused by a mutant gene called JAK2 and there's no cure and they don't know what triggers it. A mutant gene – I'm a mutant! Wait a minute, I'm an X-Man! Apparently one of the symptoms is unexpected weight loss and, when I was doing *Waiting for God*, some friends came to see it and said, 'What's up with Jeff? He looks terrible!' I seemed to have lost a lot of weight and didn't realise. So, the lad in *Brassed Off* did me a favour when he clobbered my leg, as I might not have known what condition I was in until it had got much worse.

I had no work in the book for the rest of that year, for which I was very grateful, as it allowed me to recuperate at home and get my strength back. I'm now on meds, of course, to keep my blood levels stable and happily they're working.

The first thing of any note to happen in 2018 was that Ray Cooney came to the fore once again. Judy and I were asked to go to Sonning, not for a drama this time, but for a farce.

They were doing a production of *Move Over Mrs Markham*, which Judy had done before for Derek Nimmo, but I hadn't. Judy played Linda Lodge as before and I played Walter Pangbourne, the meek mummy's boy boyfriend in bowler hat and pinstripe suit. Very me, don't you think? The title role was played by the lovely Finty Williams, daughter of Judi Dench and the late Michael Williams, and we all hit it off together immediately. Ray directed and it was huge fun! Mark Curry was in it too, with whom I had worked with Victoria Wood. To give it credence, it was set in the 1970s and the set was decorated with some of Linda Cooney's paintings. Linda is Ray's wife, and a very accomplished artist in her own right. The men were wearing flares too. We all enjoyed it very much, and I'm happy to say, so did the audiences!

Just before it opened, however, we had a trip to Ticehurst, where Spike Milligan once lived, to celebrate what would have been his 100th birthday. It was quite a celebration too, and was held at the Bell Hotel there. We also did a reading of some *Goon Show* scripts, which is always fun! After having done *Goon Again*, it was great to voice the old characters once again. Some of our friends from the Laurel and Hardy 'Sons of the Desert' in Southend, who are also Goon fans, were there to lend support, and a good day was had by all!

Another visit to the Edinburgh Fringe followed in August and proved a great success. What was good about this season was that there was a *Blue Peter* play on, featuring a lot of former presenters of the show as themselves, of course – namely, my old mate Mark Curry; Peter Purves, who had directed me in two panto seasons, one with Judy; and Peter Duncan, whom I had met before and who was also doing his own one-man play about a pantomime dame called, aptly enough, *Dame!*

Not only that, but there was a show about some missing Hancock radio shows too, three as I recall, with our old mate Kevin R. McNally doing a brilliant 'Hancock'! Kevin is best known from the *Pirates of the Caribbean* movies with Johnny Depp. Kevin and I, both massive Laurel and Hardy fans, could often be found after our shows holding up a wine bar somewhere in Edinburgh, having conversations in the voices of Stan and Olly. Kevin's 'Olly' is brilliant! Also Robin Sebastian, with whom Judy and I had done *'Allo 'Allo!*, was doing his 'Kenneth Williams', and, it must be said, he is probably the best of all those around. Those two things were the bonus of that season for me!

The Christmas Spirit?

There aren't many things in my career which have made me very disappointed and unhappy, thank the gods, but one particular thing that did happened at the end of 2018.

I had a call from Jean to say that this production company I hadn't yet heard of wanted me to play the title role in a Christmas show, not a panto, but a musical play, called *Santa Claus: The Frost Files*. This was to be mounted at the Royal Hippodrome, Eastbourne, a favourite place of ours. Well, having spoken to Jean, we did a deal with the producer, whom I will not name! I rented a flat from some people who were in the brass band there when I did *Brassed Off*, which was very nice. Rehearsals went according to plan, and we opened. It ran for just under three weeks, during

Always Have a Great Finish for Your Act

which time I didn't see any money. Sometimes companies can be late paying when theatres are late handing over their share of the box-office takings, so I let it go.

Well, it went on and we closed and still I hadn't seen any money! Jean was forever on the phone, chasing and chasing, and getting no reply. Eventually we got on to my union, Equity, and they did what they could, even took the company to court, but because they were a company in name only with no assets, there was nothing they could do to enforce payment!

At the end of the day, I didn't get paid by a man who knew full well that he could get away with it because, as it turned out, it wasn't the first time he had done it. He still works in the business as a panto performer, but I hope he has stopped his criminal activity by now! How can you sleep at night when you know you are depriving someone of their livelihood? How would he feel, I wonder, if it happened to him?

Putting all negativity aside now, I did quite a few *Mr Laurels* around the country during the first few weeks of 2019. Then, of course, as I mentioned before, we went to Dublin and took him all around Ireland. That took the whole of April and then there were a few more when we got back.

For me, the most unexpected venue to book the show was Dubai. Yes, Dubai! I had an email from a man who had set up a cabaret venue in what used to be an old warehouse, and it was big and bare and quite uncosy, to say the least. He did music and tribute acts there, he told me, but he wanted to attract an audience who could appreciate theatre too. Well, we did our best and the show went all right, despite me having to enter and exit from the back of the audience, there being no 'wings' as such. He flew us over and we were billeted in the Radisson Blu, which was very nice. It was a very unusual gig for me but one I will never forget. It was in the middle of June and the temperature was 45 degrees, so we were very grateful for air conditioning!

Back to Pastures Familiar

Later that year we were back at Sonning. Yes, another Ray Cooney, directed by the man himself, but guess which one? 'No, it can't be!' I hear you cry. But yes, it is! It's *Run for Your Wife*! How can this be? We're far too old! But, every time we say this to Ray, he just pooh-poohs us. He still thinks we're in our 40s! So who are we to argue? It was a chance, a *final* chance, it must be said, to do this wonderful comedy just one last time. Ray said that, as he had aged all the parts up, it would still work. He was right. It did!

A switch for Judy this time, though. I don't know how the decision was made, but she was cast as Barbara, having *always* played Mary in all previous incarnations. Lovely Michelle Morris played Mary, Delme Thomas played Bobby, Nick Wilton was John, I gave my Stanley, David Warwick was Porterhouse and Lizzy Elvin was a uniformed Troughton. Quite new, but Ray's idea. We called it 'the geriatric version', but strangely enough it was the triumph it usually is! It is such a sound piece and I have always said that, for me, it is Ray's finest work. I did feel rather uncomfortable with the line, 'I can only just about find enough energy to satisfy the girlfriend and sign on at the Labour Exchange!' at the age of 73. But that's showbiz, folks!

We had a big *Hi-de-Hi!* get together for our fortieth anniversary at the Phoenix Arts Club in Tottenham Court Road on Sunday, 20 October, it being forty years since we had made the pilot episode in 1979. A lot of the boys and girls from the stage show came too and it was lovely to see them all. The Croft family were well represented and Mary Husband was there on Jimmy's behalf too. It was a marvellous evening!

Su and I were about to embark to Wolverhampton Grand to do the panto. At a sumptuous night out earlier in the year, at the Wolves Molineux Stadium to celebrate the Grand Theatre's 125th anniversary, it was announced to those assembled that we were going to do *Dick Whittington* later that year. Adrian Jackson wanted people in it who meant something to the theatre, and I, with my local connections and being president of the 'Friends' too, meant something!

The irony for me, after twenty-six years playing the dame and having decided that after forty-five seasons this would be my last panto, was that I was going to be playing a man! I would be Alderman Fitzwarren! I really didn't mind a bit. It was so much easier for me and I loved being able to watch the brilliant Ian Adams strut his stuff! Ian has established himself as a regular dame at the Grand, and having worked as I have with so many, he really does remind me so much of Jack Tripp. Ian not only played Sarah the Cook but also wrote the panto – something he is becoming very accomplished at.

Because he is, and always has been, a huge fan of *Hi-de-Hi!*, he wrote a special moment in for Su and me at the end. When Su, as the wicked Queen Rat, was vanquished by good over evil, she was suddenly surrounded by fairy dancers; as the lights go out, she was transformed in the blackout and, when the lights snap back up, there's Peggy! It always got a massive round of applause from the audience. Then, out of vision in the wings, came my voice, 'Are you there, Peggy?' and then I walked on wearing a yellow coat and white trousers and shoes, and suddenly we were Spike and Peggy again. We shouted 'Hi-de-Hi!' a couple of times and the audience replied with 'Ho-de-Ho!', of course, to which I said, 'Oh, it's like old times!' That was a special moment that I will always treasure – even though I was 73 years old!

There must have been a lot of explaining going on to the younger kids, but the mums and dads loved it, and so did we. It was very special for me to finish my last ever panto with a *Hi-de-Hi!* moment!

The First Rule of Comedy..!

The History Boys and Lockdown

When we closed on Sunday, 12 January 2020, I started rehearsals the following morning for Adrian's next Grand Theatre in-house production of Alan Bennett's great play *The History Boys*. What a show that was! A brilliantly written play with not a weak character in it. I was playing the slimy headmaster, and we had the amazing Ian Burford playing Hector, the part made famous, of course, by the wonderful late Richard Griffiths. Ian has gone on to play Dumbledore in the hugely successful *Harry Potter and the Cursed Child* at London's Palace Theatre!

The timing of *The History Boys* couldn't have been better as, just as we were finishing our run, it was announced that there was a deadly virus which had begun to spread rapidly from a place called Wuhan. Everything hit the fan, as it were, and we barely had time to get on a train back to London – but we managed it. I still had a *Mr Laurel* to do at the Playhouse Theatre in Stratford-upon-Avon on Saturday, 7 March, and just after we got home from that, within days 'lockdown' was declared. Wow!

There is absolutely nothing in my diary for the rest of the entire year! Apart from, that is, a couple of hospital blood check appointments, which were very strictly monitored, and when we were tested for COVID at the same time. This was the time that everyone, including Judy and myself, discovered the wonderful Zoom that could keep us all in touch, even if we couldn't meet in person.

The absence of diary entries continued, with the exception of the odd dental and blood appointment, until 19 September 2021, when we had a luncheon appointment, albeit rather late, to celebrate Charles Garland's 70th birthday. He called it '70 plus VAT'! I also had a *Mr Laurel* booked for the Stables Theatre in Hastings on 3 October and both of those dates seemed to pass without incident.

Moving into 2022 was no different. I was beginning to enjoy my 'semi-retirement', as I was starting to think of it. Things were relaxing somewhat, particularly with the advent of various vaccines which had materialised from certain laboratories. Everyone began to get much more careless, ourselves included, and masks began to get forgotten or ignored. We paid the price, though, when we decided to go to see Su at the Pizza Express in her one-woman show. We went with Rob Ross and Gemma, and the room was very crowded with many of Su's fans, and a great night was had by all. A few days later, however, after a bit of a splutter and a cough, we both tested positive! Fortunately, as I am on the vulnerable list because of my blood condition, I was entitled to put in a claim for anti-virals, or so they called them, which were delivered to my door by the NHS. I took them as prescribed and they kept me out of danger with no particularly bad symptoms, and I was clear within a few days. Judy had a bit of nastiness and a cough, but that didn't last long either. We were very lucky, I think!

A month or so later, although things were still somewhat unpredictable, we took the bull by the horns and did a show. We went to stay with David and Jean Webb in Mistley and had a *Hi-de-Hi!* event at the Harwich Museum, which I'll describe later, but things were beginning to get back to a semblance of normal, if we will ever be normal again! They say COVID is here to stay, so keep looking over your shoulder. You never know!

Rob and I got our show, *Comedy Friends and Heroes* (the genesis of which later), up and running and had two back-to-back dates in late July in Birmingham and then Holborn, where we had seen Su previously and Judy and I had contracted COVID. All was well on this occasion, though, and we did really well at both venues. We did one at The Tabard too, in September, and it was a great night!

I had a *Mr Laurel* at the Lighthouse Studio in Poole on Saturday, 26 November, and apart from reading some poetry at a carol concert in December, that was it for 2022. Not much happening professionally! The theatre, and showbiz in general, was still smarting from lockdown and many people were still unwilling to go and sit next to a stranger in a theatre.

It seems I was going to be busy with *Mr Laurel*, on and off, for a couple of months, in February, March and April 2023. Also there was a *Comedy Friends and Heroes* thrown in. We did another *Hi-de-Hi!* event at the Harwich Museum too, with Su this time, which was another triumph!

Funny Turns and Funny Places

Then, having been to see Mansel David, an old actor friend of Judy's, doing his one-man show about the poet A.E. Houseman, a conversation ensued and we found a new play to do! We had seen Mansel in another new play called *Funny Turns* at Jermyn Street sometime before and he told us that they were supposed to be doing it again at the Grove Theatre in Eastbourne. It is set in 1935 in a theatrical boarding house somewhere in the north of England. We liked it very much, and Judy mentioned to Mansel how much she had enjoyed the performance of the actress who played the landlady. When he told us that she had sadly died, it was suggested that Judy could play it and also that I would be ideal as the 'failed comic' character. I wasn't sure how to take that! But it seemed like a good idea, nevertheless. He said he would speak to the writer and producer and come back to us, so we left it at that.

The Perry and Croft weekend was coming up in mid-May again, and Rob and I were booked to do our *Comedy Friends and Heroes* show for their Friday entertainment at the Carnegie Rooms in Thetford. It went brilliantly well for everyone there!

In the meantime, I mentioned a while ago a play called *The Art of Concealment* that Judy had done about the young Terence Rattigan by Giles Cole. Well, Giles had *After All These Years*, a play in three acts about two older couples who had known each other all their lives and used to be in showbusiness together. We called it 'a play for the older actor'! We were engaged to do this too, and in three separate venues. Firstly, at the Lantern Theatre in Brighton, as part of the 2023 Brighton Festival, for which it won a best new play award. Secondly, at the Minghella Theatre in Newport, Isle of Wight. And thirdly, for two weeks at the Jermyn Street Theatre. It's a very clever play where the first scene is about two men in a pub putting the world and their lives – and wives! – to rights. The second scene is similar, with the two ladies in one of their flats, having a girly evening with unexpected consequences. And the third scene is two years later, when everything in their lives has changed!

We were booked to do it at The Tabard for three weeks in early February 2024, and we had a great number of friends come to see it there. It really was a great role for me, stretching *all* my acting muscles this time, and I was very satisfied to be playing such a worthwhile part.

Paul Shane's Death

There are some experiences in life that you never forget, whatever the reasons, and Paul Shane's passing is one of those for me.

We had been told of his admission to the Rotherham Hospice by his daughter, Janice, a few days before. The doctor had been called and was astounded that Shaney was even still alive! Apparently he was in the final stages of cancer, which had spread throughout his body. He had apparently been diagnosed with it some ten years earlier and had done nothing about it. He was a 'head in the sand' sort of person and thought if he ignored it, then it would go away. Well, unfortunately, it hadn't.

Janice rang me and said that he hadn't got long, and would I also inform Su Pollard? I duly did, and she got herself on a train that very day and went to see him. I couldn't go just then, but opted for the next day, hoping and praying I wouldn't be too late. I rang

The First Rule of Comedy..!

Nikki Kelly, who lives not far from us, to ask if she would like to come with me. She was devastated, naturally, but said she would accompany me, hoping that she could hold it together. We set off in my car the following day, a Wednesday as I recall, eventually arriving at Rotherham Hospice.

We were directed to Shaney's room, where he was lying in bed and holding court to a roomful of family and friends like nothing was wrong! I soon realised, however, that this was not the case, and I had never seen him looking so thin. I gave him a hug, which he found difficult to respond to, and I soon realised that his motor functions were shutting down. He always was a great hugger, and this was very sad to see.

We took our places among the other visitors and tried, as one does, to make light conversation with him and everyone else. Well, it soon livened up when he started telling tales about Nikki and the other girls while we were away filming *Hi-de-Hi!*, and a lot of 'dramatic licence' was used to great bawdy effect. We all had a great laugh!

After a few hours had passed, it became apparent that Paul was beginning to flag and needed to rest, so as Nikki and I had a long drive back, we decided it would be wise to take our leave. Saying cheerio – or goodbye, as we knew it was – was almost impossible. I can't remember how Nikki left the room, but I hovered at the foot of his bed for a while, and then he said, 'Tarra then, mate!' and I said something like, 'Do as you're told now!', meaning they were looking after him and had his best interests at heart. I passed through that door into the corridor, where Nikki already was, and we both burst into inconsolable tears. We knew we would never see him again.

The following day, and I was *so* glad I'd made it the day before, I got a message to say that, at a few minutes past six o'clock that evening, Paul had opened his eyes from a deep sleep, taken a look around at all his family that were around his bed, smiled broadly at them, and then just passed peacefully away. That was Thursday,

16 May 2013, and he was just a few days short of his 74th birthday. He was a part of my life for thirty-four years and I still miss him very much.

My Speech at Shaney's Funeral

I first made this speech as a tribute to Paul at a lunch held in his honour for the Heritage Foundation a couple of years earlier, and having kept it on file, I thought it would be very appropriate to repeat it at his funeral service in Rotherham Minster on Friday, 31 May 2013, when I was asked to pay tribute to him there:

George Frederick Speight! – Juddy! or Steven Paul (as he always wanted to be called Paul!) or Paul Stevens – and then – Paul Shane!

I was privileged to work with 'Shaney' for the best part of eighteen years in all. First in *Hi-de-Hi!*, then after that, in *You Rang, M'Lord?* and later, in *Oh, Doctor Beeching!* – and in all that time, the one thing that sticks in my memory, is FUN!

The first time I met him was in the BBC rehearsal rooms when he had been summoned to read for the part of Ted Bovis in *Hi-de-Hi!* I was already cast as Spike, and after Jimmy and David had chatted with him for a while, I was called in to read a scene with him. I remember walking into the room with my hand held out, saying, 'Hello, Paul. Lovely to meet you!' – or words to that effect – and he responded much the same, but then he froze, and looked at me with a very knowing look and said, 'Have we worked together before?' The answer was 'no', but I too felt he was just as familiar to me! You see, the chemistry was already there! We clicked instantly! I think the proof of that is in the work we did together over the years. But also, off the screen, we were great pals too.

I said we had fun! – we did! We had a very naughty sense of humour and we loved to play tricks on people!

The First Rule of Comedy..!

I remember the time we sneaked up on an unsuspecting Barry Howard, and scooped him up, physically taking an arm and a leg each and running the length of the room with him squealing like a schoolgirl! We had a lot of laughs with Barry!

Then there was the occasion when the two of us were sitting in the canteen with a couple of the others, and lovely Kenneth Connor arrived. He filled his breakfast tray and paid at the till, and, having spotted us, we waved him over. Then, as he made his way down the room, on a given cue, we all stood up as one man and left! We looked back to see his reaction, and there was Kenny barely able to hold his tray, crying with laughter! That was typical of us!

There was, however, one occasion that nearly backfired! We were at an after-show party in Blackpool, I think it was, at the home of a very nice lady. This was during the summer season of 1984 with *Hi-de-Hi!* We were in her garden, and Shaney was there with his lovely wife, Dory, who, at that time, was using a couple of walking sticks to help her get around. They were both sitting on a bench with a drink and a bit of food, and the sticks were safely leaning on the seat next to Dory. Well, Shaney tipped me the wink, and suddenly I snatched up both sticks, saying, 'Give me those!' And I threw them roughly into a nearby hedge! What I didn't know was that the very nice lady whose house it was had taken a VERY dim view of this, and had a VERY stony look on her face! If it hadn't been for the fact that both Shaney and Dory were both screaming with hysterical laughter, I think I might have been asked to leave!

But we did have fun! We had a lot of SILLY fun, but we had a lot of professional fun too! We were very lucky with all the wonderful stuff that Jimmy and David wrote for us to do, both as Ted and Spike in *Hi-de-Hi!* and more seriously as Alf and James in *You Rang, M'Lord?* We had some wonderful scenes to play together in that, and his Alf Stokes was a formidable piece of work!

It has been a great joy to work alongside him for all of those eighteen years, and to have watched him grow in stature and confidence, from the terrified Club Comic in the first episode of

Hi-de-Hi! to the SOARING Mr Bumble in the musical, 'Oliver!', on the stage of the London Palladium!

Shaney, it has been an honour for me to be able to pay tribute to you here today! Being Ted and Spike in *Hi-de-Hi!* was amazing. Being Alf and James in *You Rang, M'Lord?* was fantastic and being Jack and Cecil in *Oh, Doctor Beeching!* was just a bonus!

Thank you for those wonderful times, but most of all – thank you for all the *fun*!

That was the speech. It brings tears to my eyes, reading it again for the purpose of including it in the book. I know Paul would love it to be included, in its original state. And that fun that I spoke about continues to this very day. Even though we have to soldier on without Shaney, the shows we worked on together are still extremely popular. I'm reliably informed that *Hi-de-Hi!* has made an appearance on Britbox – albeit with a warning about period attitudes that may offend. Please! *Hi-de-Hi!* Offend? I think the Guv'nor and Jimmy would spin in their graves!

There has been a trend lately towards shows from the 1980s because of a popular show called *Stranger Things*, I'm told. Well, go for it, say I! Even for a show set in the late 1950s and early 1960s, it is a 1980s show, in truth. Indeed, one might say the very apotheosis of a 1980s show! If they love it for that reason, then they love it. After all, as we have always said, it's just good, clean, old-fashioned family fun. You see, there's that word 'fun' again!

You Rang in Budapest

Back in 2017, I did an interview for a radio station in Budapest as, believe it or not, *You Rang, M'Lord?* is immensely popular in Hungary! My interview was to be translated into Hungarian and my answers to their questions were to be voiced by the actor who

The First Rule of Comedy..!

had dubbed my James Twelvetrees voice in Hungary. They say that the popularity stems from the fact that Hungarians were under the Communist thumb for decades, before they were freed, and the people still recognise the injustice on the two social levels that the show represents: the upstairs aristocracy and the below stairs servants and underdogs!

When we were winding the interview up, they asked me what we were doing next year (2018) to celebrate thirty years since making the pilot episode, in 1988. I suddenly had an inspired moment and said, 'Why don't we come to Budapest and celebrate it with you?'

After a very pregnant pause he said, 'Leave it with us!'

So we did – and the next thing I knew they had organised a huge event which had been very secretly put together. Tickets were sold, and only the ones who bought them knew where the event would be taking place. I told you it was top secret! These lucky ticket-holders were told to keep quiet, as they didn't want any gatecrashers.

We were flown over and put up, and even we didn't know where they were taking us until we were ferried there by coach on the day. Sadly, Su Pollard and Perry Benson couldn't come because of work commitments, but there were five of the main cast there: Susie Brann, Amanda Bellamy, Catherine Rabett, Michael Knowles and me. The event took place in a huge room, which was a lecture hall at the university in Budapest, and there were over 900 people in there!

The show was divided into two parts, with the first forty minutes being devoted to the Hungarian actors who dubbed our voices. They were all very well known over there, and they were telling their own stories and the crowd loved it! It was compèred – or rather commèred! – by a lady who was appropriately dressed as a 1920s 'flapper'.

At the end of that particular section of the proceedings, she called for a refreshment break, rang a little bell and said, 'Can we have a drink, please?'

At this point, enter me! Now, I had bought my costume when the series ended and I thought they might like to see it, so I got into my striped jacket and black trousers, white shirt and black tie, and on I came as James Twelvetrees, carrying a tray of champagne. Well, as soon as I came into sight, they went ballistic. I've never heard a sound like it! The scream took the roof off. I could have been Elvis or one of The Beatles for all the noise they made!

When they did eventually calm down and let me speak, I very correctly said, 'You rang, m'lady?' and off they went again! I was eventually allowed to leave the stage and I made my way into the safety of the wings, where I promptly burst into tears. It was just so totally overwhelming, the love in that room for our show. I will never forget it as long as I live!

We are lucky enough to have it on YouTube, so if you want to see it, go to YouTube and enter 'You Rang M'Lord in Budapest' and it should come up. What an extraordinary experience that was!

Cruising to a Finale

There is a fairly new opportunity for employment that has been created for us actors in recent years, not only to work, but also to travel to exotic places – namely, on cruises! Judy and I have done quite a few working cruises over the last twenty years or so, starting with two Ray Cooney farces, *Run for Your Wife* and *Funny Money*. Ray himself starred in them and also directed, as no one knows his plays quite like he does! The wonderful Henry McGee played opposite Ray and they were great together. We had quite a job the first time, in 1999 on the *Marco Polo*, putting up a theatre set for *Run for Your Wife* in what was a cabaret space, but somehow we managed it.

We had another chance a couple of years later, in 2001, when we did the two plays for P&O on the *Aurora* and the *Oriana*! It was a wonderful trip for us as we flew to San Francisco to pick up the *Aurora*. We found, when we got there, that we had a whole day in port before we sailed, so we were able to go and visit Alcatraz. That was one thing checked off the bucket list! Next day we sailed for three weeks to Australia, via New Zealand and visiting Auckland, and on the way we went to Bora Bora and Honolulu in Hawaii too. Then we ended our journey in Sydney, where we changed ships to the *Oriana*, but had three leisurely days there in a hotel first!

While we were there, we managed to link up with Ray Meagre, who plays Alf in *Home and Away*, with whom Judy had done panto in Darlington the Christmas before, and he took us over to Bondi Beach, and all round the Sydney area, in his car for the day. It was a great day out!

Then, after our three days off, we sailed back to San Francisco via Auckland again, Pango Pango this time and then Tahiti and Honolulu once more, before we called briefly for a night at Vancouver. In the morning, I took Judy for breakfast at my old favourite haunt from my visit in 1988, The Elbow Room, before we sailed on to San Francisco to get our flight home. It was a cruise we will never forget. We were out of the UK for the whole of February and half of March, so missed all the bad weather!

One of the hilarious joys of cruising is docking at Lanzarote. There is an amazing statue there of some politician, or rebel leader or something, but the hilarious thing is that this statue of a long-dead dignitary is the spitting image of the Joe Maplin statue featured in *Hi-de-Hi!* Talk about a photo opportunity! Wonderful! The funny thing is, of course, that Joe Maplin never actually appeared in the series. For many years, David and Jimmy were threatening to write him in, but it just never happened. The nearest we got was when that wonderful actor, Ewan Hooper, came in as the irregular threat character of Alec Foster. You remember the one who tries to string poor Peggy along and seduce her? Horrible man. Lovely actor! It's the sort of behaviour that one can imagine Joe Maplin getting up to. Still, I think David and Jimmy thought there was much more mileage in keeping Joe out of the show and just in the mind of the viewer, through those brilliant, illiterate letters he would send in and force Jeffrey Fairbrother to read out!

However, I do know that they got as far as casting an actor to play Joe Maplin. Over the years I've heard all sorts of names bandied about, but the one star guest who was actually lined up to play Joe Maplin was Charlie Drake. Now, I've got no personal axe to grind where Charlie is concerned, but his reputation for being difficult in this business is well established! Anyway, it didn't happen, but just think of Charlie Drake in that part. A tiny little man with all that power. Perfect! Strangely enough, his son, Chris Drake, was one of our supporting artists, one of the campers, for all the years of the show. Have a look for him next time you're watching. He's taller and slimmer, but has Charlie's red hair, so not too difficult to spot – but I've digressed again!

They stopped doing plays on the ships shortly after that as it was uneconomic for them. Shame! However, we were asked by Chris Gidney, who runs a company called That's Entertainment!, to go on another cruise line, Cruise and Maritime Voyages, to do chat shows about our careers in comedy. One, a celebration of comedy legends, included myself and Judy alongside such lovely chums as Sue Hodge (little Mimi Labonq from *'Allo 'Allo!*) and fellow David Croft and Jimmy Perry actor Michael Knowles.

Michael had done almost as many shows for Jimmy and David as I had done, probably more, including *Dad's Army* several times. He was also in a little-remembered science-fiction comedy series called *Come Back Mrs Noah*, which saw the dithering housewife, played by Mollie Sugden, blasted into outer space! Michael had been brilliant as Captain Ashwood in *It Ain't Half Hot Mum*, and he played an even more silly ass character, the Hon. Teddy Meldrum, in *You Rang, M'Lord?* Michael loved playing this character. He was pure P.G. Wodehouse, with his monocle and his passion for the shiny scrubbed faces of young chambermaids. Hilarious! One of my favourite lines of his is when Teddy is at breakfast. His appetite is as large as his lust for life and, piling up his plate with food, he gushes and says, 'I want heaps and heaps!' It's a line I often use at home, which always makes Judy laugh! But, believe me, on those cruises you do get heaps and heaps of food. Never was it more appropriate!

Yes, those cruises were great fun for us and very, very successful too. As a result, Judy and I went on several of these over the next few years, and fortune smiled down upon us because, on one of them, we were to meet our dear friend Robert Ross, the comedy historian, and straight away hit it off big time. Rob always says, 'It was comedy-love-at-first-sight between us!', and he is right. There is nothing that Rob doesn't know about comedy on both TV and the big screen, and he has written several books on the subject.

We started by challenging each other with silly questions like 'who played so-and-so in so-and-so?' I like to think of myself as rather good on actors who played various historical characters in all those wonderful ITC serials of the 1950s that I loved so much as a boy. You know the ones? Conrad Phillips in *The Adventures of William Tell*. Robert Shaw in *The Buccaneers*. Richard Greene, with whom I worked on stage in my debut in 1967, in *The Adventures of Robin Hood*, etc. So, come on then, which actors played Little John and Friar Tuck?

Robert is brilliant at those wonderful character actors of Hollywood and British cinema. He can spot a Franklin Pangborn or a Michael Ward at thirty paces! He knows the lot: directors, dates, every detail. Quite astounding, and great fun for a challenge! This lovely little game of ours has never ceased, and here we are together in this book, where there are plenty of challenges. We are very lucky to be in a profession where we can go on trips like that, to entertain and see some wonderful places too.

Indeed, so much fun did Rob and I have on that cruise that the idea for a touring show, *Comedy Friends and Heroes*, was discussed, and soon after getting our feet back on *terra firma*, it was created. It's a conversation piece, with classic clips, and allows Rob to ask me about my career and the people I have worked with, alongside a comedy history lesson in which we can chat about people whom I love and who have inspired me, such as Stan Laurel and Peter Sellers. It's such a fun show, and no two performances have ever been exactly the same. We like that relaxed, impromptu feel to it, and to be able to just chat. There is a sort of structure there, of course, but Rob is such a good interviewer, and we both know each other so well, that we can trust each other to free-fall a little. Exciting and funny! The trouble is we have to keep our eyes on the clock as we could talk for hours!

Over the last couple of years I have been amazed that I've become something of a cult figure. Not only in terms of lovely audiences coming to the stage door with photographs from comedy successes twenty, thirty, even forty or more years ago. No, I mean that contemporary and very talented people in the business have taken to referencing me in their shows. That Chatty Man himself, Alan Carr, relates his own very funny and very poignant childhood, in the 1980s, in the situation comedy *Changing Ends*. In the series one episode 'Sick as a Parrot', young Alan (played brilliantly by Oliver Savell) is avoiding school – and the shower after games – to watch television. He's looking forward to the *Hi-de-Hi!* team being on *Pebble Mill at One*, while he also mentions *Russ Abbot's Madhouse*. Can you believe it? Even more personal was the weird and wonderful *Inside No. 9* episode 'Wise Owl', written by Steve Pemberton and Reece Shearsmith. The fabulous Ron Cook, playing an old actor who was once beloved as the voice of a cartoon owl in children's information films, talks about having done some great theatre work, including a 'two-hander with Jeff Holland'. Now, it was the fact that Steve and Reece called me Jeff, as an old theatre mate would. Wonderful writing, and quite a pleasant shock when I heard my name mentioned. It's just a pity they have brought the *Inside No. 9* series to an end. I would have loved to have appeared in an episode!

Goodnight Campers

The very sad part of this wonderful business is, of course, when you lose a valued colleague. Ruth Madoc left us a short while ago, and was working until the very end. I had a phone call from her and we chatted not long before it happened. She was rehearsing for the pantomime *Aladdin*, at the Princess Theatre in Torquay, for the 2022/23 season when she had a terrible fall and damaged her knee badly and was forced to bow out of the production. Tragically, she never regained consciousness and passed away during an operation. This was on 9 December 2022, the day before the show opened. She was 79 and had a wonderfully full diary of shows and appearances for the following year. It was so unfair!

As is sadly usual at these times, lots of my *Hi-de-Hi!* friends and I were called up by various radio and TV producers and asked whether we could come on to their programmes and talk about Ruth. This is never easy, but it is a duty that I feel honour bound to fulfil, to pay tribute to the people with whom I have worked so closely and so well in programmes that the great viewing audience love so much. One of these producers made me shudder when he said, 'Well, you know, you are the senior cast member now!' It hadn't occurred to me up to that point, but they went on to say that with Paul Shane gone and now Ruth, being third in the cast list, I was now the senior survivor. Golly! We were a great team, though – and we still are! We will always be a part of that wonderful show that David Croft and Jimmy Perry had gifted us all those years before.

Ruth's memorial service was held at St Paul's, the Actors' Church in Covent Garden, and was, as you would expect, a star-studded celebration of this highly acclaimed actress. The Welsh choral singing was heartbreaking in just the right way, and our show was represented by addresses from Linda Regan – who gave a wonderful speech on the many charities Ruth tirelessly supported – and Su Pollard, who stopped the 'show' with a heart-felt and hilarious rattle through Ruth's brilliance in *Hi-de-Hi!* Su being Su, there was just a little fruity language along the way. Some words even shocked the Reverend Simon Grigg, who has heard it all before!

I was particularly pleased to be able to chat with Ruth's children, Rhys and Lowri, both grown up now, of course, whom I hadn't seen for such a long time. I wasn't able to attend the funeral in Swansea, but the memorial service more than made up for it.

All in all, it was a perfect send-off. Sadly, I couldn't stay for the drinks afterwards because I was committed to a personal appearance for the Laurel and Hardy Appreciation Society down in Southend-on-Sea, but that struck me as very apt too. Ruth was working until the very end, and I intend to do the same! So, dear reader, whether it's Stan, *Hi-de-Hi!* or any of the comedy heroes and shows I've been lucky enough to be associated with, laughter and celebration is all that matters. It's an eternal celebration, whether the actors and performers are still with us or not.

As well as Ruth, 2022 was also the year we lost that lovely actor Frank Williams. Frank was the vicar in *Dad's Army*, and our bishop in *You Rang, M'Lord?* David and Jimmy loved him, and the feeling was mutual.

Now, Thetford, in Norfolk, where we had filmed *Dad's Army*, has long hosted an annual gathering of fans, organised by the Dad's Army Appreciation Society. There's an amazing museum there now, and a life-size statue of Arthur Lowe as Captain Mainwaring. It's quite an experience attending these events, as I try to do each year, but every year we are losing more and more originals from the cast and crew, 2024 being no exception with the passing of Ian Lavender and of David's then production manager, who became a successful producer himself, Harold Snoad.

At each of these events, though, David and Jimmy were very supportive, as were Clive Dunn and Bill Pertwee. Bill would always turn up in his ARP warden helmet and be in character for the delighted fans. On the Sunday there was always a

The First Rule of Comedy..!

gathering in Bressingham, a lovely village a little over 10 miles east of Thetford, where there is a steam museum and now they have a permanent exhibit displaying all the main locations of Walmington-on-Sea. You can really believe you are there among the members of Mainwaring's platoon, back in the more austere days of the 1940s!

Back in the day, it would be me and Jimmy and David and Bill and Clive and Frank and Pamela Cundell ... I could go on! We would all sit in a row and sign photographs and books and whatever for these wonderful *Dad's Army* fans. A lovely lot of food and drink would be laid on for us too. Those wonderful days, through the 1990s and on into the early 2020s, were some really happy days for us all. Now, it seems, I'm the last old solider on parade!

With Frank's death, and more recently Ian's too, the organisers decided to make the 2024 gathering the last one, but it was such a success that they have since changed their minds. It will always be a joy to visit that lovely hotel, The Bell, where we stayed when I shot my episode in 1977. It's still there, steeped in *Dad's Army* history, and we're all billeted there for these fun weekends. Well, it seems we will now be back! Although now there are so few originals left that the *sons* of the originals are starting to make an appearance, to keep the flag flying and the flame burning! Wonderful friends like Jonathan Pertwee, son of Bill, and Nicolas Ridley, son of the marvellous Arnold who played Private Godfrey. It's *Dad's Army – the Next Generation*. How fabulous is that?

Thetford is an amazing place, particularly on that weekend of *Dad's Army* celebration. Lots of the locals dress up! You can buy meat from Jones the butcher in the High Street, there's his van parked outside the museum, and you can even buy *Dad's Army* biscuits and *Dad's Army* beer! A pint of Stupid Boy, anybody? Wonderful! This last time, when Judy and I were walking round the streets of Thetford, we saw a gaggle of six or seven family members, all dressed up in their 1940s gear. The most delightful sight of all was a little lad of 6 or 7 years old, dressed up as

Jones the butcher. What an amazing impact that show has had, and continues to have! How could they ever stop celebrating *Dad's Army* there?

It's true to say that, by the same token, we can never stop celebrating *Hi-de-Hi!* either. The same wonderful people who mount the *Dad's Army* weekends do a similar one in salute to *Hi-de-Hi!* at Harwich Museum, where they have a marvellous exhibit. Myself, Su and David Webb, as well as others involved with the show, attend when we can. Thinking back to that little lad in Thetford, I have a very real and tangible sense that our shows are going to be enjoyed for ever and ever – certainly long after we are all gone!

I was approached by a young mother who told me that her little daughter, also aged about 6 or 7, was so fond of *Hi-de-Hi!* that she would watch all the episodes over and over again. She watched them so much, she knew every single storyline, every single line of dialogue pretty much ... and her absolute favourite was Spike! Having heard about our reunion weekend and understanding that I, the actor that is or was Spike, would be there, this little girl had begged and begged her mother to take her to meet me. Now, this lovely mother tried to explain to her little girl that the show had been made quite a few, well a lot, of years ago and, maybe, just maybe, the man who played Spike might not look quite the same as he did when he was in the show. The little girl was adamant! She loved Spike and she wanted to meet him and me ... and she didn't care if he did look older. He was still Spike!

Anyway, sure enough we met and she was an absolute delight! I signed her pictures and books and posed for photographs, and, do you know what, at that moment it all made perfect sense to me. Spike and *Hi-de-Hi!* have always meant the world to me, but to this young girl it also meant the world – and more – even more than forty years after we had filmed it. Incredible! I mean to say, her mother wasn't even born when we were making it! I felt humbled and emotional and very, very grateful to David and Jimmy.

But, dear reader, this is where you came in!

The First Rule of Comedy..!

Amidst all the previous pages, while attempting to remain interesting, and worthy of your time and patience, I have endeavoured to describe my life, my family, my career, its ups and downs, and the many things that have happened to me in the last seven to eight decades – things that have shaped the way other things have transpired. Decisions I made, whether they were wise or otherwise, and the resulting outcomes! We don't always get everything right, but one thing I do know for certain: whatever I have done previously in my career and whatever I may be blessed to do in the future, the one thing I know for sure is that I will always be 'that bloke from *Hi-de-Hi!*'.

AFTERWORD
BY ROY GOULD

I first met Jeff when I joined *Hi-de-Hi!* as an assistant floor manager, as they were about to embark on the fourth series of the show. I vividly recall being very nervous walking into rehearsals at the BBC North Acton Rehearsal Rooms on my first day, as all the cast had come from relative unknowns to household names over the previous three years and I hadn't met any of them before this, so I had no idea whether, as a newbie, I'd be welcomed into the fold. As it turned out, my insecurity was happily misplaced as I was greeted by a sea of friendly faces, none more so than Jeff's, who I recall coming straight over to me and welcoming me to the show. Our friendship blossomed during the four weeks we did on location at the holiday camp, owing to our combined love of *The Goon Show* – from that moment on we would greet each other in *Goon Show* characters with silly voices and calling each other Ned or little Jim and quoting The Goons with phrases such as 'You silly twisted boy'. Some evenings after we'd returned to the unit hotel, we would get our pints and sit in Jeff's car in the car park and listen to one or two of the *Goon Show* cassettes which he took everywhere with him, and the good people of Dovercourt would give the two of us strange looks as they passed by the car while we were laughing uncontrollably at the antics of Secombe, Sellers and Milligan.

I was lucky enough to work with Jeff on three sitcom series, *Hi-de-Hi!*, *You Rang, M'Lord?* and *Oh, Doctor Beeching!*, rising from my junior position to director, and from that standpoint I was able to witness Jeff's talent and appreciate what a wonderful actor he was (and still is). David Croft, who was a wonderful man but not one to gush over actors, once told me that he knew he was always safe if Jeff was in a scene, as his performances were always rock solid and he never had to worry about him – David called Jeff the hub of the company, and when I came to direct him myself, I found this to be totally true and he saved me on more occasions than I care to remember when I wasn't sure how to direct a scene. As David Croft always said, 'If in doubt, cut to Jeff'!

Over the years Jeff and I have stayed close friends and I am honoured to be asked to say these few words in praise of a lovely man.

Note, no money has changed hands in order to force me to write this gushing afterword ... but I will expect him to buy me copious pints of ale from now on.

Roy Gould
Director

ACKNOWLEDGEMENTS

I must begin this pledge of gratitude for help with this book by thanking my friend Nicki Edwards. It was her, and her husband Jon's suggestion in the first place several years ago that I should write a book! Nicki and Jon have continued to look after and maintain my website and Nicki is always there to help if I have a moment when I need assistance on the internet! I haven't yet managed to tackle my technophobia! Nicki even got me started all that time ago by taking some quite in-depth interviews on tape to start it all off. But, life being life, other things tend to get in the way of good intentions which, with the best will in the world, sometimes get shunted on to the back burner. Being a philosopher of 'things always happen when they are meant to', as I have illustrated within this story of mine, I was content to let nature take its course in its own good time.

Then I met Robert Ross and his wife Gemma. Rob and I met on a comedy-themed cruise and we became instant friends. We found we had so much in common that it was like we had known each other forever! Rob met Gemma a little while later, fell in love and married her, and she has become a serious guiding light on this literary journey of ours!

Robert, being undoubtedly the most renowned of comedy historians in this country, has published several definitive books on many subjects in the comedy world and very kindly offered to lend a hand if I ever chose to write the book. His input has been invaluable as his knowledge of the backgrounds of so many of the people in the business with whom I have worked has allowed him to flesh out the pictures and detail the experiences of so many of them. He has put in so much extra stuff in order to colour the pictures so much brighter. His contribution has left me lost for words, literally, on several occasions and I certainly could not have done this without him. Thanks to him, the extra bits in my life have come to light without me even trying! Thanks Rob! And thanks to Gemma too. She has a very clever knack of knowing how to get things done – and boy, do they get done! This book would have taken a lot longer to reach the shelves if she hadn't taken the helm. A natural leader who gets the people who matter listening to what she says – and woe betide them if they don't!

A very special mention to Penny Croft, the ever-resourceful and ever-helpful daughter of my Guv'nor, David Croft. My sincere thanks to her for her lovely reply to my question of whether I could use 'The First Rule of Comedy..!' as my title: 'Of course. Dad wrote that for you and Shaney. It was his gift to you.' Penny's affectionate and pugnacious curating of her father's legacy of laughter has been invaluable.

My thanks must also go, of course, to my publishers The History Press: thanks to Mark Beynon, who set it all going in the first place only to move on to pastures new, leaving it in the capable hands of Claire Hartley and Chrissy McMorris, and not forgetting publicity king Graham Robson! Thanks guys! It's been quite eye-opening for me to see, for the first time, how the wheels of publishing roll along from concept to bookshelf. Well done!

The final thanks go to my darling wife Judy who, without any fuss whatsoever, kept the tea, coffee and toast coming while I sat tapping away for all those weeks! It's been a wonderful experience

Acknowledgements

writing this book and I hope, dear reader, that you agree that it was well worth it!

Photo Acknowledgements

All the photographs included in this book are from Jeffrey Holland's personal collection, with grateful thanks to the creative talents involved. Any omissions or corrections will be rectified in future editions.

INDEX

...And This Is My Friend Mr Laurel (play) 102, 126–34, 211–12, 213–14, 215, 221, 224, 225–6

Abbot, Russ 138, 152–4, 176, 205, 237
Adams, Ian 77, 223
Adams, Tony 174
After All These Years (play) 226–7
Aitkens, Michael 217
Akabusi, Kriss 163
Aladdin (panto) 72–3, 179–80, 196–7, 209–10
Alderson, Anthony 130
Alexander, Lindy 125
Alexandra Theatre, Birmingham 61, 101, 112, 147, 168, 196
Alibi for a Judge (play) 61
'Allo 'Allo (stage show) 77, 183–4, 185–6, 189, 220
'Allo 'Allo (TV series) 14, 78, 141–2, 172, 185, 186, 235
Andrew, Prince, Duke of York 28
Andrews, Chris 30
Andrews, Eammon 23
Archer, Karen 164
Are You Being Served? (TV series) 29, 184–5

The Art of Concealment (play) 210
As You Like It (BBC Television Shakespeare) 89, 91
Ayckbourn, Alan 177

Baker, Hylda 145, 181
Baker, Kenny 18
Bannister, Trevor 179, 180
Bardon, John 15
Bare Necessities (play) 164
Barrie, Amanda 170–1
Barron, Richard 175
Barrymore, Michael 152
Bass, Alfie 185
Bates, Alan 89, 122–5
BBC 31, 84, 89–91, 112, 129, 135, 139, 146, 152, 189, 195
  'net curtain' comedy 207
  pay 164
  radio 140, 147, 170, 205
Beagley, Susan 29
Beck, James 15, 16
Beck, Paul 77
Belgrade Theatre, Coventry 21–2, 63–9, 71, 72–5, 80–1, 83, 124, 152
Bell, David 153–4
Bellamy, Amanda 232

Bennett, Alan 10, 224
Benson, Perry 232
Bentine, Michael 135–6
Bettinson, Rob 164
Birmingham 43, 59–60, 68, 104, 106, 225
   Alexandra Theatre 61, 101, 112, 147, 168, 196
   Chappie's drama school 59–60, 111
   Hippodrome 161–2, 193–4
Blair, Joyce 74–5
Blake, Susie 152
Bolam, James 91
Bournemouth Pier 98, 172, 173, 176–7
Bowness, Felix 23
Bradley, Pat 71
Brann, Susie 232
Brassed Off (play) 77, 217–18
Bresslaw, Bernard 101, 106–9
Briers, Richard 96, 100
Brightman, Sarah 116
Bristol Hippodrome 196, 197
Bruce, Brenda 91
Bullock, Michael 104–5
Burford, Ian 224
Buxton, Judy 28–9, 125–7, 131, 132, 133, 171–84, 187–8, 193, 225
   cruises 173, 177, 180, 214, 233, 235, 236
   Derek Nimmo tours of Far East 54, 165, 172
   Jeffrey meets 162–7
   panto 76–7, 169, 172, 174, 175, 177, 178, 182, 192, 220, 234
   plays 69, 91, 162–3, 173–4, 177–8, 183–4, 192, 207, 210, 213, 215, 217, 219, 222, 226–7
   training and method 69
   TV shows 162–3
By Jeeves (play) 181

Cadell, Simon 16, 25, 27, 28, 30, 87, 147
Caine, Marti 162, 163
Calibre Productions 183
Callister, David ('Cally') 216
Campi, Marji 164
Canada 97
Cape Town 177, 180
Carr, Alan 237
Carr, Robin 74, 75
Carry Ons 68, 101, 106, 108, 139–40, 143, 144, 147, 168, 170, 195
Carson, James Robert 183
Catholicism 48, 49, 53–4
Caught in the Net (play) 179, 180
Cecil, Henry 61
Challis, John 169, 213
Chapman, John 178
Chapman, Pamela 60, 111
Charles, Craig 209
Chichester Festival Theatre 86
Chico (*The X-Factor* contestant) 213
Christian-Young, Julie 29
Christie, Allen 101
Cinderella (panto) 175
Clary, Julian 194, 211
Clegg, John 21–2
Cole, Giles 210, 226
Cole, Stephanie 217
Collin, Madge 64, 66, 82
Collins, Joan 193–4
Comedy Friends and Heroes (touring show) 225, 226, 236–7
Confrontation (play) 78–80
Confusions (play) 177
Conley, Brian 164
Connor, Kenneth 68, 139–42, 143–4, 230
Conroy, John 120
Cook, Ron 237
Cooney, Linda 219
Cooney, Ray 100, 173
   acts 130, 233
   directs 222, 233
   produces 100
   writes 96, 98, 99, 130, 165, 176, 178, 179, 180, 212–13, 219, 222, 233
Cooper, John Kaye 152, 153
Coronation Street (TV series) 10–11, 125, 206, 208, 209
Counsell, Elizabeth ('Libby') 125
Coventry 12, 64, 77, 79, 94, 152, 160

Index

Belgrade Theatre 21–2, 63–9, 71, 72–5, 80–1, 83, 124, 152
  Coventry Theatre (*was* New Hippodrome) 71
  Jeffrey lives in 63, 71, 81, 82, 88, 120, 122
COVID pandemic 132, 224–5
Coward, Noel 24
Craven, Gemma 74
Crawford, Michael 113
Creasey, Terrence 30
Cribbins, Bernard 96, 100
The Criterion, Piccadilly Circus 96, 97, 107, 198
Croft, David 11, 19, 26, 86, 103, 147, 186, 192, 203, 208–9, 244
  'Allo 'Allo! 78, 141–2, 183, 185, 186
  Are You Being Served? 184
  Dad's Army 11–15, 16, 31, 239–40
  Hi-de-Hi! 10, 16, 24, 25, 26, 27–8, 31, 33–4, 111–12, 145, 200, 234–5
  Hugh and I 195
  influence 10, 16, 31, 86
  It Ain't Half Hot Mum 17, 31, 122, 124
  Oh, Doctor Beeching! 164, 203, 204–5, 206
  Roger Redfarn 14, 66, 103
  You Rang, M'Lord? 35, 36, 37, 38
Crossroads (TV series) 67–8, 84–5, 174, 189
Crowden, Graham 217
cruises 173, 177, 180, 214, 215, 233–6
Crush, Bobby 180
Cundell, Pamela 113, 240
Cundell, Tony 120
Curry, Mark 191, 219, 220
Cyrano de Bergerac (play) 86–7

Dad's Army Appreciation Society 215, 239–41
Dad's Army (radio) 147
Dad's Army (stage show) 12–16, 86, 88, 113, 119–22, 183
Dad's Army (TV series) 12, 16–17, 22, 23, 31, 113–14, 147, 184, 235, 239
Darrow, Paul 107

Davenport, David 168
David, Mansell 226
Davies, Windsor 16, 18, 163
Davro, Bobby 95, 173, 210, 212, 213
Dawson, Les 98–100
Deakin, Julia 206
Dench, Judi 208, 219
Dennis, Les 152, 153
The Devils (play) 65
Devonshire Park Theatre, Eastbourne 181, 217–18
Diamond, Jean 154, 165, 167, 175–6, 183, 190, 195, 217, 220, 221
Dick Whittington (panto) 73, 77, 109–11, 161–2, 163–4, 166, 169, 172, 175, 176, 178, 180, 193–4, 196, 197–8, 222–3
Dirty Work at the Crossroads (play) 73
Dixon of Dock Green (TV series) 83–4
The Doctor and the Devils (play) 78
Dodd, Ken 109–13
Dog Ends (play) 216
Dolan, Leo 88
Dong Ding, Murder Me On High (play) 216
Drake, Charlie 235
Dubai 221
Duncan, Peter 220
Duncan, Robert 166, 180
Dunn, Clive 17, 183, 239, 240
Dwyer, Leslie 24, 141, 155, 200

Eastbourne 181, 217–18, 220, 226
EastEnders (TV series) 15, 125, 216
Edinburgh Festival Fringe 129–34, 214, 219–20
Edis, Richard 159
Ekland, Britt 172
Ellington, Lance 137
Elliott, Paul 98, 178, 198–9
Elvin, Lizzy 222
Emberg, Bella 152
An Enemy of the People (play) 87
Equity 61, 221
Everett, Kenny 138–9

251

Fargas, Antonio 182–3
Fergusson, Jean 181
Ferrer, José 86–7
Fields, Gracie 64
Finch, Nicki 152
Ford, Rosemary 161
Forsyth, Bruce 113
Fortuna, Brian 210
Fox, Sonia 85
Francis, Clive 175
Francis, Stu 175
Fraser, Bill 68
Freeman, Dave 170, 171, 195
Funny Money (stage farce) 233

Gallivan, Collum 134–5
Garland, Charles 142, 205, 224
Garner, Rex 178
Gaunt, William 175
Gee, Dustin 152
The Ghost Train (play) 209–10, 213–14
Gidney, Chris 214, 215, 235
Gielgud, Sir John 90–1
Giles, David 89, 91, 122
The Gingerbread Lady (play) 162
Glover, Jon 137
Goodwright, Peter 98, 129
The Goon Show 134–8, 140, 219
Gordon, Noele 67, 74, 85
Gordon, Peter 215, 216
Gould, Roy 32, 36, 205
Grace, Sally 159
Grand Order of Water Rats 145, 214
Grand Theatre, Wolverhampton 29, 75–7, 174, 213–14, 217, 222–3, 224
Grantham, Leslie 183
Gravely, Celia 58
Greene, Richard 61–2
Greenhough, Andrew 175
Griffin, David 22, 30, 147, 151
Griffiths, Richard 224
Grundy, Reg 84–5
Guilty Secret (play) 207–8
Gyngell, Michael 177

Hadfield, Mark 191
Hagger, Jill 112
Hancock, Sheila 105
Hardy, Oliver ('Babe') 102–3, 124, 126–7, 128, 148–9, 154, 169–70, 239
Harris, Anita 101, 105
Harris, Keith (and Orville) 194
Harris, Richard 216
Harrison, Gail 29
Hartopp, Eleanor 'Elly' (Jeffrey's first wife) 79–83, 86, 97, 125, 155, 164
  clothes maker 110–11, 143
  good relationship with Jeffrey 179
  in Hemel Hempstead 88–9, 91–2, 151
  marriage ends 160, 161–2, 165, 167
  meets Jeffrey 77–8
  motherhood journey 82, 83, 88, 89, 93–4, 119–21
  in Somerset 156–7, 159–62, 164
Havers, Nigel 96, 194, 211, 212
Hayes, Melvyn 18–19
Heap, Douglas 97
Henry V (BBC Television Shakespeare) 89, 91, 122
Heritage Foundation 211, 229
Hewlett, Donald 18
Hewson, Sherrie 140, 152, 153, 206
Hi-de-Hi! (stage show) 128, 144–8, 222, 230
Hi-de-Hi! (TV series) 9–11, 19, 22–35, 50, 103, 105, 111–12, 128, 141, 147, 201, 241–2
  Britbox 231
  events 20, 225, 226, 241
  panto references 197, 223
  on *The Paul O'Grady Show* 181–2
  on *Pebble Mill at One* 237
  reunion 222
  Royal Variety Shows 114
  specials 99, 143
Hill, Vince 161
Hillyer, Terence 125
Hines, Fraser 173
'Hinge and Bracket' 180, 198–9

Index

The History Boys (play) 77, 224
Hodge, Sue 235
Holland, Diane 24, 25
Holman, Paul 182, 189, 192
Hong Kong 54
Hooper, Ewan 234
Hope, Bob 37
Hordern, Michael 177
Howard, Barry 25, 71, 186–7, 197, 230
Howard, Ricky 29
Howerd, Frankie 100–6
Hubbard, Kevin 120
Hudd, Roy 217
Hughes, Geoffrey 97, 107–8, 164
Hungary 231–3
Hunt, Gareth 78, 79
Hurran, Richard 197
hurricane of 1987 31–3
Husband, Mary 28, 36, 215, 222

In Which We Serve (film) 24
Ingerfield, Ken 74
Inman, John 16, 25, 71, 140, 185
Inside No. 9 (TV series) 237
Irving, Penny 29
Israel 173
It Ain't Half Hot Mum (TV series) 17–19, 21, 22, 23, 31, 122, 124, 147, 184, 235
It Runs in the Family (stage farce) 176
It'll Be Alright on the Night (TV series) 204
Ives, Kenneth 162, 163

Jack and the Beanstalk (panto) 73, 74–5, 76–7, 174, 182–3, 192, 211, 213
Jackson, Adrian 77, 217, 222–3
Jackson, Laura 29
Jacobi, Derek 89–90
Jason, Sir David 211
Jenkins, Warren 67, 78, 79
Jewel, Jimmy 144, 145, 148–9
John, Elton 91
Johnson, Celia 177
Johnston, Bill 179

Jones, Tom 37
Jordan, Chris 181
Joseph, Lesley 161, 169

Kearns, Patric 213, 215, 216, 217
Kelly, Gene 115
Kelly, Matthew 91
Kelly, Nikki 29, 227–8
Kelman, Louis 83, 120
Kent, Brian 67–8
Kenwright, Bill 170, 195
Kiley, Jonathan 177
Kindly Keep It Covered (play) 170, 195
King, Ross 161, 163
Knowles, Michael 21, 147, 232, 235–6

La Rue, Danny 214
Laurel and Hardy Appreciation Society ('Sons of the Desert') 219, 239
Laurel, Stan 102–3, 124–5, 128–9, 148–9, 169–70, 212, 237, 239
  see also ...*And This Is My Friend Mr Laurel* (play)
Laurie, John 15
Lavender, Ian 19, 239, 240
Lavender, Miki 18
Lawton, Leslie 173
Laye, Dilys 68
Leland, David 190
Leveson, Brian ('Lev') 205
Liston, Ian 179, 180
Little, Mark 216
Lloyd, Hugh 195
Lloyd, Jeremy 183, 184, 185–6
Longworth, Toby 159
Look No Hans! (play) 22
Lowe, Arthur 17, 19, 114, 119, 121, 239
Lowe, Gail 126–7, 129
Lowrie, Philip 208
Lucy (Jeffrey's daughter) 83, 85–6, 88, 89, 94, 154–6, 161, 162, 165, 166, 186, 192, 212
Lyndhurst, Nicholas 211
Lynn, Vera 113

253

McAuliffe, Nichola 217
McGee, Henry 233
McGowan, Alistair 159
MacIntosh, Sheila 88
McKenna, Virginia 125
McNally, Kevin R. 220
Madden, Peter 79
Madoc, Philip 22
Madoc, Ruth (née Llewellyn Baker) 22, 23, 30, 31, 115–16, 181–2, 197, 238–9
Maggs, Dirk 135, 136
Manchester 145, 178
Marks, Alfred 168, 196
Massey, Anna 123
Massie, Paul 78–9, 80
Maynard, Bill 195
The Mayor of Casterbridge (TV series) 89, 122–5
Mead, Lee 211, 212
Meagre, Ray 175, 234
Mellor, June 58
Michell, Keith 79, 87
Michelle, Vicki 100, 139, 183, 211
The Mill, Sonning 179, 192
Millfield School 156
Milligan, Spike 134, 135, 136–7, 138, 219
Milton Keynes 176
Minett, Paul ('Min') 205
Minster, Hilary 172
Minster Players 58
Minstrel Show 22
Mitchell, George 22
Moir, James 136
Moody, Ron 125
Moon, George 74
Morgan, Garfield 67, 68
Morris, Michelle 222
Morrissey, Neil 208
Mother Goose (panto) 73, 91, 196
Mould, David and Marion 154, 155, 166
Move Over Mrs Markham (farce) 219
Mr Laurel (play) 102, 126–34, 211–12, 213–14, 215, 221, 224, 225–6
Mullane, Edwin 132

The Muppet Show 37–8
Murder by Misadventure (play) 179
Murphy, Brian 97

Nedwell, Robin 171
Neighbours (TV series) 84, 174, 216
Nettles, John 161, 174
Nimmo, Derek 54, 159, 164–5, 172, 173, 174, 212
Nixon, David 71–2
No Fear Nor Favour (play) 61–2

O'Driscoll, Ed 183, 184
O'Grady, Paul 181–2
Oh, Doctor Beeching! (TV series) 28, 164, 166, 203–7, 229
O'Hare, Eugene 191
O'Neil, Sheila 12
Out of Order (stage farce) 165, 212

The Pajama Game (play) 81, 82
Palace Theatre, Watford 21–2
Parkes, Doris (Jeffrey's mother) 39–51, 53–5, 57, 58–9, 62, 70
Parkes, Sam (Jeffrey's father) 40–8, 51–3
Parsons, Nicholas 167
Parsons, Tony 80
The Paul O'Grady Show 181–2
Pemberton, Steve 237
Perry, Gilda 21, 24
Perry, Jimmy 17, 31, 86, 145, 186, 192, 215–16
  Butlin's redcoat 10, 24
  Dad's Army 11–15, 16, 17, 22, 239–40
  Hi-de-Hi! 10, 22, 24, 25, 27–8, 33–4, 145–6, 151, 229, 230, 234–5
  It Ain't Half Hot Mum 17, 21, 31
  music-hall expertise 145–6
  Oh, Doctor Beeching! 205
  Palace Theatre, Watford 21–2
  You Rang, M'Lord? 35, 36, 230
Pertwee, Bill 100, 114, 172, 239, 240
Pertwee, Michael 22
Peter Pan (panto) 172
Pinocchio (panto) 73

Index

Platinum Jubilee 28–9
Plews, John 127, 215
Plymouth 95–6, 129, 167, 169–70, 177, 180, 181, 198, 212, 213
Pollard, Su 16, 27, 28, 172, 179, 181, 199–201, 208, 215, 227, 238–9
   Hi-de-Hi! 26–30, 34, 35, 181, 199–201, 226, 241
   Oh, Doctor Beeching! 204, 206
   one-woman show 225
   panto 29, 77, 222, 223
   You Rang, M'Lord? 35
Portman Smith, Kat 130, 131, 134
Praed, Michael 130
Pretty, Stan 180
Pringle, Brian 91
Pugh, Mavis 21, 22
Purves, Peter 220

Qdos 174, 177, 178, 179, 193, 194, 214

Rabett, Catherine 232
Rattigan, Terence 210
Redfarn, Roger 12, 14, 63, 66, 67, 68, 73, 91, 103, 168, 199
Regan, Linda 29, 238
Relatively Speaking (play) 177
Rice, Anneka 116
Richard Harris 216
Richard II (BBC Television Shakespeare) 89–91, 122
Ridley, Arnold 19, 240
Ridley, Nicholas 240
Ritchie, Shane 216
Robin Hood (panto) 95–6, 212, 216
Robinson Crusoe (panto) 101–7
Robinson, Sir Tony 73
Ross, Rob 225, 226, 236–7
Roughead, Hamish 15
Royal Variety Shows 113–17, 119
Rubin, Lionel 74
Run for Your Wife (stage farce) 96–100, 107, 164, 173, 180, 198, 208, 222, 233
Russ Abbot's Madhouse 138, 152–4, 205, 237

Sam (Jeffrey's son) 89, 97, 119, 155–6, 157, 161, 162, 165–6, 167, 175, 211
Santa Claus – The Frost Files (play) 220–1
Savalas, Terry 113
School for Scandal (play) 67
Scott-Lee, Lisa 182
Scott, Margaretta 79
Scott, Terry 98, 168, 170, 195–8
Sebastian, Robin 220
Secombe, Andy 137, 138
Secombe, Harry 113, 136, 138, 140
Secondary Cause of Death (play) 215
See How They Run (play) 172
Sellers, Peter 14, 37, 135, 140, 237
Shane, Paul ('Shaney') 9, 10–11, 20–1, 30, 115, 197, 227–31
   Hi-de-Hi! 10–11, 32, 34, 128, 141, 143, 146, 181–2, 230
   Oh, Doctor Beeching! 204, 206
   You Rang, M'Lord? 35–6
She Knows, You Know! (play) 181
Shearsmith, Reece 237
Silvera, Carmen 78
The Simmons Brothers 161
Simon, Neil 162
Sinden, Donald 87, 91
Sinden, Jeremy 87
Sleep, Wayne 161, 163
Sleeping Beauty (panto) 129, 198–9
Smith, Peter 49, 56–7
Snoad, Harold 147, 239
Sonning 179, 192–3, 207–8, 219, 222
Spencer, Jesse 174
Spencer, Mike 29
Spendlove, Richard 205
Spinetti, Victor 172
Spring and Port Wine (play) 192–3
Steafel, Sheila 138
Stephens, Larry 136
Stuart-Hargreaves, Barry and Yvonne 24
Sullivan, John 211
Swansea 43, 82, 239
Sykes, Eric 98, 101, 136

Talent (play) 190–2
Tate, Richard 183, 184
Taylor, Donald 78
Thaw, John 105
Theatre Royal, Plymouth 95–6, 129, 167, 169, 177, 180, 181, 198, 199, 212, 213
There Goes the Bride (play) 178
Thetford 16, 215, 226, 239–41
This Is Tom Jones (TV series) 37
This Is Your Life (TV series) 23
Thomas, Delme 222
Thomas, Dylan 78
Thompson, Stephen 59
Thornton, Frank 100, 184–5
Timothy, Christopher 137
Travels with My Aunt (play) 175–6
Trinder, Tommy 101–3
Tripp, Jack 101, 106–7
Turns (TV series) 145–6
Two Into One (play) 130, 212–13

Upstairs, Downstairs (TV series) 35–6, 37, 78

Valentine, Anthony 207–8
Vienna 177–8, 18

Wade, John 31, 32
Waiting for God (play) 217
Wakeman, Rick 214
Wallace, Jessie 216
Walsall 39, 40, 46–7, 50–1, 53, 55–6, 58, 59, 60, 62, 75–6, 104, 189

War and Peace (play) 63–5
Warner, Jack 84
Warriss, Ben 144–9
Warwick, David 222
Watford 17, 21–2
Watson, Reg 84–5
Webb, David 225, 241
Webb, David and Tony ('The Webb Twins') 30
Weekending (Radio 4 show) 159, 164
West, Timothy 29
Whiting, John 65
Williams, Finty 219
Williams, Frank 22, 239, 240
Williams, Kenneth 139–40, 142–4
Wilmot, Gary 169, 175, 176
Wilson, John 137
Wilson, Richard 211
Wilton, Nick 130, 222
Wimbledon 97, 172, 173, 176
Windsor, Barbara 143, 168–70, 196
Wolverhampton 29, 75–7, 174, 213–14, 217, 222–3, 224
Wood, Victoria 189–93

Yardley, Patsy 111
Yarwood, Mike 71
You Rang, M'Lord? (TV series) 21–2, 35–8, 142, 158, 159, 169, 181, 230–1, 235–6, 239
  in Budapest 231–3
  parrot 200–1

Zerdin, Paul 211